REA

ugal Glob

The Frugal Globetrotter

Your Guide to World Adventure Bargains

Bruce T. Northam

Fulcrum Publishing
Golden, Colorado

The information in *The Frugal Globetrotter* is accurate as of January 1996. Telephone numbers, prices and other items may change, and readers should call ahead for current information. *The Frugal Globetrotter* provides many safety tips about travel, but good decision-making and sound judgment are the responsibility of the individual. The author and publisher accept no responsibility for loss or injury sustained by persons using this book.

Library of Congress Cataloging-in-Publication Data
   Northam, Bruce T. (Bruce Thoreau)
      The frugal globetrotter : your guide to world adventure bargains / Bruce T. Northam.
      p.   cm.
   Includes index.
   ISBN 1-55591-249-4 (pbk.)
   1. Travel.   I. Title
G151.N67   1996
910'.2'02—dc20   95–47539
                                                                      CIP

Printed in the United States of America

0 9 8 7 6 5 4 3 2 1

Fulcrum Publishing
350 Indiana Street, Suite 350
Golden, Colorado 80401-5093
(800) 992-2908

CONTENTS

Acknowledgments

This book was written on a laptop that migrated south for the winter on my motorcycle: The trek was hatched in the Adirondack Mountains surrounding Chestertown, New York, and flowed through Woodstock II; an upper-west-side Manhattan brownstone (lacking a lavatory); the University of Virginia's library; Dewey Beach, Delaware; a Washington, D.C., basement sanctuary; the oak-treed suburbs north of Raleigh, North Carolina; over a windy bridge into South Carolina's Lowcountry; down to Tampa, Florida, and back to New York City (round five) for inspired editing under the lofty ceiling of Manhattan Library's main reading room.

Thanks to the comrades and kin who supported my nomadic inclination at the time of writing. And a gratuitous tip of my cap toward those who didn't, for igniting a blaze beneath the self-deluding phantom.

Carmel Huestis, Jennifer Waters and everyone else at Fulcrum Publishing for giving me a shot.

Brother Bryan, the grand storyteller, keeper of monkeys, horses, goats and disadvantaged people. Tripp Martin for the lifts, friendship and his blind allegiance to the fountain of youth. Roger Yespy, the rock-and-roll CPA. Richie Kodora, the spirited senator of New Jersey, for the laptop. Steve Millward, ever-busy engineering strategies for spontaneity, for the North Carolina nest. Peter Allen, for his ruthless forthright and Asian accompaniment. Dare Koslow's aspiring ambassadorship to Nepal. Alain Bedard. John Pentaleri, the Italian Long Islander attempting to mellow in South Carolina, for his advice. Joe Satriani and Jorma Kaukonen's *guitar brilliance*. Woodsy, for not taking me too seriously. My old dog Ben. Brother Basil, for editing and helping me discover the *moon* I'm *still* pointing at. And the sense of freedom and love beyond renown from Mom and Dad (sorry about that adolescence deal).

P.S. Lynchburg College: I still haven't figured a way to use that B.S. in physics.

A project of this nature needs revision to stay up to date. I encourage you to write with updates and intelligence you think might be of interest to readers of future editions of this book. Feedback of any sort is most welcome. Write to the author c/o Fulcrum Publishing, 350 Indiana Street, Suite 350, Golden, Colorado 80401-5093.

Things do not change; we change.
—Thoreau

PREFACE

Do we spend the first half of our lives figuring out what we want to do with the second half of our lives, or do we spend the second half of our lives wondering what happened in the first half? Tough call, traveling will help you figure it out.

You may have guessed by now that this is not your standard travel guide. Many guides are written under the assumption that you are already motivated to visit distant lands. This is a travel guide for people who haven't yet unearthed the time, money or conviction to initiate an immense global adventure. This book will transform your limiting beliefs about world exploration.

I first got into the travel-seminar business because I recognized how essential a vacation is to the happiness of nearly everyone. Travel allows people to see their goodness reflected in the image of others. For far too many people, life today can be an unrelenting series of hassles, eventually leaving most people bored, estranged, overstressed or underchallenged. This unhappiness affects their families, friends and work. I believe periodic partings (travels far away) from this pattern are beneficial.

Many of you are carrying around an important secret that you have yet to let yourself in on: **Life is short so have fun when you can.** Here are strategies and plans you can develop to realize your visions of offbeat wandering at its finest. That's the point of this book—designing original tactics for enjoying your ultimate escapade. Of course, it's really up to you; you are the active ingredient.

Some of you may be a little scared to travel to places where the language, food, customs and cultural milieu are radically unlike those of western civilization. I was also apprehensive at first. So relax, and let's begin the process of finding out just *where* you are going. ...

As my seminar audiences grew, so did my distance from any desire to backtrack into the conventional nine-to-five format. Many came to me seeking adventure counsel, wishing to seize the exhilaration of roaming. I wanted to make a difference and reach out to people where they live. I begin with the following philosophy.

Long ago in the United States, perchance during the industrial revolution, the vocation gurus forgot to pencil in sufficient vacation intervals for their workforces. Hapless plan. The consequences prevent most of us from exploring the secluded fringes of our planet. Nevertheless, you *can* afford to sidestep the prescribed

Everything must end; meanwhile we must amuse ourselves.
—Voltaire

decorum of amassing material gadgetry that ultimately narrows your chances of ever venturing into remote cultures. First of all, the following plights need to be dismantled:

- Fear of losing ground on the employment timeline,
- Hesitancy about blazing your own expedition trail,
- Inability to get some distance from your workaday life in order to strike a balance: Clearly recognizing what you do and do not value,
- Inability to ease back on the lawnmower throttle, and
- Blind allegiance to the American lifestyles portrayed by the fabric-softener commercials.

Then, you'll be primed to take a most vital step for recharging your life-vivifying power: Hitting the road ...

Welcome to *The Frugal Globetrotter: Your Guide to World Adventure Bargains*. Since you have acquired this expedition primer, you must already be intrigued by alternative transglobal travel. And so the first stride is complete. Now, turn off your vacation governor and throw a dart at the globe.

The general public's reluctance to eradicate the stultifying American vacation policy requires you to take holiday matters into your own hands. This book may as well have been called either *How to Quit Your Job and Travel the World* or *Rat Race Exit Blueprints*. Don't live to work. Work to live.

Most people have that fantasy of catching the train that whistles in the night.
—Willie Nelson

If you've ever attempted organizing an adventure vacation to an off-the-beaten-path destination, or even just tried to get the best airfare deal, you know what a hassle it is to get quick, reliable information. You can waste precious time hunting for destinations and transportation options only to become more confused as your options multiply.

My idea of travel is one human being meeting another, face-to-face, person-to-person—not tourist-to-native. One key in this process is getting into areas where the local people have not yet developed the concept of *tourist* in their mindset. Travel deals to these corners of the earth are usually well-kept secrets. This is where *The Frugal Globetrotter: Your Guide to World Adventure Bargains* comes into play. A bargain hunter can pay one-third what a typical consumer does for travel. This resource will tell you how to get a lot of excitement for a little price by comparing and combining opportunities available from air couriers, around-the-world airline ticket brokers, domestic and international air charters, auto driveaways, offbeat adventure travel companies and myriad other resources.

Initiating your *own* quest is a thrill in itself. Skeptics envision traveling, working or simply living in distant lands as difficult, risky or expensive. Even the most comprehensive travel books already on the market focus on the traveler's experience and economics once they have *arrived* at a destination. "Travel cheap" seminars tend to sway the attender into a travel agent's package, onto the often *pedestrian* cruise ships. It is difficult for an aspiring explorer to analyze all of the budget options available to escape the homogenizing influences of our corporate culture. This book clearly suggests the least expensive ways to take the first steps with examples of four very affordable "off-the-beaten-path" traveling extravaganzas. Each scenario considers the traveler's budget, time frame, air or land options and safety.

Another important ingredient for initiating an extended journey is invoking the personal power to **get up and go.** Many North Americans do not see enough of the world beyond Europe and the Caribbean. Spending less (month by month) than what you pay for your home or apartment can afford you the spiritual expedition of a lifetime. Henry David Thoreau correctly observed that humans are enslaved by their possessions. Most of the fashionable one- to two-week vacations require as much planning, preparation and cash as a two-month globe-circling odyssey—assuming that your exploratory acumen will appreciate the *bright side* of the third world. Besides, if you're not thunderstruck while voyaging, you're not having fun.

Remember, we are all one. **This is it.** Find out for yourself what a miraculous world we live in (contrary to media portrayals). Realize that, sane or loony, we are all here together, and like it or not, this is it. Boost your mental, physical and spiritual well-being—take a recess from the nine-to-five habit and chart your *own* authentic, unrefined, outward-bound escapade.

If you found out that you had one year left to live, what would your most important goals become? If traveling surfaces as one of them, why wait? Take a time-out, attend the Global University and get your Ph.D. in results! I only offer the travel wand; you are the magician who can wield it.

People tend to have an endless series of questions about affordable worldwide exploration. I developed this travelers' bible and made it rain-forest lush with information. As the global village shrinks, we become increasingly aware of our interdependence concerning the events in distant lands. Because we all play a part, however small, in the interlocking of cultures, the objective of this book is to inspire "homebodies" to gain first-hand interaction with the staggering beauty and diversity of our planet.

Travel is life. Use this up-to-date, down-to-earth data to leap off the capitalism treadmill. Design the new-frontier chal-

The world is a beautiful book, but of little use to him who cannot read it.
—Carlo Goldoni

lenge of a lifetime right now. The world's characters and camaraderie will change you forever. Make an effort to meet the real people along the way—not just waiters, tour guides and hotel clerks, who are trained to cater to tourists. The day you finish that last trip is the same day you'll begin thinking about your next one. The travel bug carries potent venom.

The book explores your adventure options in six parts. Appendix 1—Global Adventure Resources is a complete listing of every company or organization cited in the text (and more). Appendix 2—Hostel Guide is an expansive listing of inexpensive places to stay in the United States and Canada. Some chapters are introduced by a brief tale about real people who chose to try something unconventional (although they previously had no idea they could afford to!).

Undertake an elongated journey and rest assured, the rat race will still be on when you return. You might just find you've jumped into the lead!
—Bruce T. Northam

Optima dies prima fugit— The best days are the first to flee.
—Cicero

Perspective: Exploring China in 1987, I befriended Mr. Chen, who was in my opinion, the governor and spokesperson of his hamlet, Yangzhou (local *officials* might not agree). One afternoon, I joined Mr. Chen in his old rickety truck for a fifty-mile journey to a little-known village. En route, we passed an elderly man who was walking in the opposite direction and balancing two immense jugs on a pole laid across his back. It was hot; the old man was barefoot. Cars are still luxury items for most mainlanders.

Returning to Yangzhou hours later, we approached the barefoot old man again. As we were now heading his way, I suggested that we offer him a lift. We pulled over, and he and Mr. Chen had a brief exchange, after which Mr. Chen pulled away without him. Puzzled, I asked Mr. Chen about their chat. Mr. Chen explained that the man didn't need to be in Yangzhou until tomorrow, and that if he got there today he wouldn't know what to do with the additional time.

We're not *all* in a hurry—just busy digging ourselves out from beneath the workaholic rubble left behind by the industrial revolution.

In the remainder of this preamble, I will graduate from the motivational warm-up and examine the mind of a travel master. The succeeding contemplations are those of my world-wandering, oldest brother Basil. He "challenged" me as a child with beatings, by locking me in hampers, dangling me precariously off the rim of rooftops or cliffs and sending me on shoplifting missions for the goods he longed for. He taught me how to sneak out of the house after midnight and even intentionally lied to me about certain facts of life (for his own amusement). In spite of those happy-go-lucky quirks, he is an eternal, loving companion and energy source.

It's tough to bolt Basil (Baz) down. Historically, he roves for ten months out of every year. One eventide, in a charming upper-west-side Manhattan Irish dive bar, he jotted down some of his beliefs in the midst of our meandering discussion:

Stagnation—A pond without an inlet or an outlet dies. Traveling is your in and out.

We take off for different reasons. Escape, a break, the search. Whatever, you're headed into a challenging experience. Nothing like a reality check of the world to heighten the senses. So why not? Bust it up! Humdrum reality too thick? Challenge yourself, test your soul. It's time.

To start you'll be on a "pancake trail" (traveler's phrase for popular travel circuits prescribed by various shoestring guidebooks) with other travelers—mostly adventurous Europeans. Once you are comfortable with the "trail," take off. Risk reaps rewards or pain. I've explored closed areas in China, Laos, Vietnam and Burma. Easy? No, but we don't remember which flavor cream cheese we had last week. Rock your soul with adventure and you'll never be the same: Material to run on for life.

One important issue is *trust* —not too easy, not too cold.

OK, you're motivated to travel to distant, far corners. *Why* is not so important. Confront a fear and challenge it; savor the gifts later. Remember, 85 percent of your problems are self-contrived. You are living in the crème-de-la-crème and don't even realize it. This trip's a wake-up call to your soul. A mood-altering experience that will carry you through the rough troughs.

A travel education can blow away university teachings, life's rollercoaster and all else. Then again, if you cushion the country you visit with excess cash and grand international hotels, save the airfare and make a beeline for Vegas. Forget who, what and where you came from. Be a sponge. A chameleon. Let your ego go for a bit and be open to cultures that are so foreign, they're scary. Remember, being an American licenses foreigners to believe that you are wealthy and underworked. Some of them want a bit of it.

Wanderlust—A strong or irresistible impulse to travel.

Be careful of wanderlust; it can be an affliction. At sixteen, a little hitchhiking trip lasted all summer and overran my life. Since then, contentment in one spot is impossible. Sure, many great places exist, but for all year long? Tap dancing the globe can be an escape ... or an exploration. Many in-between college students who need down comforters explore this avenue. A few get addicted. I'm one of them. Settling down? Unlikely.

Keep moving.
—Hunter S. Thompson

College students, the time to go is now—before you are swallowed up by the make-n-spend monster. Make the decision, stick to it, ignore cold feet.

Curiosity and hunger for exotic stimulus drives me into time-warped tribal areas. Not so comfortable or easy, but that's the stuff that sticks with you.

A couple of rules. Pack, then take half out (you don't need it—don't do another overkill). *Rely on your intuition and instincts rather than your things, OK?* I promise that you'll return invigorated, energized, maybe robbed, but certainly more open than before you left. Money-back guarantee. We seek difficult challenges for gifts.

So, you're ready? But what about your needs? Your whole life you've been sucking in commercials and work—produce—consume—indoctrinate. OK, you're going to get culture-shocked. Like a cold, you will get over it. Let go of all the stuff you believe is reality and be open to others. Educate yourself to the world. "Ignorance is bliss" they say, but some of us like to test our boundaries. It all started with hitchhiking ...

Suddenly, Basil was distracted by something else.

The message is: DO IT, whether you do it because you can't stand the thought of regretting not doing it for the rest of your life, or just because of the wonderful things it will reveal to your soul.

Travel is one way of lengthening life, at least in appearance.
—Ben Franklin

How to Use This Book

Close your eyes and imagine that you are eighty-five years old, rocking away, contemplating your life. How would you feel if you'd never had a genuinely wild journey? Globetrotting isn't for everyone, but here you are—questioning what lies beyond this prodigious land of mountain ranges, shopping malls, plains, baseball stadiums, coastline, drive-thru restaurants, forests, MTV, lakes and 33-percent taxation. If you can't stand the idea of *not* taking a big trip, keep reading.

I tramp
a perpetual journey,
Come listen all
My signs are
a rain-proof coat,
good shoes
and a staff
cut from the woods;
No friend of mine
takes his ease
in my chair,
I have no chair,
no church,
no philosophy;
I lead no man
to a dinner-table or
 library exchange,
But each man and
each woman of you
I lead upon a knoll,
My left hand hooking
you 'round the waist,
My right hand
pointing to landscapes
of continents, and
a plain public road.
Not I,
not anyone else
can travel that road
for you,
You must travel it
for yourself.

—Walt Whitman,
Song of Myself

How to Choose the Adventure That's Right for You

The process of choosing and planning the offbeat adventure that's right for you can be defined, in a visionary sense, as creating an image of the environment you want to explore and then organizing your energies into building it. It necessitates being part dreamer, part builder. Innovation and growth result when an individual takes risks and dares to *experiment* with their own life. However, traveling doesn't always have to be unusual. In our alienated, fractured modern life we need an awareness of the sacred in the ordinary.

No guidebook can tell you how to choose your quest; it can, at best, catalyze and awaken the quest within you. You can paint by numbers (visit a tourist trap), but you'll never create a holiday masterpiece this way. Inventing a holiday masterpiece demands the spirit and impulse of an artist. To construct the adventure masterpiece of your life, you need more than travel agents and destination recommendations. You need to generate faith in *your own* trailblazing competence. Born in your heart, tempered by your mind, molded with your hands and walked with your own two feet, the trail you blaze is your remarkable gift to yourself, everyone you leave at home and whoever you encounter along the way.

Career-on-Hiatus Guilt

First things first. You must set aside any guilt you may have about putting your career momentarily on hold. Since work is what we do with most of our waking lives, we must, if we deem life precious, ponder what we are working *for*. Everyone takes their first major trip with different motivations, leaving behind a variety of employment (or unemployment) situations. Please allow me to vent my feelings about the dismal state of the American vacation.

Please do not dash into, nor feel obliged to continue, slaving fifty weeks per year. Too many Americans decline to build on their sensations of crusading and their intellectual curiosity about the other societies and creatures that populate the earth—opting instead for a yawn and prolonged trots on career treadmills. The mega-adventures spotlighted in this text can be an eye-opening flight from a state-of-mind that's diluted by an endless loop of labor, bills and worry. I cultivated the notion for this publication with an effigy of sniveling office politics fresh in mind. Its intent is to empower you to momentarily stride *out* of the cattle call, and *onto* unworn trails and pure cultures.

Why is it that Americans are granted about one-third the vacation time of our European and Australian allies? Four to six weeks of paid holiday is standard, and often the law, in most of Europe. Swedes can receive up to two months of freedom per year. From days past, the Hopi Indians took off half the year, the Ashanti of Ghana skipped work for two hundred days per year and Kung Bushmen preserved 230 days per annum for soul searching.

But today, residing in "the land of the free," we must toil for a year to earn one-, two- or *possibly* three-week's leave. Damn, it can take a week just to adapt to a new climate, diet or culture. And with job-swapping being the popular national pastime, we often have to reignite the vacation accrual process. Only the Japanese, with an average of one week off per year, are on a clearer path to self-destruction.

Extending this rant, I concede that not everyone is wired for the unknown. Employers evidently don't surmise that leisurely recesses are the mother of imagination. Some firms seem biased against employee rejuvenation and stress relief by discouraging time off. Oh, if only corporate America understood that lengthened relaxation stretches recharge the creative battery, ultimately boosting worker productivity. We may be paid well, but we don't get the chance to really savor it. Thus, my calling in life is trolling this land of workaholics, breathing life into their dim but not dead adventure subconscious.

The key reason for the disparity of an American's time off, contrasted to that of the Euros and the Aussies, is that Americans have fewer workers' rights. It's unlikely that a government legislate will transform our holiday legacy *in this particular dimensional plane*, so get busy rocking your own dream dinghy. Corporate downsizing, temporary-employee agreements, dwindling benefits and sour economics are liable to persist in limiting your opportunity to visit assorted societies. The reality is, TECHNOLOGY HAS DIMINISHED OUR LEISURE TIME. Sorry.

It is *Homo sapiens*'s nature to hesitate at the threshold of pathless woods. Just remember the ten most omnipotent words in our language: *If it is to be, it is up to me.* Don't allow our puritan conventions to groom you into a workaholic, monkey-suited robot. Ferret out your secret aspiration. In Greek times, Plato declared public festivals as "breathing spells" that were concocted by the gods out of compassion for people's unyielding drudgery; the Greeks devoted half of their year to hedonistic pursuits. So should you. **Go do your thing.**

Traveling is mightier than you; it does with you what it wishes. En route, everyday life is experienced as a heroic quest and played as a game.

Short Trip Vs. Long Trip

Before investigating a particular trip, one must consider time and money. Use this as a guideline for possibilities.

*To be a star
You must shine
Your own light,
Follow your own path,
And don't worry
About the darkness
For that is when stars
Shine brightest
—copied from a
guest-house wall in
Singapore*

*People don't
take trips—
trips take people.
—John Steinbeck*

1 week—Courier trip to either Europe or Latin America.
2 weeks—Any courier trip, including the Far East. Drive across the U.S.A. (includes night driving).
1 month—Any courier trip (depending upon return policy): Drive across the U.S.A.,
Circle-the-Pacific-Rim tour (with fewer than 4 flight segments),
Circle-the-Globe tour (with fewer than 4 flight segments),
Touring or Trekking.
2 months–1 year—All of the above except courier trips having scheduled returns.
Warning: These trips are fun and may extend themselves.

Festivals and Events

In the planning stage, be on the lookout for festivals, feasts and jamborees taking place globally. Source the Sunday travel section of a primary newspaper (*New York Times* lists an *International Datebook*) for details on festivals and events. See Appendix 1 for information on the book *Wild Planet (1,001 Extraordinary Events for the Inspired Traveler).*

Your Budget

How much money you have to spend on your excursion influences your itinerary as much as any other factor. Take time to create a realistic budget, including your pretrip costs, actual travel costs and daily expenses for food and accommodations. Daily expense estimates for the *conscientious* traveler (see below) vary depending on country and personal style. Guidebooks and well-traveled acquaintances can give you rough ideas of how much you'll need to do a particular trip without stressing about money.

Trip-Expense Scenarios

It is wise to cushion the reality of your return home by leaving at least $2,000 in your checking account. To give you a rough idea of the various trip-expense scenarios that will be detailed in later chapters, use these transportation and budget survival examples:

One-Week Courier Trip to London

$100 round-trip transportation between airport and your locale
$159 round-trip airfare New York–London
$300 expenses at $50 per day for 6 days
$559 total

↑ Drive Cross Country (fly one way and return via two-week auto tour)

> $129 one-way air charter fare: San Francisco–New York or Los Angeles–New York (either way)
> $0 auto driveaway vehicle
> $175 gas based on a wandering 3,750-mile tour
> $420 expenses at $30 per day for 14 days (2 or more persons)
> $724 total

Six-Month Circle-the-Pacific-Rim Tour

$1,800 airfare (open ticket, maximum 1 year travel)

New York (depart September, bypass winter)	Bangkok
	Singapore (overland)
Los Angeles	Jakarta (overland to Bali)
Honolulu (Mahalo!)	Sydney (overland west or north)
Tokyo (most expensive)	New Caledonia (French island in
Seoul	the Pacific)
Taipei	Auckland (both islands of New
Hong Kong (overland into China—very inexpensive)	Zealand)
	Tahiti
	Los Angeles (arrive May)

$4,500 expenses at $20 per day for 6 months
$6,300 total

Circle-the-Globe expense approximations are similar to Circle-the-Pacific-Rim expenses. Here is an example of airfare through a ticket broker: New York, Dublin, London, Istanbul, Karachi, Kathmandu, Bangkok, Manila, Honolulu and San Francisco for $1,700. (Not bad, huh?)

Hot Tip

Do a little math summing up your typical expenses over a six-month period (rent, car, bills, food, entertainment, etc.) and compare it with the six-month expense approximation for circling the Pacific Rim. Have a nice trip!

Tourist Boards

Nearly every country and every U.S. state have tourist boards (see "Tourist Information" in your *Yellow Pages*). Tourist boards furnish free information on specialized charter and tour operators running specials or promotions. Get yourself on their mailing lists. Contact these tremendous resources of each country prior to your departure. Be sure to obtain the following information:

1. Free maps, tour guides and event calendars.
2. Names of national carriers and charter companies providing low-cost airfares.
3. Names of tour operators that specialize in their country.
4. Advance notice of any specials or promotions.
5. Travel agents that focus on that destination.

6. Off-season information.

7. Other printed material about the country.

Remember: This "chamber of commerce" touristy information will not get you far off the beaten path. For more information on tourist boards, see "Domestic Tourist Boards" and "International Tourist Boards" in Appendix 1.

Adventure Travel Companies: Touring and Trekking Outfitters

Adventure travel companies optimize the adventure opportunities within your precious vacation time by strategizing and condensing the choice touring options in a particular region. Whether you're climbing into the home of an Irian Jayan tree house–dwelling family in Indonesia, on a cigar-smoking adventure in Cuba or rolling overland from England to Nepal in a converted rainbow-bus commune, these preplanned expeditions have already been troubleshot. Time wasters such as itinerary scheduling, figuring out what to pack, buying equipment, making accommodation reservations and obtaining trekking permits are eliminated. For instance, you won't be delayed by the trekking permit office in Kathmandu that's on holiday half the year.

Specialized adventure travel companies can open doors in countries prohibiting independent travel or in open countries that close certain attractions and lodgings to the general public. They're a wise choice in regions requiring a higher level of security. En route hassles are swiftly navigated, and you're in good hands in the event of an emergency. Knowledgeable, typically bilingual guides and trip leaders (often local residents) are up-to-date in their region, timing your excursion so it encounters local festivals, feasts and fair weather.

Although mapping your own excursion can be much cheaper, if you're limited to one to three weeks off, you can't afford a holiday-spoiling setback. Prices, not including airfare, average $75–$250 per day for accommodations, meals, ground transportation, your guide's expertise and the option of having a porter carry your pack. Group size averages 5–20 people, usually sharing an interest in fitness and leaving civilization behind. You probably won't meet anyone from the "cruise ship crowd." Your common experience will sprout friendships, yet it can also resemble being at sea on a small boat, where it's impossible to avoid someone who gets on your nerves. Always shop around and bargain!

Wherever touring or trekking companies advertise, there's the possibility of booking it yourself upon arrival, benefitting

Trekking is a blend of easy walking and harrowing cliff scaling.

from the experience of travelers who've gone before you. Tour companies print informative, picturesque catalogs that will be mailed to you upon request. If you choose to create your own escapade, these catalogs are a generous source of ideas. Call a few of these companies for the low-down on a territory before you hit the road. (Listings for adventure travel companies are in Appendix 1.)

The Four Basic Escapade Ideas

The International Air Courier

Ideal vacation for a flexible, solo adventurer who needs a quick getaway. Part 3 of this book addresses tactics for a duo to fly on courier flights, but the soloist will have the best luck to save big money. The daily expense estimate is $30–$50 (couriers are forced to spend more time in or near major cities). (See Part 3—Flying As an International Air Courier for information.)

Circling the Pacific Rim

Perfect recipe for enthusiasts of maximum culture shock. Concentrating your trip in North and Southeast Asia makes for the ultimate getaway from western civilization. Not recommended for cleanliness neurotics or those not willing to experiment with food. Highly recommended for those wishing to lose any extra poundage (junkfood is often hard to find). Very affordable circle-Pacific tours provide a non-stop continuum of massive cultural experience. The daily expense estimate is $5–$20. (See Part 4—Circling the Asian Pacific Rim.)

Circling the Globe

More cultural diversity than a circle-the-Pacific tours since it's difficult to bypass Europe, the Middle East and either India, Nepal or China. Circle-the-globe trips typically visit either part of North or Southeast Asia. However, Singapore, Indonesia, Australia and New Zealand are systematically bypassed. Bangkok, Thailand, is usually where the fate of a circle-the-globe or circle-the-Pacific excursion is navigated. From Bangkok it's either south, east or west! The daily expense estimate is $5–$30. (See Part 6—Circling the Globe.)

Traveling across North America

Best option for travelers placing safety and medical security high on their value list. Also logical for those with serious time and money constraints. Food-borne illness is not much of a concern either. The daily expense estimate is $20–$50. (See Part 7—Traveling across North America.)

For wayfarers of all times, the right strategy for skillfully spreading the way essentially lies in adapting to communicate. Those who do not know how to adapt stick to the letter and cling to doctrines, get stuck on forms and mired in sentiments— none of them succeed in strategic adaptation.
—Zhantang

The moment the slave resolves that he will no longer be a slave, his fetters fall. He frees himself and shows the way to others. Freedom and slavery are mental states.
—Mahatma Gandhi

BEFORE YOU HIT THE ROAD

Travel Guidebooks

Bargain hunting for global adventure is simplified by consulting a budget-travel guidebook. Events along the offbeat wanderer's trail can be greatly influenced by the guide chosen. These handbooks are useful for plotting overland transit, points of interest and unearthing hotels, guest houses or bungalows—the archetypal Bohemian lodgings of international budget travelers. The ultimate goal of these books is to provide accurate, up-to-date coverage of all the practicalities: language, currency, transportation, accommodations, food, entertainment and services.

There's a guidebook for everybody. A quality check for choosing one is to compare how easy it is to locate specific information about the same destination in various books. Fact monsters may want to buy two books anyway.

Often rather bulky, guidebooks can weigh you down. Consider a) taking notes from guidebooks at home (or while hiding in a bookstore), b) buying them as you proceed (new or used) and either trading or giving them away, c) temporarily borrowing guidebooks from other travelers or d) proceeding with your own sojourn instincts, sidestepping the *pancake trail* altogether.

Pancake Trail: Overtrekked international travel routes fed by religious followers of budget guidebooks. Can result in missing the point of exiting modern civilization since facilities along the "trail" often provide western-style comfort, convenience and food (including pancakes). Admittedly, places along the "trail" are great for partying or recharging your battery.

Each of these "bibles to the road less traveled" has an inescapable *pancake trail* element, but all are prudent places to plan your escapade. Guides (and word of mouth) will steer you to locales and cafes worthy of travelers' patronage. Consider travel insurance and PACK LIGHTLY.

You've bought your tickets, you've packed your bags, now it's time to choose your travel guide. But remember: You won't be the only one buying it. When you purchase a guidebook, you're inviting thousands of strangers along on your vacation. Depending on your selection, you'll hang out with entirely different people, sleep in different places, eat in different restaurants and experience different local cultures. This guide will help you choose the travel book that's right for you—and that will ensure your path to enlightenment doesn't turn into just another bad trip. Go do your thing.

GUIDE: *Let's Go.*
AVERAGE COST AND SIZE: About $15. Thick and heavy.
SPHERE OF INFLUENCE: Twenty-one books written by Harvard and Radcliffe students covering Europe, North and Central America, the Middle East and Asia.
AREA OF EXPERTISE: Europe.

WHAT THEY PROMISE: A youthful, intelligent, no-frills guide for the backpacking set.

WHAT YOU GET: The grunge tour.

SUFFICIENT BUDGET: College student on a parental handout.

THE PATH: Beaten and hard.

PEERS YOU'LL MEET: Fresh-faced students flirting with the plaid-and-nose-ring aesthetic.

LOCALS YOU'LL MEET: Low-budget proprietors who've learned English from the thousands who came before you.

ACCURACY: Allegedly spotty—rumored that listings aren't always culled from first-hand experience. (However, I find them decent.) Continues to be best-selling European guide.

UPDATED: Yearly.

WHAT YOU'LL EAT: Wow, there's a KFC in Bangkok!

GOOD FOR: Finding cheap accommodations and meeting casual traveling companions.

BAD FOR: Dodging conversations about *Melrose Place* while abroad.

GUIDE: *Berkeley Guides*.

AVERAGE COST AND SIZE: Under $20. Big and heavy.

SPHERE OF INFLUENCE: Thirteen books written by U.C. Berkeley students covering eastern and western Europe, Mexico, Central America and the U.S. West Coast.

AREA OF EXPERTISE: Eastern and western Europe; Ralph Nader politics.

WHAT THEY PROMISE: Straight-dirt, planet-wise instruction for cash-conscious cowpokes.

WHAT YOU GET: For the price, the time of your life.

SUFFICIENT BUDGET: Huckleberry Finn's.

THE PATH: Alternative to the overtrekked beats.

PEERS YOU'LL MEET: Earthy, politically aware vagabonds.

LOCALS YOU'LL MEET: Witty hoteliers and hip restaurateurs.

ACCURACY: Good.

UPDATED: Heavily rewritten yearly.

WHAT YOU'LL EAT: Fish & chips with guacamole on the side.

GOOD FOR: Hard-core recyclers with a sense of humor.

BAD FOR: Lightweights who care about things like personal hygiene and privacy.

GUIDE: *Lonely Planet Publications*.

AVERAGE COST AND SIZE: Around $15. At times huge (some of their guides are bigger than toasters).

SPHERE OF INFLUENCE: Over 150 titles spanning the globe, penned by sometimes cynical road warriors.

AREA OF EXPERTISE: Asia, Australia and South America.

WHAT THEY PROMISE: Adventure through the back door.

WHAT YOU GET: A new appreciation for western comforts and your Ph.D. in backpacking.

SUFFICIENT BUDGET: Thank God for unemployment checks.

THE PATH: Well-trod.

PEERS YOU'LL MEET: Americans trying to avoid other Americans (the beat generation, round II).

LOCALS YOU'LL MEET: Europeans, dropouts and others bailing out on capitalism.

ACCURACY: Very good.

UPDATED: Every 2–3 years.

WHAT YOU'LL EAT: Rice, consumed in a hut without electricity.

GOOD FOR: Meeting nude sunbathers and fellow world wanderers.

BAD FOR: Those who get testy when there's no hot water.

GUIDE: *Moon Travel Handbooks.*

AVERAGE COST AND SIZE: Around $15. Entire series is compact ($5^1/_8$ inches by $7^3/_8$ inches).

SPHERE OF INFLUENCE: Fifty-two titles covering Asia, the Pacific, the Caribbean and the Americas, composed by information junkies.

AREA OF EXPERTISE: Indonesia and the U.S. West Coast.

WHAT THEY PROMISE: An in-depth dunk into the land, the people, their history, art and politics.

WHAT YOU GET: De-westernized.

SUFFICIENT BUDGET: A New Yorker's monthly dry cleaning tab.

THE PATH: The one less traveled.

PEERS YOU'LL MEET: Philosophical travelers maintaining the "eco" in ecotourism.

LOCALS YOU'LL MEET: Natives unaware of the World Wrestling Federation.

ACCURACY: Optimum; very detail oriented.

UPDATED: Every 1–3 years.

WHAT YOU'LL EAT: Tofu.

GOOD FOR: Keeping the funk in travel. Also sensitive to gay people and the needs of the physically challenged.

BAD FOR: Jet-setters.

GUIDE: *Frommer's $-A-Day Guides.*

AVERAGE COST AND SIZE: $17 and up. Midsize, light (lightest pulp-weight in travel-genre price range).

↑ SPHERE OF INFLUENCE: Twenty-three titles in $-A-Day series covering Europe, Australia, Hawaii, India, Israel, the Caribbean and South America; written by travel veterans with a nose for comfort.

AREA OF EXPERTISE: Europe, Australia, Mexico.

WHAT THEY PROMISE: Conventional remedies for the nine-to-five blues.

WHAT YOU GET: The textbook vacation.

SUFFICIENT BUDGET: Two mortgage payments (Unless the kids are eyeballing university life).

THE PATH: No vacancy.

PEERS YOU'LL MEET: Grown-ups who've graduated from student-travel books.

LOCALS YOU'LL MEET: Families.

ACCURACY: High, consistency maintained using single author per book.

UPDATED: Every 1–2 years.

WHAT YOU'LL EAT: Buffets.

GOOD FOR: Hotels, shopping.

BAD FOR: Spontaneity.

If you come to a fork in the road, take it.
—Yogi Berra

GUIDE: *Let's Party Europe.*

AVERAGE COST AND SIZE: $13. Compact.

SPHERE OF INFLUENCE: One book covering Europe, written by four partyers.

AREA OF EXPERTISE: Alcohol. Escaping reality.

WHAT THEY PROMISE: A passport to drink, rage and swoon in strange new lands.

WHAT YOU GET: A hangover.

SUFFICIENT BUDGET: Two hours panhandling a day should cover it.

THE PATH: Enlightening (once the acid kicks in).

PEERS YOU'LL MEET: Pauley Shore types and other sophomores sniffing out beer blasts.

LOCALS YOU'LL MEET: Fellow hedonists, barmaids and late-night hostel clerks.

ACCURACY: Relax, dude. Take a hit of ecstasy, wash it down with a splash of Jaegermeister.

UPDATED: Maybe someday, after one more pub crawl.

WHAT YOU'LL EAT: A spacecake with a pint of Guiness.

GOOD FOR: Buzz seekers searching clubs, bars, pubs and brewery tours.

BAD FOR: Lightweights and people who like to sleep.

GUIDE: *Rough Guides.*

AVERAGE COST AND SIZE: Over $20. Over two pounds.

SPHERE OF INFLUENCE: Sixty-two titles covering Europe, Asia, Africa and the United States; scripted by jaded Brits.

AREA OF EXPERTISE: Europe, Africa and India.

WHAT THEY PROMISE: Rambling among the natives.

WHAT YOU GET: A bungalow near the guy reading *Lonely Planet*.

SUFFICIENT BUDGET: Jack Kerouac's.

THE PATH: Teeming with surly foreign existentialists (toting books by Nietzsche and Camus).

PEERS YOU'LL MEET: Shoestringers burnt out on shoestringing advice.

LOCALS YOU'LL MEET: Eurogrunge and maybe the Dalai Lama.

ACCURACY: Immaculately researched.

UPDATED: Every 2–3 years.

WHAT YOU'LL EAT: Try a doobie made of tobacco, ganja and hash.

GOOD FOR: Searching for global raves (underground techno-head bible).

BAD FOR: Gap shoppers.

GUIDE: *Fodor's.*

COST AND SIZE: $15–$20 Some handy, some cumbersome.

SPHERE OF INFLUENCE: Over 200 worldwide titles by British/Americanexpat journalists (most editors are female).

AREA OF EXPERTISE: Europe, Caribbean, United States and Mexico.

WHAT THEY PROMISE: Directions to Haagen-Dazs after a day of museum-hopping.

WHAT YOU GET: A poolside cocktail and a *Lifestyles of the Rich and Famous* sunset.

SUFFICIENT BUDGET: Never a worry when you carry the American Express Card.

THE PATH: The pride and joy of the Ministry of Tourism.

PEERS YOU'LL MEET: Republicans with mortgages, wearing brightly colored hiking attire.

LOCALS YOU'LL MEET: Ricardo Montalbans, smiling with outstretched palms.

ACCURACY: Fortified by the local chamber of commerce.

UPDATED: Yearly.

WHAT YOU'LL EAT: $3 glass of orange juice.

GOOD FOR: Your fourth honeymoon.

BAD FOR: Cultivating international street-smarts.

Hot Tip

Avoid the *Ugly American Syndrome*: When in the developing world, try to do as the developing world does.

Six Top Ways to Obviate Your U.S. Status While Traveling Abroad

1. High-five everyone you meet.
2. Wear high-top sneakers and baseball caps everywhere you go.
3. Talk incessantly (volume set on loud).
4. Come to the defense of America's defense policies.
5. Give 'em the enthusiastic thumbs-up sign, accompanied by a giddy grin.
6. Prefix your sentences with the words "yo" and "like" and respond with the words "totally" and "definitely." Then, high-five again.

GUIDE: *Fulcrum Travel Series.*

COST AND SIZE: $10 and up. Various dimensions.

SPHERE OF INFLUENCE: Two dozen U.S. guides written by locals.

AREA OF EXPERTISE: America the beautiful.

WHAT THEY PROMISE: A good time off the beaten path. Lots of walking and the lowdown on the birds and the bees.

WHAT YOU GET: Insider tips for natives, newcomers and visitors; cardiovascular activity and gourmet camping.

SUFFICIENT BUDGET: Midwestern teacher's salary.

THE PATH: Green and unworn with no bus tours in sight.

PEERS YOU'LL MEET: Emerson, Whitman and Thoreau on their way to a poetry slam.

LOCALS YOU'LL MEET: Shotgun Sheriffs wunderin' whatchore doin' in dem woods.

ACCURACY: Highest rating.

UPDATED: Every two years.

WHAT YOU'LL EAT: Grape nuts, skim milk, lactose-tolerance tablet.

GOOD FOR: Timing a homegrown holiday around spring blooms, fall colors or ultimate skiing.

BAD FOR: Mainstream sloth.

Tread lightly, the third world's pre-tourism traditions are hanging on by a shoestring. Don't forget to eventually lose the guidebook and blaze your own trail. That's when the *real* fun begins.

Money Matters

When budgeting, overestimate your expenses to cover the unexpected. Take 20 percent more cash than you think you'll need.

It always amazes me when people who spend at least $100 per week on food and entertainment alone, are skeptical about the feasibility of independent, worldwide exploration. On one of the "off-the-pounded-path" ventures included in this book, clean, safe accommodations normally range between $3 and $10 per night, and hearty meals usually cost less than $3.

Save some money before you go. Here are some ways to save money before your trip:

- Eat at home and take your lunch to work.
- Get a second job: earn more money and have less time to spend it.
- Live with family or friends as long as possible before departure to reduce expenses.
- Stay out of shopping malls and bars (unless it's happy hour).

- Sell anything you don't need or will eventually replace anyway.
- Minimize all domestic expenses while on the road.
- Automobile: sell or store and freeze insurance.
- Home or apartment: sublet or rent if your are tied into a lease or mortgage. Otherwise, store your belongings and find a better place to live when you return.
- Aircraft storage: Why are you reading this book?

Other Things to Do before You Go—Checklist

- Put checking and savings accounts in dual name prior to departure.
- Make a "Last Will and Testament." (Who gets the CDs?)
- Life Insurance?
- Arrange for bill payments while on the road.
- Split money between prepaid credit cards and American Express traveler's checks. (Use traveler's checks and always carry your traveler's check numbers in a separate place. Remember to get a list of American Express offices for checkholder mail pick-up).

Packing

Circumnavigate lightly. A large day pack can suffice in tropical regions. **Pack a few days before leaving and take your pack for a few test strolls around your neighborhood. Most airlines allow you to check two 70-pound bags and bring one carry-on. Hopefully, your total load will weigh under** *20 pounds and be acceptable as a carry-on.* An overstuffed pack makes for big mobility dilemmas. Don't overpack! Leave your favorite outfits at home for they will only become shadows of their former selves. Remember to list everything you bring back into the country as a gift or souvenir on your customs form.

The shopping mall sporting goods stores can make anyone presume that they're a genuine rock climber. They can also disengage you from bundles of your hard-earned moolah. K-Marts, Wal-Marts and the similar volume warehousers often sell comparable provisions for less.

Travelers aspiring to travel light should consider ordering the California-based, mail-order *Magellan's Catalog*. They specialize in gadgets and gear to lighten the adventurer's load. Accessories include leak-proof neck pouches that let you safely store your passport and other valuables while you are swimming or washing ($9.95), an anti-bug suit ($45) or a charcoal-activated anti-pollution mask ($9.95—don't laugh if you haven't taken a

Hot Tip

Get bohemian in the kitchen. Consider "E-Z Stew." Ingredients:

(2) packages dried ramen noodle soup (flavor and low-fat optional)

(1) 10-oz package frozen corn

(1) 10-oz package frozen green beans, broccoli, cauliflower or spinach

(1) 15-oz can chili

(3) garlic cloves

(4) firm shakes of hot sauce

Add any combination of available chopped, fresh vegetables. Spice as desired: oregano, black pepper, seasoning salt, Creole seasoning, red pepper, black pepper, basil, curry powder.

Boil contents 5–10 minutes. Stir and allow to cool. Good anytime and microwavable at work.

deep breath in Bangkok, Delhi or Jakarta). Order a free catalog: (800) 962-4943. Bargain hunters, order the CampMor catalog: (800) 226-7667.

I behold packing as a continual process that merely commences on the day you depart. If you set out on an escapade with the spirit of this book, you can certainly procure what you overlooked substantially cheaper on the road. Nonetheless, some strategists must design, systemize, blueprint, map out, chart and plan!

Here's a guideline for lightweight packing:

Everything Lightweight, Packing Guideline

- Internal frame backpack (medium size) with attachable day pack.

Important Papers and Cards to Be Kept in Money Belt

- Documents (and photocopies at home and with you)
- Passport and visas
- Cash
- Credit card
- Traveler's checks
- Airline tickets and rail passes
- Hostel and student ID cards
- International driver's license

Note: Be sure that your passport fits in the money belt **before** buying it.

Footwear

- 1 pair of quality sneakers or light hiking boots
- Teva-style sandals for tropical climates (easy to clean and useful in showers anywhere) (Cheap Teva knock-offs are available abroad.)

Note: Be sure to test drive and break-in all footwear.

Clothing

- 3 pairs of socks
- 3 pairs of underwear
- 2 pairs of shorts (one a versatile swimsuit)
- 2 pants or skirts (one decent for blowing through airport customs)
- 3 T-shirts
- 2 non-T, or long-sleeve flannel shirts (climate?)
- 1 waterproof poncho or raincoat
- 1 light or heavy jacket or pullover with hood (climate?)
- 1 "Hey, I'm smokin'!" outfit
- Hat, belt and accessories (optional)
- Consider pants with zip-off legs

Remember to **adjust the waist belt on your backpack** so your hips support the majority of the weight. This alleviates any strain on your shoulders. It's more comfortable when there is some play in your shoulder straps.

Remember: Darker colors hide dirt. Calculation for weekly laundry ritual: $2–$5. (Or do it yourself in a sink. Socks and undies are a cinch.)

Health and Beauty Aids (housed within a small toiletry pack)
- Prescription drugs
- First aid necessities
- Soap and tiny bottles of shampoo (Pert, an all-in-one shampoo and conditioner, kills two "packing birds" with one stone. I, however, would never kill any bird.)
- Toothbrush and toothpaste
- Comb or brush
- Aspirin or ibuprofen
- Insect repellent
- Sunscreen
- Anti-diarrhea pills (Consider charcoal pills.)
- Deodorant
- Razors (Third–world barber shaves cost less than $1.)
- Toilet paper (only if you're a wuss)
- Eye care
- Tampons
- Stretch legwear (black?)
- Tank top (hot climates)
- Casual shirt
- Button-down shirt
- Belt
- Scarf
- Hat
- Basic makeup (Ahh, leave it at home.)
- Contraceptives?

Note: Always minimize bottle and container sizes and use Ziploc bags.

Miscellany
- Money belt
- Water bottle (campstyle)
- Sturdy journal and address book
- Pens
- 1 or 2 paperback books (trade for other books en route)
- Day pack (attachable to main pack an excellent option)
- Waist belt or fanny pack
- Towel that doubles as beach towel (A wet towel can be hung outside backpack while mobile.)
- Walkman and five 100- to 120-minute cassettes (Buy, sell or trade tapes as you migrate.)

I always take abroad with me one really soft pillow— to me it makes all the difference between comfort and misery.
—Agatha Christie

- Batteries (cheaper in nonwestern countries)
- Guidebooks (or ripped-out sections of them to lighten your load)
- Maps
- Small luggage lock (discourages petty theft)
- Plastic laundry bag (Transfer dirty clothes into this bag until you're out, then it's time to do laundry.)
- Small sewing kit

Optional Miscellany

- Bedsheet
- Clothesline and clothes pins for hands-on launderers
- Laundry soap (Individual packets are easy to buy en route.)
- Watch with alarm
- Swiss Army knife or pocketknife (good for peeling, cutting fruit)
- Lighter
- Safety pins
- Flashlight
- Pocket calculator (handy for currency-exchange neurotics)
- Umbrella (a luxury item)
- Camera (small, durable, point-and-shoot, automatic everything, 35mm) **Develop film on the road—mail negatives home** (safeguard in case of theft), or store film separately in Ziploc bags.

Note: In some foreign countries the people believe that being photographed takes away their soul, *or earns them money*, so get permission first.

The Overplanner's Packing Checklist

_ Airline tickets	_ Light gloves
_ Traveler's checks	_ Medical tape
_ Backpack	_ Neosporin
_ Journal	_ Ibuprofen
_ Frisbee	_ Bandages
_ Photos of family, friends, home	_ Cotton balls
	_ Lighter
_ Passport with visa	_ Sewing kit
_ Photocopies of passport, visa and plane tickets	_ Cash
	_ Swiss Army knife
_ Sunglasses	_ Address book
_ Contacts, solution, case, mirror	_ Camera (receipt copy)
	_ Film (cheaper in Asia)

_ Extra camera battery
_ Walkman (receipt copy)
_ Cassette tapes
_ Extra tape recorder batteries
_ Local instructions
_ Kids' giveaways (pens and small writing tablets for local schools)
_ Sea shells (great gifts for re-mote, land-locked peoples)
_ Time zone map
_ Vitamins (acidopholus)
_ Flashlight (pen-sized)
_ Extra flashlight batteries
_ Anti-diarrhea pills (for bus, train and plane rides)
_ Antiseptic
_ Mercurochrome
_ Antibiotic powder or dry spray
_ Calamine lotion
_ Thermometer (alcohol, not mercury)
_ Lip balm with sunscreen
_ Sunscreen
_ Insect repellent (with deet) (Better yet, take daily gar-lic pills 1 month before departure.)
_ Water purification tablets
_ Loose-fitting cotton pants
_ Long shorts
_ Wool jacket
_ Thermal underclothes
_ Wool hat
_ Waterproof jacket
_ Extra glasses
_ Socks
_ Underwear (Turning them inside-out on day 2 is an option.)

_ Shirts
_ Electric razor
_ Electrical adapters
_ Water bottle
_ Sandals (Teva-style)
_ Sneakers (quick-dry)
_ Passport photos
_ International health certificate
_ Chain lock
_ Health guide
_ Malaria pills
_ Toilet paper (Remove inner cardboard tube and flatten.)
_ Towelettes
_ Q-tips
_ Shampoo
_ Soap in soap box
_ Toothpaste
_ Toothbrush
_ Dental floss
_ Deodorant
_ Moisturizer
_ Nail clippers
_ Small calculator
_ Ziploc bags (3 sizes)
_ Baseball cap
_ Belt
_ Extra shoelaces
_ Antihistamine (Benadryl)
_ Calculator
_ Folding umbrella
_ Antacid (Pepto-Bismol tablets)
_ Personal medication
_ Playing cards
_ Binoculars
_ Space blanket
_ Watch w/ alarm

↑ Home Matters Checklist

_ Arrange mailing of mortgage checks
_ Pay medical insurance
_ Medical insurance coverage instructions
_ Long-distance overseas instructions
_ Finalize international emergency contact plans
_ Immunizations
_ Freeze dating service membership
_ Freeze health club membership
_ Automatic payment on utilities

_ Hold mail and paper
_ Assign yard upkeep
_ Car start-up instructions (save battery)
_ Lend house plants to neighbor
_ Mutual fund drafting
_ Move savings into checking account
_ Waterproof specific trip items
_ Arrange mailing of birthday cards on time
_ Living will, "Last Will and Testament" (can be a tough one)

Things to Plan to Do While Traveling

Simplify.
—Henry David
Thoreau

Secure your money in your money belt before leaving the bank. Cash large denominations on arrival, small denominations before departure. Keep leftover hard currency for the next country. Don't trade back to dollars (avoid high money-changer commissions). And use your credit card for expensive purchases. Consider importing and exporting local crafts for profit.

Cash

Carry at least 10 percent of your money in cash. Keep an emergency $20 or $50 bill hidden separate from your valuables. Very few countries in this world are reluctant to accept U.S. dollars.

You can sometimes get much better exchange rates on the "black market" for cash (some people will pay more than the bank exchange rate for U.S. dollars). Exercise the utmost caution when dealing with the black market. Beware of slight-of-hand, counterfeit money and setups. Countries with black markets for cash include Burma, China, India, Nepal and Venezuela. Be careful.

Overseas ATMs

One way to minimize costs in exchanging foreign currency is to make cash withdrawals at overseas ATMs. The usual $1–$3 fee for accessing the interbank rate is considerably lower than the commission, fees and traveler's check rates charged by hotels, private money changers and bank exchange desks. But the lid may blow off on this tactic soon. Wells Fargo Bank has raised its overseas ATM cash withdrawal fee to $5. That fee means that you must withdraw over $200 in order to justify conversion fees. Contact your bank to find out what the service charges are to use their ATM network overseas. Also ask for a list of specific ATM locations.

Credit Cards

Should you take one? Yes. A prepaid credit card can be a convenient asset, and it can save you money while traveling. Unless you have a mammoth unpaid balance, I recommend you overpay your last statement prior to departure by $500–$1,000. Then you needn't worry about missing a payment. Credit cards can be emergency lifesavers. Many foreign banks will cash a personal check if it is backed up by a major credit card. Credit cards lost or stolen overseas are quickly replaced. If you lose airline tickets that were charged on a credit card, inquire about the credit card company's loss protection plan to avoid paying ticket reissue fees. While overseas, you can call Visa and MasterCard collect in the event of an emergency.

Particularly in underdeveloped countries, most offbeat hotels and restaurants don't accept credit cards. The travel themes in this book hope to take you to these places where credit cards are not accepted. However, you will be flying into airports near major cities. When using your credit card in foreign third-world cities, the billing process can take more than three months. Your bill statement from credit cards used during a earth-circling odyssey becomes another official testimonial to your experiences.

Keep in mind that cash advances accrue interest from day one unless your bank offers a debit card that deducts credit card purchases directly from your checking account. If you're in a jam you can have cash wired from home using American Express Moneygram or Western Union.

Most domestic airlines sponsor credit cards giving a mile of frequent-flier credit for each dollar charged to the card. Most airlines require 25,000 miles for a free trip within the lower forty-eight states. That benefit can be worth up to $500.

If obtainable charge a rental car using a "gold" credit card; then you are automatically covered for collision protection (which costs $7–$13 a day in the United States, $13–$20 a day in Europe). If you rent a car for only three days a year you will offset the annual fee, which costs $20–$30 a year more than regular credit cards.

Traveler's Checks

The safest way to carry money is in traveler's checks. American Express is the most universally accepted. They are also available from Thomas Cook, Citicorp, Barclays Bank, Visa and BankAmerica. Don't forget to record the numbers of every check spent or still in your possession. Purchase denominations of $100, $50 and $20 (a few). (The smaller denominations come in handy when you are about to exit a country.)

Calling Cards

AT&T's "USA Direct" service is the best option for calling the United States while abroad. English-speaking operators are always available anywhere on the planet. Call (800) 874-4000 for a free calling card.

Don't make calls from any hotel without asking about surcharges.

Telephones are excuses for not writing postcards. Postcards from abroad are gems to be enjoyed by you and your pen pals *forever*. (One of your own prize photos with a stamp on the back is the ultimate mail treat.)

Suggestion: Develop a few job prospects before departing to cushion the blow of "reality" upon your re-entry.

Chief Economic Indicators

Pick a staple item and record the price to compare the cost of living in various countries. Staples may include the price of breakfast, a massage, lodging, local transport or a bottle of beer or water.

Working As You Go

A tight budget does not have to limit the length of any exploit. Consider these employment options while on the road: teaching English, proofreading, editing, baby-sitting, bartending, waitroning, acting, working as a movie extra, doing construction work.

Organizations providing job and internship opportunities can be helpful. "Home-grown" jobs are best acquired on site: Consult with other travelers, look for advertisements on guest house and hostel bulletin boards and check the local papers. Often the actual guest houses and hostels can provide work-stay arrangements. Working abroad gives you the inside-out view of any culture.

Taiwan, Korea and Japan are excellent places for voyagers to make money as English teachers (no Japanese required). (Unfortunately, gender-based wage discrimination plagues many parts of the world.) While on an extended trip it is wise to work in an economically healthy country, such as Japan, and take a "vacation from your vacation" in a country where your money goes a long way (Thailand, India, etc.).

Jobs are also listed in local English-speaking newspapers. See "Working Abroad" in Appendix 1.

Hot Tip

When in doubt about packing something, buy it cheaper on the road. While traveling, if in doubt about purchasing nifty gifts for friends, **buy them** and carry or ship them home by sea mail. A $2 Balinese wood or stone carving packs a far fiercer gift-punch than another $75 sweater purchased at Bloomingdales.

Mail

Poste Restante—You can address a letter to any post office in the world c/o Poste Restante, and the post office will hold the mail for one to two months. Tell pen pals to underline your last name and also write "HOLD" on the envelope.

American Express Mail—American Express credit card or check holders are entitled to use any of their worldwide offices to receive and forward their mail while they're on the road.

Airports

If you take photographs or happen to compose electronically while on the road, what you don't know about x-ray machines and metal detectors at airports could be hazardous to your equipment. Some passengers are reluctant to place their laptop on the security conveyor belt, deducing that the computer and disks, like a camera and film, might be damaged by the x-rays. No worries. X-rays, a form of light, might affect film, especially the high-speed kind, but computers and disks, which are written by a magnetic field, aren't sensitive to light. What computer equipment might be sensitive to are the magnetic fields of the metal detector in the security arch and the handheld wand. So passing the laptop through or by the arch or near a metal-detecting wand is more likely to mess up your files.

So the best way to get through airport security is to put the laptop computer on the conveyor belt and to ask about the safety of your camera film.

Customs

One of the less adventurous aspects of world touring is flying in and out of airports. In the United States, and in many other countries, a traveler coming from a foreign country usually passes through two federal checkpoints: immigration, which checks passports and ensures that a person has a legitimate right to enter the country, and the customs service, which ensures that people aren't bring anything illegal or harmful with them. (They are looking mostly for drugs, however.) Customs also acts on behalf of other federal agencies in their search for medfly-laden oranges, illegal animal pelts, Cuban cigars (United States only), gold bars and knockoffs of copyrighted clothing or computer software.

Customs services are sensitive to reveal their profiles of possible smugglers. However, traveling alone, acting agitated, walking quickly, looking grungy or wearing clothing that may conceal contraband may increase your chances of a search. The law of the land gives customs full latitude on searches in order to keep the countries' borders secure. Customs agents don't need

Aside from calling a common third party back home, the best way to communicate with fellow travelers also en route is to leave messages for each other on guest house bulletin boards. Sometimes airline reservation computers have a space for personal messages for ticket holders. When temporarily splitting up with your travel partner, always have a backup communication plan, perhaps through someone back home.

A free way to say "I'm OK" to people back home is to call collect as Jimmy Hoffa. (And then they, of course, refuse the charges.)

"probable cause" to order a search, nor must they read a passenger their rights.

A strip search cannot be ordered unless the pat-down turns up reasonable cause, in the supervisor's judgment, that the traveler is concealing something. A traveler may request to speak with a higher supervisor if they are being treated unfairly—but the bottom line is that customs can force travelers to undergo a search.

If you have indeed been treated unfairly, register an immediate complaint to the highest manager at the airport. Further action may be taken with the local government.

Keep receipts of all purchases you make while abroad. You will be required to declare these items before you re-enter the United States. The first $400 worth of goods is duty free. A 10-percent duty is imposed on the next $1,000. You can't be taxed on gifts or souvenirs. (Claiming 130 silver bracelets as napkin holders for your sister's wedding is stretching it.)

For more information about U.S. customs, write: Know Before You Go (from U.S. customs), Box 7407, Washington, D.C. 20044. (202) 927-6724.

There are only two emotions in a plane: boredom and terror.
—Orson Welles

P.S. from the author: On long-distance plane rides, the partiers tend to wander to the rear of the plane.

Plane Talk

Airplanes are excellent places to gather information, befriend natives and hook up with temporary travel partners. For tips on starting conversations with business people, order the free booklet *Plane-Talk* listed in Appendix 1 under "Travel Magazines and Newsletters."

Vital Documents

Passport

Proof of citizenship that permits you entry into the other nations of the world.

If you don't already have a passport it's best to apply for one at least forty-five days in advance. U.S. passports are valid for ten years. The least expensive route is to deal directly with one of the U.S. passport agencies (Boston, Chicago, Honolulu, Houston, Los Angeles, Miami, New Orleans, New York, Philadelphia, San Francisco, Seattle, Stamford, Connecticut or Washington, D.C.). If you don't live near one of these agencies, your post office can provide an application. You can get your passport in one day, for a substantial fee, if you can prove that you're leaving the country within seventy-two hours. I've accomplished this by stating that I'm booked on an international flight and won't receive the ticket until departure.

You must apply for your passport in person and you will need

>*Proof of U.S. citizenship*—A certified copy of your birth certificate from the county or city where you were born or a naturalization certificate or, if you were born abroad, a consular report of birth of a U.S. citizen.

>*Proof of identity*—A valid driver's license, government ID or a certificate of naturalization of citizenship. You can also use an expired U.S. passport.

>*Two recent, identical passport photographs*—2-inches-by-2-inches, black-and-white or color. Background must be white. Photo booths are no longer acceptable. Always carry extra passport size photographs on extended excursions for visa applications. Also have extras made because they're often requested for other foreign permits, such as trekking permits.

>*A completed DSP-11 form*—Wherever you apply they will have one of these simple forms.

>*Payment*—Current fee is $55 along with a $10 processing fee for first-time applicants. Call in advance: You may need to pay cash (exact change). For more information send $1 for this government brochure: *Your Trip Abroad*, Superintendent of Documents, U.S. Government Printing Office, Washington, D.C. 20402. (202) 783-3238.

Visas

Dictate your permitted length of stay in a particular country. To obtain visas one must call the necessary consulates involved and fill out a visa application form. A visa is the endorsement that a foreign government stamps into a passport. The length of stay for a visa can vary from two weeks to one month to six months. Visas are necessary to visit most countries. When visiting certain countries for less than specific time periods (i.e., two weeks) you don't need a visa. It's always best to take care of visas prior to departure but if you take an unexpected side trip, you can occasionally obtain a visa at the border. You need two photos per visa; photo booths are acceptable and less expensive than photo shops. Visa services (see "Passport and Visa Services" in your local *Yellow Pages*) are a fine place to start gathering general information on varying visa requirements. If you actually use a visa service, there are moderate fees. Ask them for general information and their visa requirement booklet. Otherwise visit or contact the embassy or consulate of the countries you plan to visit. Overseas, a visa service can be worth the added expense.

Note: When diplomatic relations exist, foreign countries typically have one *embassy* in the capital city and possibly *consulates* in other major cities.

Foreign visa requirements. Copies are available for 50 cents from The Consumer Information Center, Pueblo, Colorado 81009; (719) 948-3334.

For the European continent, the only countries that still require a visa prior to entry are the former Soviet Union and Romania. Visas for other East European countries can be obtained at the border. For Africa, the countries without visa requirements are Morocco, Tunisia, Egypt, Zimbabwe and Namibia. Visas for South Africa can be issued on a sheet of notebook paper. All Middle Eastern countries require visas with the exception of Turkey. In Asia, visas are required in Pakistan, India, Myanmar (Burma), Cambodia, Laos, Vietnam, Taiwan and China. Australia has the only visa requirement in the South Pacific. Central and South American visas are only required for business travelers.

If traveling around the world, your airline consolidator will probably have visa forms, which they can mail to you. It is also often possible to obtain visas on the same day while en route by visiting individual consulates.

If you choose to process visas yourself by contacting the individual consulates, see "Governments–Foreign Representatives" in your *Yellow Pages* to inquire about fees (some visas are free), documentation and processing times.

Discount Cards

International Student Identity Card. One advantage of being a student traveler is that you can often get discounted prices when traveling. However, showing your own college ID isn't accepted as valid proof of student status in most foreign countries. A wise move is to invest $16 in an International Student Identity Card (ISIC). You will get access to student discounts, student airfares, sickness and accident insurance, plus access to a 24-hour traveler's assistance hotline in case of a medical, legal or financial emergency. For a sample of the services provided by this hotline call (800) 626-2427. ISIC's now provide discounts on phone calls made back to your home.

P.S. Fake student ID cards are easily obtained on Khao Sarn Road in Bangkok.

International Teacher Identity Card and the Go 25 Card. If you are not a student, but are a teacher or person twenty-five or under, you can get many of the same benefits with the *International Teacher Identity Card* ($17) and the *Go 25: International Youth Identity Card* ($16).

Order by Mail: CIEE, ID Dept., 205 East 42nd St., New York, NY 10017-5706. Or visit any Council Travel Office.

International Driver's License

These give you legal permission to drive in the other nations of the world and are available from AAA or your local MVA. Your accommodators (guest houses, etc.) will hold this document, in place of a passport, while you are checked in. That gives you the option to keep your passport on you at all times. If you feel comfortable with the staff where you are staying, then you may wish to leave your passport and traveler's checks in their safe anyway.

Health

Have your teeth checked before departure! Dental technology in the third world is an oxymoron.

Before you hit the road, be certain that you have sufficient health and accident insurance for the entire length of your adventure. Understand the travel provisions of your current insurance (if you have it) and make sure you understand both the coverage and the procedures you are required to follow if necessary. If your existing insurance does not cover foreign travel, or if you want additional coverage, you should purchase a policy prior to departure. See Appendix 1 for a listing of trip insurance companies.

If you are taking a sabbatical, maintain your health insurance policy. If you are leaving a job (or were "laid off"), extend your coverage (COBRA), paying for it in advance. (COBRA is a legal six-month extension of health insurance at employee rates after leaving a company.) Individual insurance policies are expensive (most insurance companies provide individual policies). In some countries they will provide health care at no charge, but don't bank on it. Others have coverage loopholes.

Aside from medical insurance, various trip plans are available, providing inexpensive comprehensive protection against trip cancellation or interruption, lost baggage, stolen property and emergency evacuation.

Students carrying International Student Identity Cards who travel outside the United States are covered for basic sickness and accident insurance.

Hot Tip

Staying healthy is very much a matter of what you eat. Here's what you should eat each day for robust health:

10 carrots = 20 mg beta-carotene

1 bunch of broccoli = 400 IU vitamin E

3 1/2 glasses of orange juice = 500 mg vitamin C

3 cloves garlic = 200 mg selenium

1/2 head of leafy green lettuce = 10–20 mg B-complex

1 glass of milk = 500 mg calcium

Some countries require or recommend vaccination certificates or other personal health information, including the results of an AIDS test, before entry. Contact your local public health department for specifics on the countries you plan to visit.

On the road, bring your own "health and beauty aids," such as antiseptics, aspirin or ibuprofen, and motion and altitude sickness medications. Prescription drugs should stay in their labeled containers and carry a written copy of their prescription. Many prescription drugs are available at a fraction of the cost in the United States.

Most local or county health departments have public health service immunization clinics specific for foreign travel. On average, their fees are 50 percent less than private clinics. Certain vaccines interfere with other vaccines or require multiple injections, so plan ahead. In most cases, a vaccination is a controlled dose of the disease you want to prevent. The shots and pills can cause adverse reactions ranging from muscle soreness to nausea. Some vaccinations last for years.

Request an International Certificate of Vaccination (as approved by The World Health Organization). Immunization certificates are only demanded by immigration officials if you are traveling to or from an infected area.

How involved you become with the inoculation circus is up to you. Your public or private doctor will most likely request a Centers for Disease Control and Prevention (CDC) printout, which will recommend that they prescribe a full course of inoculations. Many experienced travelers, who sidestep getting shots and ingesting pills, maintain perfect health while traveling abroad. Safety first is always the rule, but remember that medicine is big business.

Drink only bottled water or other bottled drinks in the tropics and be sure that any ice in drinks is made from purified water. *Don't even brush your teeth or wash fruit with tap water.* While in the shower, keep your mouth closed.

Avoid fresh milk or ice cream and eat only fresh, well-cooked food. If possible, avoid meats, shellfish and eggs (except hard-boiled) if you have doubts about their preparation. Don't eat food that has been on display for too long. The more crowded restaurants catering to travelers are your safest bet (although local street stalls are more adventurous). Don't be overly paranoid, a bout of diarrhea is not the end of the world.

For information on vaccinations and health concerns, call the CDC hotline at (404) 332-4559 for information on recommended vaccinations and especially to find out if there are any disease outbreaks in countries on your itinerary. (You can also

Hot Tip

Street vendors: The hotter the flame, the safer the food.

keep yourself informed on plague outbreaks by paying attention to the media and calling your embassy.) Request the CDC's free information booklet. Also consult with a doctor for a second opinion. As I mentioned, chances are that a doctor's first recourse will most likely be contacting the CDC herself.

Be sure to inquire about yellow fever, typhoid, tetanus, diphtheria, polio, measles, meningococcal meningitis, malaria, hepatitis A and B, dengue fever, rabies, Japanese encephalitis, cholera or anything else that's brewing. These shots are usually not covered by insurance since this is "optional" preventative medicine.

Staying Healthy in the Tropics

Even experienced travelers venturing into tropical realms often do so with some apprehension about their health—and understandably so. After all, lots of bacteria, parasites and other microscopic bugs are just waiting to strike. That's why you are well-advised to keep your immunization record up to date.

But worries about catching a tropical disease—or suffering from traveler's diarrhea—shouldn't deter anyone from a visit. Indeed, travel to the tropics really isn't difficult, and it isn't something to be feared as long as good health habits are carefully practiced. Although many exotic diseases and other health hazards in tropical locales are not found in the United States or Europe, most of these illnesses are preventable by maintaining sanitation and using common sense.

Diarrhea. An estimated 50 to 70 percent of travelers to the developing world suffer a bout of diarrhea. The most common sources are contaminated food, water and beverages. While most people are aware of the major precautions—don't drink the tap water or eat unpeeled raw vegetable and fruits—they sometimes get tripped up on oversights, which include brushing your teeth with contaminated water; ordering a drink with contaminated ice; sipping a diluted fruit juice or eating cold meats.

Cold foods and salads may contain impure water and are much more likely to be contaminated by the hands of infected food handlers. Leafy green vegetables may contain bacteria and parasitic cysts, and simply washing in clean water—if a restaurant can be counted on to make the effort—won't eliminate the health risks.

To spare your stomach, make it a practice to consume only hot-cooked food, fruits that can be peeled, carbonated beverages (they inhibit the growth of bacteria), coffee, tea, beer and bottled water. Boiling water for five minutes kills all dangerous organisms, including hepatitis viruses. You can carry iodine or water purification tablets or small, portable water filters with an io-

Hot Tip

The Universal Health Tips: Boil it, cook it, peel it or forget it. Use insect repellent and sunscreen when necessary.

dine component. But be aware that may available water filters cannot be considered reliable for removing all infectious agents. Also, make a point of washing your hands frequently—especially before eating.

Pepto-Bismol tablets, taken as a preventative, have been found safe and effective in warding off diarrhea for many people, though the dosage of two tablets four times daily for up to three weeks may prove toxic if you already are taking aspirin-containing compounds or the anticoagulant coumadin. Generally, tropical medical authorities don't recommend taking antibiotics as a preventative unless you have other medical problems that could be worsened by diarrhea.

The best treatment for diarrhea is replacement of lost fluids and electrolytes (or salts). For fluids, drink tea (which upset stomachs seem to tolerate better than coffee), broth, carbonated beverages (without caffeine) and fruit juices. For electrolyte replacement, carry packets of rehydration salts, which are available commercially. As your stomach improves, eat such bland easily digested foods as rice, bananas, gelatin, salted crackers and dry toast. Avoid alcoholic beverages, fatty and spicy foods and dairy products, which may aggravate the problem.

If you suffer severe cramps and frequent bowel movements consider taking liquid Pepto-Bismol or an antimotility agent such as Lomotil or Imodium. If the diarrhea continues or worsens three days after these measures have been taken—or if there's blood or mucus in the stool or high fever with chills—see a doctor. If diarrhea or other gastrointestinal symptoms occur after you return from a trip, you may have picked up a parasitic infection that must be treated.

Note: Seasoned travelers recommend riding out the common diarrhea storm without drugs.

Hepatitis A. Considered a significant risk in developing countries. Hepatitis A can be acquired by consuming contaminated food, water or shellfish taken from contaminated waters—all of which are sometimes hard to avoid in the developing world. Immune globulin (IG) is the current recommended vaccine. A new vaccine (now licensed in Europe) provides longer protection than IG.

Cholera. For most travelers, cholera immunizations are no longer recommended. The only vaccine currently available is not considered very effective and the injection can cause a fever and headache. Instead, if you are going to an area of active cholera outbreaks, such as South America, your best protection is to be cautious in what you eat and drink. Improved oral vaccines may be available soon.

Typhoid fever. Since 1989, an oral typhoid vaccine has been available in the United States for travelers age 6 and older. A version of it is in development for younger children. Previously, prevention of a typhoid, a bacterial infection caused by contaminated water and food, required a series of injections.

Sleeping sickness. In tropical Africa, sleeping sickness is a potential hazard, particularly in the game parks of East Africa. But infection has been rare in American travelers. The disease is spread by the large tsetse fly, and the best protection is to wear insect repellent, long-sleeved shirts and pants to avoid bites.

Malaria. Travelers to developing countries should review their itineraries to determine if they will need to take anti-malaria pills—generally chloroquine, where it is effective, or mefloquine hydrochloride in chloroquine-resistant areas. The treatment begins one to two weeks before departure and continues four weeks after you have left the malaria area. The drug lariam provides protection against most malaria strains, but word on the streets is that it can have some nasty side effects.

Most major cities of Asia and Latin America do not have malaria, so prophylaxis usually is not necessary. But malaria is a risk in most cities of tropical Africa as well as in the rural areas of Asia, Latin America and tropical Africa. But if you plan to be in the countryside only during daylight hours, when the malaria mosquitoes don't bite, you can probably skip the pills.

Nowadays, however, prevention requires greater attention to personal protection measures designed to prevent mosquito bites. If you are in a malaria area in the hours from dawn to dusk, you should remain in well-screened areas, use a permethrin-impregnated mosquito net (Permanone), wear clothing that covers the body, use an insect repellent containing deet (35-percent concentration) on exposed skin, spray a permethrin insecticide on clothing and use a flying-insect insecticide in your room, such as an incense coil.

Malaria-causing mosquitoes are becoming increasingly resistant to anti-malarial drugs in some parts of the world and no present-day anti-malarial drug regimen guarantees protection against malaria. Malaria is regarded as one of the most devastating infectious diseases in the world, striking more than 250 million people a year, and is a major risk for travelers in infected areas.

AIDS. Hopefully, you already know how devastating this situation is. The National AIDS Hotline is (800) 342-2437.

The Centers for Disease Control and Prevention Hotline, (404) 332-4559, lists areas where there are outbreaks of yellow fever, plague, etc.

Here are three suggested health precaution readings:

Health Hints for the Tropics, American Society of Tropical Medicine and Hygiene; 60 Revere Dr., Suite 500, Northbrook, IL 60062. Send a check for $5, Attn: Secretariat.

Directory of Physicians (primarily United States and Canada) specializes in traveler and tropical medicine. Send a stamped ($1), self-addressed envelope (9 by 11 inches) to Dr. Leonard C. Marcus, 148 Highland Ave., Newton, MA 02165.

Health Information for International Travel, Superintendent of Documents, U.S. Government Printing Office, Washington, D.C. 20402. (202) 783-3238. $5.

Travelers' Clinics

The following clinics specialize in the medical problems of travelers, offering immunizations, pretrip advice on health concerns and treatment for exotic infections acquired by travelers abroad. Contact your local community health center; they often provide the same services as "travelers' clinics" for far less money.

Traveler's Medical Service of Washington, 2141 K Street NW, Suite 408, Washington, D.C. (202) 466-8109

Traveler's Clinic, George Washington University Medical Center, 2150 Pennsylvania Avenue NW, Washington, D.C. (202) 994-8466

International Health Service, Georgetown University Hospital, 3800 Reservoir Road NW, Washington, D.C. (202) 687-1872

Foxhall Immunizations, 3301 New Mexico Avenue NW, Washington, D.C. (202) 362-4467

Traveler's Clinic, 3289 Woodburn Road, Suite 200, Annandale, VA 22003 (703) 280-2836 or 560-7900

Find A Doctor (IAMAT)—a passport-sized directory of English-speaking doctors worldwide, 736 Center Street, Lewiston, NY 14092 (716) 754-4883

Where to Stay

International flights frequently land in the morning, leaving you the day to hunt down the ideal accommodations. Because the focus of this book is the initiation of adventurous wandering, I opted to not get specific regarding accommodations outside the U.S. and Canada. Getting there inexpensively is the most strategic part anyway.

Each of the four unconventional undertakings promoted by this peculiar book necessitate different tactics for locating safe, low-cost, clean, comfortable, *entertaining* places to stay. When considering any of these scenarios, the question "Where do you stay?" is *very* common. Well, our planet is bursting at the seams with inexpensive lodgings. Setting camping temporarily aside, the terms for inexpensive lodging around the world vary: guest houses, pensions (family-owned inns), bungalows, hostels, dorms, hotels, motels, losmen (cheaply run but livable hotels) and bed & breakfasts are the most popular. Conditions vary widely, from heavenly to hellish. In any case you will have the chance to meet new friends, and that is the key to touring. Unlike Americana, the other westernized countryfolk have been mingling in the world's offbeat wandering arteries for decades. Ask one of them where to stay!

Spontaneity has its merits, but planning ahead for your first night's accommodations, especially couriers who tend to arrive on their own, in each new country is recommended. If traveling long term, your airline consolidator may be able to make reservations for you in conjunction with the purchase of your airline ticket. Regional guidebooks (discussed in the beginning of Part 2) will also direct you to the inexpensive neighborhoods as you proceed.

International sojourners tend to meet one another easily and share their secrets. Whenever possible, you might want to share room costs with a trustworthy touring comrade. Eventually, instinct will tell you when you've found the bohemian region where the true, *unprocessed tourists* amass. Hostel memberships are not necessary throughout the third world. However, if more than a week in Europe is on your itinerary, consider signing on with Hostelling International (see Appendix 1 under "Accommodations").

Hostels

Once you've persuaded yourself to abandon the relative charms of hearth and home, a bit of familiarity with hosteling will make the transition into *bohemia* easier.

The biggest drawback to some hostels (notably Hostelling International) are their curfews, early morning checkouts and "light-chore" requirements. A plethora of independent hostels, rid of any summer camp–style hassles, have sprung up and are proving to be stiff competition for Hostelling International. (For U.S. wayfarers, Part 7—Traveling across North America provides information and listings of hundreds of inexpensive, alternative places to sleep and meet other spiritual people.) Hostel-

The term *youth hostel* is outdated as the prefix, "youth," is being phased out. People of all ages continue to discover the modern *hostel*. The concept of a youth hostel was developed by a German school teacher named Richard Schirrmann. On weekends, he brought his students from a coal mining city into the countryside to nurture their communion with nature. The idea caught on as a way for students on limited budgets, and other young people from different countries, to assemble in the spirit of international peace. This archetypal notion of hosteling embraced a peripatetic ethic for moving on one's own fuel: walking or cycling.

ing has evolved beyond the backpacker, and it can stretch *anybody's* jaunt-fund to the border.

Today, it's best not to have prejudged the site or service of a hostel. Modern hostels have fewer rules, no age restrictions and vie to provide a safe place to sleep, shower and gather masses of information. Studying hostel bulletin boards, along with your efforts to network with other voyagers, will multiply your rollicking possibilities. Private rooms are often available, or you may opt for the animated environment of a common room, where tales between people-on-the-move drift indiscriminately—none you'd chance to hear in a costly hotel. Common rooms routinely have bunkbeds and are not always segregated according to sex.

Hostelers share the entire space of the hostel, including the kitchen and bathrooms (not always segregated either). Although it may be burdensome for those requiring a high grade of modesty, the hosteling population is adapted to sharing space and ordinarily won't invade your privacy.

Hostels are often located within low-rent, minority communities that are usually safe and brimming with grass-rooted good times.

Some hostels limit their population to specific groups, such as international travelers carrying passports or ongoing tickets. Others will not accept local residents, who defeat the concept of providing boarding for transcontinental travelers.

Carrying your own bath towel and bed sheet is a good idea if you frequent hostels. Some hostels provide bed sheets free of charge. Some hostels do not permit sleeping bags for hygienic reasons.

Numerous wanderlusters save money by taking overnight trains, buses or ferries. For extra comfort you should get a berth or couchette. Train and bus options are examined in Part 7—Traveling across North America. See Appendix 2—Hostel Guide for an extensive listing of hostels in the United States and Canada.

Camping

Camping is always another option, but guest houses are so cheap throughout Asia, South America and Africa it's not worth the hassle of lugging the gear unless you're going on a trek. Tropical bungalows, which are wood or thatched bamboo huts elevated upon the beaches of Southeast Asia, provide very inexpensive, down-to-earth living. Sometimes a shower is pouring a bucket of water on your head.

Camping in Europe

Camping is a budget-travel tradition among Europeans. You and your campmates will get a more intimate look at the landscape than you will from a hotel room. May and the first half of June are the best off-season times to camp throughout Europe. Purchasing your food in European supermarkets and preparing it yourself is adventurous in itself. A European supermarket is usually a gourmet experience by American standards. Adding regional specialties (cheese, olives, smoked sausage) to typical camping food will breathe new life into your old kerosene-fired standbys. Regional wines can also spice up your outdoor excursion.

While many European campgrounds are in urban areas, most have some rural flavor. Campgrounds in the mountainous countryside tend to be highly scenic and well-maintained, as opposed to the campgrounds in southern Europe, which can be far less charming and overcrowded.

Campgrounds are often within walking distance from European train stations. Buses usually provide access to campgrounds as well. Check with the tourist information centers, which are typically adjacent to train stations. However, just as in the United States, the best way to camp throughout Europe is with a rental car. It allows you to hunt for the least accessible campsites with an abundance of gear.

Nearly all of Europe's organized campgrounds offer bathrooms and showers (hot water can be limited). Laundry facilities, swimming pools, restaurants and convenience stores are also common. A tent and a sleeping bag are all you really need. Some facilities offer small huts. A backpacker-style stove will be necessary to prepare meals. Remember that most airlines do not allow you to bring a fuel container, full or empty, on board.

Most European campgrounds charge fees per person, per tent and per vehicle. Total fees for a group of four ranges between $8–$30 a night.

Two good books about camping in Europe are *Europa Camping and Caravaning* (published by Drei Brunned Verlag) and *Camp Europe by Train,* by Lenore Baken (published by Ariel Publications).

New Country Arrival Strategy

Whenever possible, try to plan your arrival early in the day; that way you'll have an easier time finding local transport and budget accommodations.

Recognize and befriend fellow travelers in the airline terminal prior to the flight or while socializing on the plane (work the crowd!). Get an idea of where to go once you arrive through networking and consulting your travel guide.

Consult the airport information desk for maps, events, local transport, etc.

Exchange some money at the airport bank and ask the cashier for a currency lesson. Downtown banks often have higher exchange rates.

In underdeveloped countries, be **very wary** of the taxi drivers and hotel-hawkers who will mob you once you step out of the airline terminal. Their free transportation deals are typically accompanied by a high-pressure sales pitch into specific, overpriced hotels that will pay the taxi drivers a commission for their services.

Take local transport into the *bohemian* section of town and check out a few suggested accommodations. Don't commit to any lodging until you see it. If necessary, you can leave your baggage with a trustworthy hotel desk clerk while you shop around. (A tip may be in order.)

Don't panic.
—Douglas Adams

Continue to network with other travelers whenever possible, wander around, get the lowdown on the country and plan your itinerary.

Departure Strategy

Many travelers post ride-share-to-airport notes on guest house bulletin boards. Get the lowdown on cheap airport transport from your guest house staff or other travelers.

After a while you will recognize the underground current of offbeat travelers. Networking will make your future new country arrivals easier as you progress.

DON'T FRET OVER THE LOOSE ENDS HINDERING YOUR JOURNEY. JUST GO.

Spend your last local currency at the airport communications office. Airports are also the safest places to mail postcards and letters.

Homestays

Homestays are another accommodation option. These international organizations unite hosts and travelers. This no-cost arrangement allows the host and traveler to learn about each other's culture. The application process can include an interview and screening. See Appendix 1 for listings.

Safety

If you suspect any political trouble in a country you plan to visit, call the state department for any warnings. (Prior to a recent adventure, I inquired about any traveler warnings in Turkey or Pakistan, which are both Muslim countries. At that time my Manhattan apartment had recently been robbed and I'd witnessed both a purse-snatching and a near-fatal shooting on my street, so the state department's vague warnings about possible anti-western rallies didn't phase me. As it turned out, I was never in any danger in either country. I didn't even get diarrhea.)

The thrill of travel, along with the culture shock from the new environments you visit, makes it easy to become distracted or careless. There are no guaranteed ways of eliminating the risks, but here's a list of rules that can reduce your chances of falling victim to an attack on you or your property:

- Research the customs and political situation of every country on your itinerary—U.S. State Department, newspapers, radio and TV. Also, benefit from the insight of friends who have visited the countries you plan to visit, and anyone you know who is from a country you plan to visit.
- Some banks have safe deposit boxes available for short-term renting.
- Secure and hide your valuable documents and money close to your body—wear a money belt or neck-wallet under your clothes.
- Document Copies—2 photocopies of all documents (passport, credit card, driver's license, plane tickets): Leave one set of copies at home with friend or family member. Carry one set of copies with you, separate from original documents. If your documents are lost or stolen, having copies of these vital facts and figures will expedite the continuation of your adventure. Always file a police report documenting any losses.
- Always keep an eye, hand or foot on your pack—one second of inattention, anywhere, could result in the loss of everything you own. (Remember, while on the road you are like a snail, your house *is on your back.*)
- Be aware of your surroundings at all times.
- Never leave anything unattended; never put all your important items in one place.
- Secure a second wallet inside your clothing so if you lose the one you work with during the day, you still have money, checks, a credit card, etc.
- While sleeping on trains or buses, keep one leg looped through a strap on your pack.
- In dormitory situations, put money belt and small valuables in your pillow case while you sleep. Some of us can sleep through a 747 takeoff, but you'll notice a thief rummaging into your pillowcase. If you don't feel secure, bring your valuables into the shower with you.

Fall down seven times—get up eight.
—Buddhist quote

- A small lock securing the main zipper on your pack, purchased for $1 on the road, discourages pickpockets and other unsavory souls.
- Avoid rallies and political demonstrations—Americans are not all that popular in some countries.
- Just say NO to illegal drugs—you are subject to the laws of the country in which you are traveling. Malaysia, for instance, carries the death penalty for drug dealers. Scores of careless American travelers spend time in prisons worldwide for carrying, using or being suspected of using drugs. And the American embassy's hands are basically tied under these circumstances. Wise up.
- Be leary of who you accept candy (or tea) from—a favorite con-artist ploy is drugging an unsuspecting tourist into a slumber and then robbing them. Or worse. It happens.
- Trust your instincts—Be cognizant of your surroundings, especially if you have been partying at night. In the evening it's best to travel with a companion, staying on well-trafficked routes. If you suspect danger, keep your wits about you and **move on**.

The State Department Travel Advisory Hotline is (202) 647-5225 or (202) 647-5226. Call for updated travel advisories.

Thieves and Con Artists

Here are some tips on how not to be a target in dangerous places:

- *Monitor your partying.* Trouble occurs primarily while you are either intoxicated or sleeping. Know your limits; when you've exceeded them, you're a vulnerable target.
- *Have a plan.* Before going out, know where you're going, how much partying you plan to do and how you're getting back to your place.
- *Protect your valuables.* Secure your money and valuables before leaving your dwelling. Don't carry extra cash or credit cards when you don't have to. If you bring friends back to your place, don't leave your wallet, cash or valuables in plain sight. They could disappear while you are in the bathroom or asleep.
- *Ask new friends a lot of questions.* Ask their name, residence, workplace, etc. If you ask a lot of questions, the con person will find someone else who won't.
- *Beware of common routines.* Listen for nosy questions a criminal can use to gather information about you, such

as: "Are you visiting here alone?" or "What have you brought along with you?" Also beware of sob stories, such as, "I just moved here from somewhere else and don't have a place to stay," or "I was just robbed." If your gut feeling is that someone is bad news, don't stick around to find out.

Travelers are commonly targeted by con artists. Con artists, unlike standard criminals who usually favor "quick hits," allot plenty of time (often a full day) to win your trust before the shakedown. Some cons have acts that are convincing enough to earn an Academy Award. Like everything else, their tricks continue evolving. Here's a few classic scenarios:

Calling Card Surfers

Skulking about the pay phones in the airports and traveler centers of the world are people who make their living by selling stolen telephone calling card numbers. Police report that binoculars and telescopes are commonly used by such criminals. Whenever entering your calling card number on any phone, look over your shoulder and use one hand to cover the push button pad.

Staged Gambling Casinos

A friend of mine had just left Australia after saving $10,000 working construction. In Singapore, a new companion brought him to a small, crowded gambling casino where they both won a few hundred dollars. In the course of the day, the excited traveler made a few visits to the bank as the winning streak ended and he eventually lost nearly all of his money. When he suspected fraud, he ran out of the casino and called the police. By the time he returned with the police, the casino circus had folded up and left town. Oops.

Drugging

Travelers have been slipped sleeping pills (or worse) and robbed (or worse—had a kidney removed). Use the same common sense you had on Halloween.

Vehicle Rental

Occurring occasionally in Asia, travelers have rented motorcycles or jeeps from ad-hoc dealers who have then allegedly stolen the vehicle back from the renter, leaving the renter liable for replacement. Ouch. Ask around (travelers, shopkeepers, police, etc.) to locate the legitimate rental shops, and read the contract before you sign it.

↑ Gem Scams

Happens all the time. Know or don't go.

Handkerchief Switch

A man who can't read or write asks for your help in seeking a hotel or rooming house. He's a seaman or visitor from out of state settling matters for a deceased relative. He shows you a large sum of money and offers to pay for your assistance. Another man approaches and cautions the stranger to put the money in a bank. This newcomer also notifies the stranger that the hotel he mentioned has been demolished, but that he knows of a room.

The "seaman" does not trust banks and suggests that you hold his money until he gets a room. It is again suggested that he put his money in a bank. He replies again that he does not trust banks, but if you can prove to him that you can make a withdrawal, he will put his money in that bank. You go to a bank and make a withdrawal. He insists that you hold his money and gives it to you tied in a kerchief and begs you to be careful. The second man suggests that you place your money in the same kerchief for safety.

The "seaman" opens the kerchief and puts your money in with his and ties it up. He will show you how to carry it, either under your arm or in the bosom pocket. He also opens his jacket or shirt and inserts the kerchief (and switches the kerchief for another identical one). Once you have left the strangers, you examine the kerchief only to find pieces of newspaper.

> The major cause of problems are caused by a drug interaction between alcohol and testosterone.
> —Philosophical Venezuelan Policeman

The Lawyer Says

A stranger, usually a woman, opens a conversation with you in the street. Shortly after, another woman appears with an envelope containing a large sum of money that has just been found. You do not get a chance to examine the money. The question of what to do is discussed and resolved when one stranger states that she works for a lawyer who will know what to do. She leaves and returns, stating that the money was lost by a gambler who was trying to avoid taxes. The lawyer said she must share the money equally with the other two people, but they must show that they have money of their own.

The first stranger states that she has an insurance award with her, she leaves to show it to the lawyer, returns and states that he gave her one-third of the found money. They instruct you to go to the bank and withdraw cash. The woman who works for the lawyer says that she will take your money to him. She returns saying that the lawyer wants to talk to you; he is counting your money. You follow directions to his office, only to find that he does not exist. You return to the spot where you left the strangers to find they are gone. Sometimes the con artist works alone, having the victim speak to "her boss" over the telephone.

If you ever find yourself on the short end of the negotiating stick, stay calm, be direct and threaten to involve the police.

Dos and Don'ts on the Road

There are several things you can do (or not do) to avoid hassles. Here are lists of dos and don'ts.

Do

- Copy tickets, passport and other vital documents, and leave them with someone responsible.
- Buy a few traveler's checks in small denominations.
- Bring a calling card, or better yet, memorize the number.
- Obtain an international student ID if possible.
- Become a youth hostel member if you plan to spend any time in Europe.
- Pre-pay your credit cards if you plan to travel with them.
- Bring a sturdy journal and pens.
- Do your homework concerning vaccinations and health issues.
- Obtain an international driver's license, even if you don't plan to drive.
- Take malarial pills as prescribed, before and after visiting infected areas.
- Pack less than you plan to.
- Distribute valuables and documents around your body.
- Wear your "difficult-to-pack" clothing on the plane.
- Get as much information as possible (phrases) on the plane when en route.
- Where alphabet is different, have survival notes written by someone bilingual.
- Upon arrival, put aside departure tax in local currency with your airline ticket.
- Pick up additional maps at the airport.
- Travel at night to save time and money, but secure your belongings.
- In April and October beware of time changes.
- Arrive in the morning; avoid night arrivals whenever possible.
- Shop around and bargain for everything: tickets, accommodations, treks, etc.
- Ask plenty of questions: Additional or hidden fees? Tax? Service charge?

- If traveling solo and feeling lonely, stay in busier dorm-style accommodations.
- Carry important items with you in a day-pack or waist belt.
- Watch your back.
- Mail film negatives home or keep developed rolls with you at all times.
- Get off the beaten path. (That's where the fun is.)
- Be open, curious and positive.
- Spend any leftover money on postcards and postage at the airport.
- Take action and go on a long trip despite your training (or lack of).
- Take everything in moderation, including moderation.
- Ride out sickness, infections and fevers in a comfortable spot with a lot of clean water.

Don't

- Keep all important items together.
- Let your bags out of your sight or touch while in transit.
- Ignore your spending habits. (Keep a log.)
- Over pack.
- Forget about home. (But do get over it for a while.)
- Trust everyone right away.
- Mention *Baywatch*.

Travelers with Disabilities

A little homework opens up much of the world to the disabled traveler. For useful information about travel and study abroad write or call for a quarterly newsletter, Over the Rainbow ($10), or a booklet entitled A World of Options ($16): Mobility International, P.O. Box 3551, Eugene, OR 97403. (503) 343-1284.

Traveling Solo Vs. with Partners

When you travel alone you are totally approachable. Most experienced travelers will agree that you will never be alone for long on the road, unless you truly desire solitude. In short, traveling solo allows you to do as you please. Travelers are acquainted easily; you may very well amend your itinerary depending upon the characters you meet.

Of course, the solo traveler can be a bigger target for con artists and thieves.

Short Short Stories

Indonesia

Cremation is accepted after death in the United States, but it's not the festive, yet solemn, event it is in Bali. Large colorful creations are erected to receive the wrapped body. Then the structure is carried through the village by pallbearers who occasionally make figure-8 patterns, hoping to confuse the departed soul so that it can't find its way back home and will move on. The body is placed upon large scorching flames as the congregation reflects on the departed and contemplates the journey to the afterlife.

India

Streets in Indian towns and cities are overflowing with cars, bicycles, motor scooters, pedal-rickshaws, pushcarts, sacred cows and animal-driven carts. Auto drivers on two-lane roads without dividers play unending games of chicken, and accidents are common. Since there is no unleaded gasoline in India, trucks and buses belch black smoke.

While visiting a "hospital" in Delhi, India, I observed a mother carrying her dead infant down a long dim hallway, out the front door of the hospital and into her gruesomely impoverished neighborhood. Her face was like stone.

More than half a century ago, independence-minded Mohandas K. Gandhi urged Indians to wear homespun cotton instead of buying factory-made garments from India's colonial master, the British. Today, India's economic nationalism, or *swadeshi*, is alive and well. India does have a lighter side. In the state of Goa, you can relax to the point of collapse on Anjuna Beach with the flower-power subculture.

The nineties retro thing never caught on in Goa, India, because the sixties kept on happening. A former Portuguese–Roman Catholic settlement hugging India's central west coast where nomadic, western hippies *tuned in* to Goa's enchantment in the sixties, and where the peace-and-love legacy lives on. Visiting this "divorce-the-west," pantheistic subculture—busy elbowing the edge of the psychedelic frontier—may change your perspective on the shopping malls back home.

The Shore Bar on Goa's Anjuna Beach is a lived-in, bamboo-thatched dancing hut where earthy, western expatriate mothers move lavishly to the rhythm *while* simultaneously breastfeeding their babies. It's also the place to get the lowdown on the techno-music dance-a-thons. These untamed *cotillions* last all night, either under a full moon on the beach or in large houses

To be sure that your friend is a friend, you must go with him on a journey, travel with him day and night, go with him near and far.
—Angolan Proverb

(hidden somewhere in the jungle) where multiple rooms blaze in psychedelic light reflecting on surreal-painted walls. Partygoers, wearing minimal clothing and glow-in-the-dark face paint, undulate within the techno-sensurround. Great exercise. Not a typical day in the office.

Squatting low within a Goa, India, outhouse I was frightened by a sudden slosh and clatter. Curious, since third-world style *toilets* don't "flush" western-style. The noise below, identified by peering between my legs, was an odd, pink device flapping about wildly. I, exited, darted to the rear of the structure and barrelled into a humongous pig that was voraciously groveling its snout deep into the outflow pipe of the *restroom*. These pig-toilets are clever spin-offs of traditional Asian bathrooms, wherein you hunker down, resting your buttocks upon your ankles, hovering above an opening in the floor.

What distinguishes a pig-toilet from traditional third-world toilets is the ravenous pig that eats your shit, without delay. The sound of flushing, common in western bathrooms, is replaced by a hog slurping on the other side of a wall. Indeed, there's a sensation of a closed-loop ecosystem when your waste has recycled back into the food chain before you've even left the site. Flushing and personal cleansing are done by hand (left) with a few splashes of rainwater held in a nearby vessel. *Don't shake hands lefty in Asia.*

"If you had to boil it down to a single phrase, what is the philosophy behind techno music?" I inquired. The enlightened one smiled and replied, *"Power."* Mindless rococo or not, it's uncomplicated fun.

For ever and ever the memory of my distant first glimpse of the Taj will compensate me for creeping around the globe to have that great privilege.
—Mark Twain on the Taj Mahal

China

China has some less-than-touching aspects. Prepare yourself for throngs of Chinese people, snacking on a greasy chicken carcass, who seem amused by drooling profusely upon themselves, randomly expelling any undesirable foodstuffs. No napkins in sight. Coughing up and spitting phlegm onto any surface (including restaurant floors) is orthodox in this part of the world.

Chances are you'll go somewhere on a train. Any ride on Chinese rails provides graphic insight into the culture. On the floors of night trains there are scores of snoozing Chinese families (even in the spaces between the cars). Also on board may be flocks of live chickens stowed in the bathrooms and huge sides of butchered meat hanging from the overhead luggage racks. Mothers periodically pose their babies outside of the moving train windows so the young ones may defecate. Black diesel engine smoke blows into the car (never traveling faster than 40 miles per hour) all the while odd vendors pace back and forth, endlessly peddling their distinctive crustacean snacks. Are we having fun yet?

China's allure is a combination of haunting, rugged beauty and culture shock that's tough to beat. Often, you'll find yourself staring at someone or something without realizing it. Likewise, you get used to being constantly stared at. Requiring more of an adjustment is getting your first glimpse of a freshly lacquered, skinned, beheaded beagle and other dogs. More than one of your dining affairs may be botched when bus-tubs (shallow buckets) of dog and cat heads come into view. You soon realize that anything moving on the mainland is edible. There seem to be colonies, or at least entire streets dedicated to the slaughter of anything not human. You may find yourself sprinting to the end of more than one of these streets of carnage, deep in the throes of nausea.

While on a long bicycle journey to nowhere, I happened upon a sole Chinese woman tending to a crop. She was as surprised to see me and I was to see her. I got off my bike and she leaned on her shovel. For a moment, we scrutinized one another. The two of us couldn't have been from farther corners of the world (rural China and Manhattan). I wondered how she kept her white smock spotless while working the soil, while she puzzled over why I might be riding a bicycle across this field. After a silent, timeless minute, we simultaneously burst into smiles. Feeling self-conscious yet lighthearted, we continued smiling at one another without words for what seemed like an eternity. I waved good-bye and rode away. Before coasting out of view behind a hilltop, I glanced back at her. There she stood, still leaning on her shovel, beaming, waving. With her, I shared one of those inestimable, aesthetic flashes. Her benign image echoes within my mind long after the vaunt of many museum portraits diminish.

Japan

Japanese are trusting people, hitching is not a problem. A truck driver gave me a lift from Tokyo to Osaka, buying me lunch midway and continuously trying to illustrate the immensity of Mount Fuji to me. The only word we had in common was "Madonna." Arriving in Osaka after midnight, I had difficulty explaining to the driver that I needed to find a very cheap place to sleep. The confusion continued until he drove me to the police station in search of an interpreter. After a momentary exchange with the police, he waved good-bye. A policeman then set folded blankets and a pillow on a cot that was inside one of the jail cells. He motioned me into the cell, returning with a snack and a glass of juice. Smiling, he said, "Morning," exited and locked the cell door behind him.

Morocco

Deep in the heart of Morocco's Riff Mountains I was hiking on a rocky hillside, shadowed by olive trees. I befriended a 30-year-old shepherd, wearing a ski cap with a pom-pom. He was the

Acupuncture works! Where western medicine prescribes pills, ancient Chinese practitioners heal by stimulating the bodies dormant energy centers. Examples of an acupuncturists housecall to a western guest house in China included treating a woman who was having terrible menstrual cramps by placing four needles in her abdomen and wriggling them slightly. Upon removing the ultrathin needles, she was completely relieved. Other travelers line up, seeking relief for their ailments. One by one, the acupuncturist cures other westerners with differing ailments: A victim of constant fatigue received needles in his knees and elbows and was thereby invigorated; a "thrown-out-shoulder" patient was repaired with a series of needles to the affected area; lower backs are left painfree for months by having one needle placed in the upper buttocks and one placed behind either knee. One treatment is usually not a cure-all. Be sure the needles are clean. Successful acupuncture treatment requires a maintenance schedule.

No description of China's unromantic side would be comprehensive without a dab on the public restrooms, so hold your breath: Dimly lit cement cavern stalls are bisected by a V-shaped trough. Large numbers of defecators, usually facing in one direction, squat simultaneously over the trough, where a small trickle of water running from end to end supposedly carries away the plummeting human waste. No TP in sight. Beware: The floors are slippery; unsuspecting travelers have slipped and fallen into such cauldrons.

commander of fifty goats and twenty sheep. After a lesson on flock-control fundamentals (tree-branch coaxing, throwing pebbles, grunting and hissing), we exchanged butter rum Lifesavers and cashews. I helped bring the herd to his dwelling, lost somewhere in the narrow, windy byways of Chefchaouen. We drank Moroccan whiskey (mint tea) and smoked kayffe, employing a 60-inch pipe (pipa). The peace pipe ceremony gained momentum when his mother, brother and sister arrived and we all played the Arabic-English "name-that-kitchen-utensil" game. Meanwhile in the next room, the livestock bhaaaahd, grunted and mooed. Moroccan sunsets forever on my mind.

Venezuela

When referring to *Down Under*, do not limit yourself to merely Australia and New Zealand. Venezuela, South America's Down Under, is geographically staggering, yielding 1,800 miles of Caribbean coastline, countless palm-treed isles, the northern spine of the snowcapped Andes, the world's highest waterfall, American West–style mesas and plains, deserts and plenty of dense, Amazon-basin jungle, which is a sanctuary for several indigenous Indian societies. Oil money has catapulted Caracas into modern times. It's the least expensive *contemporary* city in the Northern Hemisphere, overflowing with exotic people, fashion trends, varied dining opportunities, museums, cafes, shopping, nightlife and potable tap water. Every dimension of Venezuela's diverse landscape relaxes with a continuous warm-climate, mañana attitude.

This bargain hunter's paradise, sharing borders with Guyana, Brazil and Columbia, has more opportunities for adventure than California. If taken by the metropolitan allure of Caraqueño flair, ramble into the Gran Parrillada El Rosal (a gut-level dance hall, 1/5 mile south of the Chacaito Metro station on Avenida Pichincha). Not exactly a blueprint of 1950s *Happy Days* nostalgia replica, but there's plenty of live salsa, merengue, ballenato, gaita and rock music blasting. An icy bottle of Polar Beer (Venezuela's national brew) costs under a buck (170 Bs).

Usually, the higher up on the socioeconomic ladder one travels, the likelihood of meeting an English-speaking acquaintance increases. In local, easygoing joints, like the Gran Parrillada El Rosal, your chances of encountering an amigo capable of speaking English are slim. No worry, lacking Spanish skills makes your search for a dance partner a bona fide challenge. One option is to persuade one of the more senior señoritas to familiarize you with the hand and foot placements. Even a language-impaired visitor soon realizes that dancing, like eating, is routine here, a national sport, where everyone's clued in! Albeit exciting, dancing faces remain expressionless, as dreamy eyes hover calmly aloft dimly-lit torsos, slyly meshing their midsections. It's somewhat like a thriving high school gymnasium dance, minus the U.S.-style cotillion theatrics.

Venezuelan charm truly hit me listening to music performed by a familial trio on the renowned, downtown pedestrian stroll mall, Boulevard de Sabana Grande. An adorable five-year-old girl played maracas in front of two men, one finger-picking an arpa (harp with attached sound cabin), the other singing while playing a cuatro (a small, four-string guitar). The vibrant tone and mesmerizing vision was Latin symphony at its best.

Woman Traveling Alone: Melanie's Story

Solo and Smiling

When I am asked what it's like to travel through strange countries by myself, as a woman and an American, many memories spring to mind—from those of sexual harassment and the difficulties of enduring menstruation every month to thoughts of discovering unique cultures and intriguing romances. There are tremendous advantages and unfortunate drawbacks to this type of travel, which has always been, and will always be, a learning experience.

"Aren't You Afraid?"

"Aren't you afraid to be alone?" The group of Balinese men and boys asked me while I was passing through the Bali Strait.

A common question. However, this particular memory is vividly etched in my mind more than most. My bus ticket from Denpasar, Bali, to Surabaya, Java, included a ferry ride across the Bali Strait. Predictably, the bus didn't start when we reached Java. I refused to part with my belongings in the galley beneath the bus and stayed on the boat while it pulled away from my intended destination and returned to Bali. Two hours later, at 11 P.M., I returned to Java for the second time that night—aboard the boat still escorting my bus. The hour had gotten so late that there were only fifty people on this ferry and all were men.

"Aren't you afraid to be alone?" They asked for the third time in five minutes. "No," I replied, "but the fact that you keep asking me is raising concern. Should I be?"

After spending several months in Asia, I eventually came to understand this was a cultural difference, not a sexual one.

Mopeds in Taiwan: Mopeds are often the family car in Asian cities. Taipei, Taiwan, has wide, busy streets where there seems to be no rules. Traffic lawlessness, such as ignoring signals, is exacerbated by leaning on the horn. Low-grade fuel emissions cloud the air. It's not uncommon to see up to four people crammed onto one moped. They move freight as well. I once saw a Taiwanese fellow weaving through traffic on a small scooter while having a king-size mattress and boxspring tied to his back.

Love on the Road

- **Romance vs. economy:** Couples usually care more about where they stay than someone traveling alone.

- **How to convince your counterpart that camping in the sub-freezing Himalayas is an unmatched experience:** Say, "We'll be home soon."

- **When departing from the homeland to foreign lands with someone who is meaningful to you—you will return alone or with a stranger (the best traveling companion you never knew). Traveling abroad creates the ultimate compatibility centrifuge.**

- **Love on the road can be tough and there will be quarrels, but as the Chinese say, even a typhoon doesn't last a day.**

Asians don't like to be alone. In general, they function together by traveling in groups, living with the family until marriage and operating in the workplace and school environments in teams, not as individuals—very unlike western cultures. They wanted to understand why someone would *want* or *choose* to be alone. In our culture, when a group of fifty men ask such probing questions, you could get ten-to-one odds they're not conducting social science interviews for a Gallup poll.

The Learning Process

My first summer studying in Greece was enlightening. Some people traveled with airline tickets in hand and a hotel reservation awaiting at the other end. However, while under the protective wing of experienced travelers on an educational tour, I took every opportunity to learn about independent budget travel.

My earliest memories of being alone during an overseas jaunt are of the summer of '84. I stumbled upon an opportunity to stay in a vacant apartment in Athens (the tenant lived in a village three hours away and would not return until the new university term in September). I also discovered a modeling assignment with an international agency seeking Americans with a "European look."

What I remember most, culturally, is attending a wedding that took an entire weekend to celebrate and ultimately endure. Typically, those who have moved from the village travel back home on Saturday. On that night the center of town becomes a lively entertainment center as residents empty their homes of chairs, lights and alcohol. Anyone with remote talents will sing, play musical instruments, dance and entertain the village until at least three in the morning.

The next day, before the church ceremony, particular traditions are followed. The groom and his family walk through town to the bride's home, where she waits behind the fenced gate, front door and bedroom divider of her house. With the assistance of his dear ones, the groom offers gifts and other dowry-like items at each entrance so that he may bribe her protectors into retrieving her. It's a jovial experience and a process that could take upwards of an hour. Once the bride is reached, the two lead a procession to the religious site where a beautiful, yet tiring ceremony is held for the entire village to observe. As everyone files out of church, meals prepared by locals are presented on dozens of picnic tables. Thus, a village wedding celebration.

It was an exciting experience traveling with my learned professor and his teaching assistant, both of whom were fluent in Greek, and fellow students. Although locals were friendly, there were no opportunities to intimately absorb their culture. Without this group, however, I realized the depth in which I could learn about a culture *because* I was alone and hospitality was heightened, *because* I am a woman and was assumed to be less of a threat and *because* I am American and most foreigners were curious about me.

The Good

A year later I returned to Europe and traveled solo through most Mediterranean countries. My free apartment in Athens the previous summer was not my only experience with Mediterranean hospitality.

On a bus from Athens to Paris, I met a middle-aged woman and her son. Upon our evening arrival, I began to seek directions for a local youth hostel, whereupon they insisted I stay for the night. They were pleased to have me there and to learn about America while I was just as excited to have an opportunity to see inside life in Paris, so I stayed the duration of my visit.

Soon after my arrival in Rome, I wandered the pension area seeking inexpensive accommodation. It was June, a very busy time in Italy. I repeatedly strolled about the same plaza, above the Spanish Steps and met a man who managed a restaurant there. By midday his empathy for me began to build and he offered an empty apartment in an exclusive area. I declined until the close of the day, feeling defeated. It was a beautiful place, ideally located, FREE and incredibly tranquil.

These two experiences amuse me because now I teach a class on independent travel and cannot refer students to specific accommodations in Paris or Rome. However, I do feel I understand more about life in these cities because of these opportunities.

The Bad

In the Learning Annex class I teach, my typical response to the question, "What are some of the problems of traveling alone as a woman?" goes something like this: "The most significant problem is what comes with being a woman and having a body that menstruates every twenty-eight days. Planning an itinerary around possibly feeling sick and needing tampons and pads is a hassle." Most students expect me to talk about safety or loneliness and are embarrassed as well as surprised at this response.

Every woman is affected differently by her cycle. Up until the past few years, I experienced nausea, dizziness, shortness of breath, extremely painful stomach cramps and every traveler's favorite, diarrhea. My mother recently reminded me of an awful experience in Greece when I had to bite on a towel and twist my hair in order to deflect my attention from the cramps. Needless to say, I revisited Poseidon's temple at Sunion.

Luckily, one horrendous day in Israel I had some good travel buddies care for me. In Indonesia (following my eventful ferry ride) I ended up checking into a five-star hotel to care for myself. The problem is that my weakened body from menstruation had decreased my immunities, so in Israel I got the flu and in Indonesia I almost caught strep throat.

Added to this heartache is the necessity of increased hygiene, which may or may not be available wherever you go. I stock up on modern amenities and have my family ship additional packages when I am on long journeys. In Tanzania I met a woman who climbed Mt. Kilimanjaro just before I met her. She told me of her tedious and difficult five-day climb *without* tampons or pads while she had her period. She managed with a pair of underwear she used in a clever fashion, which was almost as challenging as the five-day inclined walk up the continent's highest mountain.

The Ugly

Women have to be prepared for a level of sexual harassment ordinarily not experienced by men.

Of course, these things may happen no more or less than they do walking through the streets of say Boston or Chicago, while attempting to avoid construction sites and dodge athletic practices. Basic rules of safety should always be followed, male or female, in tandem or alone.

In notoriously machismo societies found in Mediterranean and Latin cultures, harassment can be unbearable. However, there are plenty of locales—the Far East and Scandinavia for example—in which men are discouraged from verbally harassing women in public. In short, it's best either to avoid high risk areas and unpleasant situations, or be aggressive.

We stopped in Bologna at 3 A.M. As the train pulled out, a broad older man opened my door and stood there for some time without moving. This scared me. I wanted him to leave; however, he finally sat in the seat next to the door while closing it tightly shut. "Shit," I thought to myself "no quick escape." Within seconds his pants were unzipped, and I heard the faint sounds of rubbing and rustling clothing. I pretended I was sleeping, then I ineptly attempted to fall asleep. I hoped he would eventually do his thing and it would all be over. What seemed like fifteen minutes passed, and I became petrified that he would jump me—either in frustration or ecstasy.

When this became more than I could bear, I invoked the international communication technique: panicked outrage. No language barriers here. None at all.

"You crazy bastard!" I yelled, "what the hell do you think you are doing? What a disgusting man!" I went next door and plopped myself down between a middle-aged couple in the midst of an exciting (yet ironic) game of hearts while I heard every curse word in broken English imaginable as he disappeared to another car.

Boys Will Be Boys?

This tactic also worked for me in Egypt. After being there about a week, I quickly lost my patience hearing twelve-year-old boys and grown men tell me they wanted to "fuck me" and perform other graphic things.

Men aren't likely to change their behavior, but perhaps boys can still be molded. While walking through a flea market in Luxor, a young boy attempted to either intimidate or excite me with his verbal sexual abilities. I grabbed his wrist, pulled him violently from behind his table into the middle of the street and screamed at him. "You want to *fuck* me do you? Do you even know what it is to *fuck* someone? Do you think I like to hear that garbage? Would you like strange men to say these things to your *mother* or *sister* or to *you?* You should *never* speak to any woman that way. It's disgusting and it's why people don't want to visit this country."

I know my strategy worked because the locals were looking at him with scorn. After all, tourism is Egypt's number one source of income. At the very least, he'll think twice about speaking that way to someone again.

I've Got to Be Meeeee

Being the youngest in my immediate and extended family has always left me easily impressed by my family's opinions. Likewise, being the "social coordinator" among friends resulted in doing what was best for the group and not for me. This time alone helped me discover what truly is important to my development because of me, not my family, not my friends. As a woman, no discovery is greater.

I remember being in Greece when President Bush made the decision to raid Libya. Arguments flew about, whether we should keep out of others' business or play world policeman. With a liberal sister and a conservative brother at home and ten months on the road alone, I know I offered my own political position that day.

Romances far removed from the influences and judgment of family, friends (or anyone else who offers gratuitous dating wisdom) can be quite rewarding. In fact you can learn more about other cultures. A superb thing about traveling alone is discovering yourself socially, politically and even sexually. With the passing of a few weeks or months, influences from home dissipate, and you'll discover underneath more of your own opinions and thoughts. Time is spent exactly as you want it.

No other experience compares. Living alone means you still interact with friends and family. Vacationing alone is so brief one's true self doesn't blossom. Traveling for weeks and months at a time allows for exposure, reflection, self-awareness and eventual growth.

On the Road Again

While sitting on a beach of the Greek island of Rhodes, I was reading *Cosmopolitan* and came upon a two-page perfume spread, which turned out to be a personal omen.

I was in La Scala, a popular crowded night club. Among hundreds of women in one of the largest nightclubs in Greece, Lorenzo extended a few dance moves vaguely in my direction. Then I turned around to sneak a glimpse of the lucky woman who was the recipient of his flirtations and realized it was me he was pursuing. Something like this had never happened to me before, and I wasn't sure if there were unwritten rules I was required to follow.

Italian man meets American woman. He comments on her perfume. They fall in love. Once reunited his first words are about her scent.

Lorenzo was a dream. It's not merely that he was gorgeous— brownish, wavy Roman hair, green hazel eyes, golden skin tone, defined muscular body, dressed like a fashionable Italian—or that his face glowed and eyes sparkled when he spoke English with a sweet Italian accent, but that he had a confident, warm, friendly way of addressing people and doing everything with utmost style.

Initially we danced, first apart and then dirty dancing style. After we worked up an enormous sweat, he offered me a drink at the bar, but I refused, asking only for water. The next thing we knew, it was 3:30 A.M. and his group of Italian friends (some of whom I had met the night before and who had actually introduced us) were going to get something to eat. I was invited. I went along.

At this point, I decided to accept any offer to spend the night with him, afraid of losing a once-in-a-lifetime opportunity since I had already assumed he would be conceited.

In traditional southern European fashion, the night went on and on, but eventually ended with us spending some time alone. We started off skinny-dipping in the moonlight and ended up at his place just near the north coast. It was fun, exciting and romantic.

The next night at the club, Lorenzo came up from behind and wrapped his shapely arms around me while whispering in my ear, "when I showered to go out this evening, my robe had your scent and I *loved* it." It was then that I thought about the *Cosmo* article and realized I was living the dream of many young American women.

I discovered I couldn't have assumed further from the truth about him. Lorenzo was working in Rhodes as a chef in an Italian restaurant (for most Europeans, working, even for a brief moment in August, is sacrilegious). His friends were visiting while I was there, yet he spent as much time with me as he could spare—not in bed at night, but taking me around the island on his dirt bike, double dating with his sister, and making meals for us when the restaurant was empty. I learned he was an intelligent, multifaceted, extremely considerate man. He recently had spent time "at University" and "in the Army" in Italy. His adorable habit of looking up every unknown English word I used, and then using it in a sentence the next day was appealing.

Each night we watched the moon sparkle over the ripples of the Mediterranean Sea from his bedroom window. Each morning we watched the sun warm the colors of the sky with golden orange and yellows. Our time was spent as constructively, energetically and romantically as possible. This was not *Cosmo* magazine advertising perfume, this was me living life!

Places to Go, People to See, Things to Do

Reluctantly, I left the island to meet my sister and her husband in Mykonos. (See what I mean about not having limitations when traveling alone?) They encouraged me to return to Rhodes when they discovered that I had passed up an opportunity to work on a yacht and travel the Mediterranean islands. Additionally, my sister was getting frustrated with my longing expression while pining over Lorenzo. So I did the worst thing imaginable and returned to a fantastic place, where I had experienced a wonderful time weeks earlier, unannounced. I was breaking rule #1 of independent budget travel. (No matter how wonderful a trip might be, the worst thing you could do is return in an effort to recreate the experience.)

Fortunately for me, breaking rules usually pays off. Lorenzo was alone when I knocked on his door at 7 A.M. After an affectionate hug he commented, "I've missed your scent." He asked if I wouldn't mind if he sought work *with* me, if we could get a job on the same boat. (My previous offer would have been a solo stint.) For days we wandered the docks and found a stupendous yacht that would have taken us, but had just been staffed the night before. The passing of a few weeks significantly decreased our employment opportunities. Facing reality, I returned to Athens to attend another Greek wedding with Michele and Marc, and Lorenzo returned to Mantova, Italy. We send Christmas cards every few years.

No article on women traveling alone would be accurate without candidly covering sexual harassment and possible romances while on the road. Women are motivated to travel, and do so alone, because while enduring sexual harassment problems and stumbling upon exciting intercultural romances, one has a myriad of superb, exhilarating, tantalizing, once-in-a-lifetime experiences that joyfully seep into memory forever.

Why, Oh Why?

My first day in China went something like this:

I arrived early in the morning after an overnight boat and train ride, petrified to be alone and in a communist country for the first time in my life. After hanging around fellow travelers and determining we had different itineraries, I walked out of the train station alone looking for a place to shower. That night I had another sixteen-hour train ride to Beijing scheduled to depart at 10 P.M.

I had walked only a few blocks when I was approached by a young Chinese college student. "Hello, can I help you?" He explained how he had followed me since I left the train station. He had lived in San Francisco for a while and spoke English rather well. Assuming my towering height and facial features meant that I probably didn't speak much, if any, Chinese, he decided to make sure I was okay.

We chatted as we walked along the street. Soon, we passed by one of his college buddies and all decided to visit a nearby museum in Canton. Each of them insisted on carrying one of my bags while I walked freely and explored the area and antiquities. When the afternoon tour was over, we parted ways for they had to get to work.

So there I was again, seeking a shower, back in the area near the train station. Deciding to try my luck on a B-class hotel, I approached the manager and offered $5 (what some make in a day) to use a vacant room (that had not been made up yet) for 15 minutes. He declined. Defeated, I left and wandered the adjacent shopping area seeking another hotel. "Hello, can I help you?" she sweetly asked with a smile.

Lena Chin, an adorable sixtyish Chinese woman who works in the travel industry and is fluent in English, tried to help me. She thought perhaps a friend, who owned an establishment not far from where we were, could help. We went for a cup of tea there and while we awaited his arrival at work, she asked me to edit a letter for her that she was writing in English. We had a wonderful time, drinking and talking. He didn't arrive.

Lena insisted that she take me home to shower there and give me a hot meal. More time passed and I accepted her offer, but she wouldn't let me pay the bill before we left.

Her apartment, which she shares with her less able husband, was small and simple, yet clean and cozy. The modest kitchen somehow accommodates a small shower tub. We boiled water and spilled heated pots over my body. This was followed by a hearty and comforting dinner. We parted when she put me in a taxi headed for the station to meet my train. I asked her to write a note to my mother that she had seen and cared for me.

Would these people have been so sympathetic had I been with a companion? I don't know, but that was my first day in Communist China. Alone—yet not alone at all.

Solo and Smiling, Oh Yeah

For me, these rich and rewarding experiences far outweigh the unique risks of traveling alone as a woman.

Hospitality—Constant travel partners are less apt to be invited to the home of a local or to an island ceremony. Hospitality is heightened for those who travel alone, more so for the seemingly less threatening female.

Freedom—Freedom is in its truest form when the world is yours to explore alone. The independence is a tremendous experience and one not limited to travel.

A Reason to Go—Everyone has their own catalyst that propels them into the world of travel. For me it was being born of immigrant grandparents and having grown up in a neighborhood where one's nationality is important, no matter what it is. Without these elements in my life, perhaps I never would have left Commack, Long Island (N.Y.) to discover more about my heritage and ultimately, unintentionally, me. I will forever be thankful.

Women and their travel experiences will always be different from men's; at times there seems to be no difference at all.

N

W

E

FLYING AS AN INTERNATIONAL AIR COURIER

Ben's Story

Ben, a thirty-year-old Manhattan-based salesperson, was under the gun. Management was frowning, constantly demanding higher sales, busier telemarketing and more aggressive client cold calling—*or else*. Ben, vowing to improve the situation, was operating on a self-deluded auto pilot. Quotas had rendered him unable to realize that his heart wasn't in this job. (*He hated it, actually*.)

Ben adjusted his work ethic, increasing personal telephone calls, visits to record stores, diners, movie theaters, his friends' offices and anywhere else having nothing to do with selling. He played hide-and-seek with his company until one March morning when he got fired. After surrendering to his manager and visiting the pile of pulp on his desk for the last time, he stepped onto the street. The sudden sense of freedom was overwhelming.

A friend had told Ben about flying cheap as an air courier. A few phone calls later he was booked on a flight to Bangkok, Thailand, departing the next day. Round-trip airfare was $199 for a two-week stay. (Ben didn't realize that these frequent flyer miles would later reward him with a free domestic flight.) Even more difficult than last-minute packing was explaining the sudden shift of events to friends and family. They believed he was running away from a problem. Ben begged to differ.

Two surrealistic days after the career hiatus, Ben was drinking a beer (cold bottle for 80 cents) with his new comrades, a Swede, a Canadian and an Australian, at an outdoor cafe on Bangkok's famed Khao San Road. The entire street is a mecca of music-playing cafes (meals for $1–$2), guest houses ($3–$10 a night), featuring nightly videos bars, shops, travel agencies and money changers all eager to assist off-the-beaten-path travelers. After discussing adventure plans with the international consortium, he decided to ride a bus north to Chiang Mai, rent a motorcycle ($35 a week) and visit the fascinating hill-tribe villages tucked away in the hazy mountains.

Later that week Ben was having lunch with a Thai family (spanning four generations) in a remote trailside village he had discovered near the Burmese border. Seated on a woven bamboo floor inside of their stilted teakwood home, he attempted to describe his Manhattan lifestyle until pausing to chuckle. The thought of sweating in a business suit while riding cramped in a urine-scented subway car suddenly seemed hilarious.

The Facts about Air Couriers

Couriers do not transport drugs. They do not ride in the cargo section of the aircraft. Couriers are not handcuffed to their shipments. Now I've answered the most *infamous* questions regarding courier travel.

What Does a Courier Company Do? Air couriers provide high-speed delivery service around the world. When Federal Express, DHL or the other express carriers aren't fast enough, shippers look to air couriers.

Courier companies purchase blocks of round-trip coach tickets in advance from airlines so their customers' packages (documents, computer discs, film, etc.) can fly as your baggage, and they can take advantage of the same expedited international customs clearance procedures as regular passenger luggage. Courier shipments can be anything time sensitive that can't be e-mailed or faxed. If courier shipments flew as regular cargo, they would be subject to time-consuming customs bureaucracy including duty, tax, inspection and possibly pilferage. *Some* countries require entry bribes. When a package is sent minus courier accompaniment, it is processed as regular international freight to be inspected and cleared in the customs house before being released for delivery. The courier procedure nearly guarantees an expedited customs clearance.

The on-board courier (OBC) flies as a passenger on commercial airlines and checks in the courier baggage as personal baggage. As passengers, they are able to avoid earlier flight closeout times associated with cargo handling or small package services that are strictly controlled by the airlines.

On arrival at the destination, the baggage is immediately cleared through customs at the passenger terminal. This streamlined and routine procedure saves an enormous amount of time when compared with shipments traveling in dedicated aircraft, which must undergo a lengthy procedure of inspection, documentation, handling and final clearance.

Air courier companies are established, legitimate businesses. You will not be escorting any illegal contraband. The Air Courier Conference of America (ACCA) is dedicated to upholding high standards in the industry. Even if illegal contraband is found in the shipments, couriers are not allowed to touch the baggage and will not be held personally liable for it. Also, customs officers know that the courier does not touch any of the shipments and that they were inspected and manifested by the courier company prior to departure. To be ultra safe, prior to departure you can verify with the courier company what precautions they take on behalf of the courier such as bonding and insurance.

Courier companies typically sell only round-trip fares. They offset part of the ticket costs by charging couriers a percentage of the actual fare. Couriers are discounted a large portion of their ticket cost for giving up their luggage space to the courier company, who make the majority of their profits by charging their shipping customers by the pound. Traditionally, trips to Europe were for a seven-day stay and trips to Asia and South America were for two weeks. The trend is becoming longer stays with open-ended itineraries.

Supply-and-demand also dictates ticket cost. Depending upon advance registrations, the inability to sell tickets or another courier's cancellation, prices vary between 50 and 85 percent off the normal ticket price. In the most extreme cases, the ticket is free. Travelers ready to travel on a moments' notice receive the best deals by either signing onto a courier company's last-minute emergency list or by calling in frequently for updates.

A courier can fly as frequently as she or he desires. While accompanying courier packages, you are a freelance courier similar to an independent contractor (not an employee). The courier does not come into contact with the "load" and fly as if they were a full-paying passenger. A representative from the courier company will meet the courier prior to departure at the airport or at the courier company's office adjacent to the airport. A courier company representative will handle all of the baggage.

In most cases, you will be instructed to meet a representative of the courier company at the airline counter inside the airport. He or she can be identified by either a uniform, hat with a logo, a badge or a predetermined article of clothing. The representative will give you your airline ticket, further instructions and a manifest of the courier shipments. The courier bags you accompany weigh up to 70 pounds each and travel in the baggage compartment of the aircraft. The only thing you actually carry for the courier company is a document pouch containing the manifest, baggage claims and your arrival instructions. The manifest lists the exact contents of the load. The pouch normally weighs less than 3 pounds and should be kept with you at all times.

Attached to the courier's ticket will be several baggage claim tags, which correspond to the courier company's consolidated "master" bags in transit. Upon landing, another representative from the courier company meets the courier at a pre-designated spot (after the courier clears immigration) to receive the manifest pouch and retrieve the cargo. Do not leave the customs area without meeting the courier company representative. If you can't locate a representative, call one of the phone numbers listed in your information packet. The scheduled return, usually one or two weeks later, proceeds in the same manner. Courier companies usually request that you call them the day before the flight to reconfirm the details.

Because the courier company uses your luggage space to transport their cargo, you are restricted to a maximum of one or sometimes two carry-on bags. Some airlines will allow you to check a bag for free. Other airlines will charge you their standard excess baggage fee. If you have more than a carry-on bag, ask the ticket agent if you can check a bag at no extra cost. If the plane isn't full, they may oblige. Otherwise, you'll have to pay. Keep it simple by packing light.

One tactic for skipping excess baggage fees, especially if you are traveling to a chilly destination, is to wear any heavy or bulky clothing and boots when boarding the plane. This clothing, that wouldn't fit into your carry-on bags, can be removed once the flight is in the air and stored in a handy plastic bag. Flight attendants can always find a place for one more bag.

Nearly all travel is on major carriers, and frequent flyer miles can be rewarded on the actual international carrier or on their domestic flying partner. Most international carriers have U.S. domestic airline frequent flyer partners.

Courier companies develop their passenger rosters up to three months in advance. To secure an advanced booking, it's best to call early in the month. Whatever your intention, the best time to call courier companies is one-half hour after they open in the morning. Collegiate courier travel soars in the summer. Since supply-and-demand dictates ticket price, summer specials can be limited. On the other hand, global events such as war and natural disaster tend to free up many courier schedules. Customer service is not a priority with many courier companies, so make it clear that you are an informed courier candidate (that is, once you've finished this section!), and you will get better service.

As I mentioned, couriers are not handcuffed to their shipments. This image, known as a hand-carry shipment, rarely occurs for the freelance courier. A hand-carry shipment is transported in the possession of one person from shipment to delivery point. Firms, such as Tiffany's and Sotheby's, that move precious cargo tend to send their own employees on such missions. Retail companies often reward their own employees with a hand-carry delivery "vacation." Freelance couriers probably won't stumble into many hand-carry delivery situations.

Companion Scenarios

Sometimes, dual travelers can benefit from courier travel. Here are four options:

1. Fly on the same day or alternate days with one company.
2. Fly on the same day or alternate days with different companies.
3. Fly on the same day or alternate days from different cities.
4. One traveler flies as courier, other traveler pays excursion fare. Split the difference.

♠ Courier Flights within Courier Flights

As the courier industry continues to relax the requirements on length of stay, it becomes easier to fly with foreign courier companies while on a U.S.-based courier trip. London, another courier hub, is especially handy for double-leg courier expeditions. If you have the time, look into flying from London (or any other hub city) as a courier to other destinations.

Foreign cities, such as London, also present the opportunity to purchase inexpensive airline tickets with no penalty for last-minute reservations.

A Step-by-Step Guide to Flying As an Air Courier

First, choose a courier company according to the destinations it services. Then, check available dates and prices for selected destinations, or choose from a list of last-minute flights. The best flight selections are available early in the month. Next, pay for your round-trip flight (and, in some cases a membership fee) with a credit card, cash or money order. Some firms also require that you fax a copy of your passport. Generally flights are non-refundable. Some companies will give you a partial refund if you cancel more than four weeks in advance. If you plan to travel with a companion, check on other flights available that day or those arriving on consecutive days and reserve accordingly.

As per directions from the courier company, meet their representative at company headquarters or at the airport several hours before departure. Receive the airline ticket. Arrive with one (maybe two) carry-on bags and pick up the baggage claim and manifests for the packages you are accompanying. The courier representative will also give you the necessary documentation for customs and your return-flight instructions.

When you arrive at your destination, give the baggage claim and documents to the courier representative who will be waiting for you. Call to check in with the courier company the business day before your return-flight date. If you are not accompanying any packages on the trip back, you can usually check in the standard baggage allotment.

Courier flights originate from the major U.S. gateway airports:

New York	Los Angeles
Boston	San Francisco
Chicago	Dallas
Miami	Houston
Washington, D.C.	Seattle
	Montreal

Here's a list of popular overseas courier destinations:

Amsterdam	Monte Video
Bangkok	Panama City
Brussels	Paris
Buenos Aires	Rio de Janeiro
Cairo	Rome
Caracas	Santiago
Dublin	Sao Paulo
Frankfurt	Seoul
Geneva	Singapore
Hong Kong	Stockholm
London	Sydney
Madrid	Taipei
Melbourne	Tel Aviv
Mexico City	Tokyo
Milan	Zurich

There is courier travel to other cities (i.e., Delhi, Bombay); however, they tend to use company employees as couriers and require fluency in the particular language.

This is an example of a courier-trip cost breakdown of a one-week courier trip to London from New York:

$50 transportation to airport using an auto driveaway (See North America chapter).

$50 allocation for bus or gas round-trip between your home and airport ($50 not applicable from cities near courier companies)

$159 round-trip airfare New York–London

$350 expenses at $50 per day for 6 days

$609 total

Courier Service Listings

See Appendix 1 for courier companies and the destinations they service. Appendix 1 also lists auto driveaway companies, which can provide inexpensive driving options for those who don't live close to a city with courier companies. Also, look under "Air Courier" or "Air Transport" in the *Yellow Pages* of any city with an international airport.

Considerations

Dress neatly: Present yourself as someone an immigration agent would let into his or her country!

- Always inquire about the courier company's last-minute flight specials, and join the frequent flyer club of the airline you fly with and provide the necessary information when checking in.

- You must be at least 18 years old (a few courier firms request that the courier be at least 21) and have a valid passport. Ensure that you get a visa if required. Ask the courier company.
- Be prepared to pay airport taxes in both directions. It is not always included in your fare.

What to Ask the Courier Company

When you call an air courier company, it may be helpful to have a list of questions at hand so that you don't forget to ask something:

1. Are there any courier cancellations today?
2. Do you have any last-minute specials?
3. Do you keep a list of couriers available for last-minute departures?
4. Which cities do you fly to?
5. On which days of the week do you fly to _____?
6. Is the return schedule flexible?
7. Can I check a personal bag without paying an excess baggage fee?
8. Is the price negotiable?
9. Is a deposit necessary? (Sometimes leaving a $100 check deposit is required.)

PART 4

CIRCLING THE ASIAN PACIFIC RIM

Have you ever flown cross-country or to Europe and yearned to carry on? Perhaps someone else on your flight was heading for Bali, Kathmandu or Buenos Aires and you assumed they must be prosperous. *Wrong.* For as little as $1,200 you can circumnavigate the Earth. As you read the two subsequent chapters, keep in mind that only your imagination (and a few disgruntled politicians) limit your globetrotting prospects.

Pete's Story

Pete couldn't find work as a journalist. Granted, he had written extensively in college for student publications, but the search for a salaried position was a futile one. His financial condition degenerating, Pete migrated home to launch an all-out job hunt and began leaning into piles of newspaper classified debris. He was eventually enticed to interview for a position peddling ad space in a lawn-care trade paper. Otherwise, no other compelling offers surfaced.

Mr. Melancholy took hold. Pete's cohorts were opting for careers as salespeople or insurance brokers, had completed training programs, been placed in jobs, given company cars and were taking people on dates. "The only writing I'm qualified to do," Pete noted, "is on what compels an unemployed person to vault in front of a dump truck."

Finally, a newspaper requested writing samples. He landed the job, moved to Connecticut, set up his stereo and reported for work. The pay was low but he grasped the business. His assignments involved covering local bake-offs, entertainment at the senior living centers and the student elections at a nearby high school. He managed to sock away a bit of cash with modest sacrifices, such as heat that winter, and by substituting happy-hour snacks for supper.

Meanwhile, Pete had a friend wandering in Southeast Asia who sent him bizarre postcards that strived to allure him to the exotic jungles and beaches along the Pacific Rim (*where it was difficult to spend more than $10 a day*). After working late one evening on a review of a toddlers' band practice, he received yet another postcard from beyond and decided to join his roving comrade—the dawn of an odyssey he would eventually transcribe with passion. With the guarded blessings of friends and family, he purchased a circle-the-Pacific-Rim ticket sequence from an airline consolidator—visiting Los Angeles, Hawaii and then hunting down his partner in Japan. His circumstances would never be the same.

About the Asian Pacific Rim

Stadium-loads of Americans visit Europe annually, mobbing the Eurail network, yowling about *Baywatch*, the Knicks and keg bashes. But, Europe's allure comes with a hefty

price tag. Contemplate the cheaper, truly mind-expanding adventure option of visiting the third world, visiting exotic countries that demand a fraction of the cash required to assail Europe. Interacting with non-western cultures will transfigure your outlook, leaving you unable to perceive the ol' U.S.A. as you once had.

No region on earth is growing faster or expanding its role in international affairs more quickly than the Asian community of nations. From Japan and New Zealand in the East to the Central Asian republics and Iran in the West, this region is home to three billion people, more than half the world's population. Relations between the Asia-Pacific countries and the United States are becoming closer but more complex. To the offbeat wanderer, this means: Visit traditional Asia before its gone.

The Pacific Rim is a term referring to the countries lining the western shores of the Pacific Ocean. Australia, New Zealand and the coastal countries of North and Southeast Asia comprise most of the Pacific Rim. Visiting several countries along the Pacific Rim is easy for *pilgrims* on tight budgets if they take advantage of the commercial airlines' regular stopovers. Capitalism is exploding throughout Asia, so the twenty-bucks-a-week days are gone (unless you really dig). Regardless, circling the Pacific Rim using a series of flights purchased from an airline ticket consolidator will always prove to be an amazing cultural wake-up call. Depending upon the time of year, you can enjoy beautiful weather on a Pacific Rim tour by touring in either a north or south direction.

The Countries

Australia

Everyone wants to visit Australia. This is understandable, for it's an amazing westernized country. Like America, Australia is a far-fetched byproduct of British and other European colonization. Australia and New Zealand need to be explored, but if you're spending the time and funds to soar to the other side of our sphere, it would be a pity to forego beholding the nearby Asian terrain (such as Indonesia or Fiji).

Indonesia, for instance, affords explorers an alluring array of cultures, landscapes and islands, for a pittance of what you'd spend in Australia. Take advantage of your latitude and longitude if you visit Australia or New Zealand.

Japan

Few foreigners visit Japan. With a population of 125 million, it is the third most populous nation in East Asia (economically the largest). Yet, it ranks just twenty-fifth as an international destination, well behind Thailand, China and even the minute Portuguese colony of Macao, near Hong Kong. Because of the astronomical costs, Americans lucky enough to visit Japan usually go on business or seeking employment. If you decide to go, you need a budget game plan.

The trip from Narita airport into Tokyo can set you back what it would cost you to live in India for two months. Voyagers' word of mouth and a shoestring guidebook will point you to inexpensive lodging and street-corner noodle shops. Crime is practically non-existent, and hitchhiking is very easy.

Don't fret if you lose your way. Japanese people tend to be hospitable to the point where it can become awkward for a westerner. It is common for a Japanese person to personally escort a tourist to the proper train or accommodation. One traveler saw it this way: Ask a Japanese person for directions and they may reply, "Wait a moment while I go quit my job so I may best assist you!" Young Japanese students are instructed how to greet tourists and are encouraged to improve their English by engaging in conversation with foreigners.

For the Japanese, there is no doubt that the United States is a kind of dream destination. Kindness prevails toward Americans in Japan. While some folks are still fighting the Civil War back in the States, the Japanese steer clear of topics involving World War II. Gift-giving is a ritual in Japan, with the giver offering "a silly little thing" and the recipient hesitating to accept such a magnificent present.

A budget traveler in Japan will likely live on a diet of noodles. There are two basic types: *soba* (thin spaghetti-sized noodles) and *udon* (thick, chunky noodles).

China

China can be a very rough place to travel. It also can a great place for travelers to have clothes tailor-made, browse bizarre markets and enjoy conveniences such as straight-razor shaves.

Flying on any of China's domestic carriers can be a hassle and occasionally dangerous. Limited fleets, often lacking computerized reservation systems can result in your getting bumped even if you have a confirmed reservation. The planes vary from older Russian aircraft to new Boeing. A shortage of skilled pilots and maintenance personnel contribute to the infamous problems of "difficult" customer service personnel.

Have notes of "survival questions" written for you in Chinese by people who are bilingual, especially to ease transportation ticket purchases.

Young Japanese students are occasionally subject to an interesting attention-getting device. The teacher, armed with a tennis ball, plays catch with random students as the class progresses. The unalert student, not ready for the incoming ball, is soon snapped out of their daydream.

In Chinese history, disasters are said to foretell the end of dynasties or the deaths of great leaders. Many Chinese saw the Tangshan earthquake (1976) as an omen of Mao Tse-tung's passing (he died a short time after the quake), just as some Chinese believed that the quake in Kobe, Japan (1995) presaged the death of Prime Minister Deng.

The Changing Life of a Dog in China

Once seen here only as a source of food, dogs are the newest status symbol in China, another sign of this country's embrace of capitalism and the things that money can buy. A 1994 government survey found that six of ten city dwellers already have a television set, a refrigerator and a washing machine. For many newly affluent urban families, a pet dog comes next on the list.

Nowhere are dogs more of a passion than in Shanghai, a metropolis of 13 million people that is China's biggest, richest and most cosmopolitan city. With the opening up of the economy, Shanghai has reclaimed its role as the country's financial capital. However, the enthusiasm of Shanghai's dog owners is not shared by the poorer rural regions or by the old-line Communists who still run the country. Because

Hong Kong

Excellent medical and dental care is available. Plenty of fast-food restaurants to binge in following a "limited delicacy" adventure in China.

Indonesia

Nearly 80 percent of Bali's population make a living in one form of the arts. Women sit sidesaddle on scooters.

Singapore

Ultra clean and controlled society. Excellent medical and dental care available.

Thailand

Northern mountains motorcycle tour—southern Thai party-leisure scene. Regulations on vehicle emissions and traffic-alleviating construction is supposedly in the works.

Vietnam

Big boom in tourism (on the heels of Thailand). Great food, people and beaches, with a lingering French-colonial flair.

Impressions

As a college student I didn't even know how to spell "the Philippines." I didn't know that Argentina was quite similar to a European country. I couldn't have imagined that an acupuncture treatment I received in China would fix my back. I had no idea that I would become a huge fan of Indian food. I did not expect to learn how to play the guitar in Indonesia.

Here are some ideas of what you may expect to find while circling the Asian Pacific Rim. This is what lingers in my thoughts of visiting these places.

Burma—time warp. Military dictatorship ruling peaceful Buddhist citizens.

Hawaii—my first exposure to Japanese culture; lushness.

Japan—kind, helpful people (who gave subway directions).

Taiwan—families cruising on mopeds.

Hong Kong—good food; multidimensional; the gateway to China; the Times Square of Asia.

Thailand—luxury; rice in leaf bundles; leisure subculture.

Malaysia—curious mix of Malays, Indians and Chinese; guard geese (Muslims don't have dogs). (I was struck by loneliness.)

Singapore—ultra sterile; good medical treatment.

Indonesia—wonderful music and art; motorbiking; great food.

Korea—dried crustacean snacks.

China—endlessness.

Australia—gut-level hospitality; jealous that the United States steals their talent.

New Zealand—environmentally conscious; lots of sheep.

Tahiti—$12 for a Heineken.

A special appreciation for music, dance and gym class in every country.

Airline Ticket Consolidators

These ticket brokers, sometimes called "bucket-shops" or "ultra-airline discounters" buy blocks of unsold coach or economy seats from the major commercial airlines. When an airline's lowest fares can't fill their planes, ticket prices are slashed again and then "dumped" onto a consolidator. Individual, one-way flight segments are linked together, producing a continuous string of flights in one direction (usually either around-the-world or Pacific Rim loops) and resold to the public. In most cases, several different airlines are used. There are unbelievable multidestination deals sold by consolidators, with unlimited routing possibilities.

Because the consolidators resell unsold tickets below market value for commercial and charter airlines, the airlines don't readily admit that they sell tickets to consolidators. Consolidators don't normally name the airlines in their promotions, so you have to call them for airline information. Consolidator tickets are not in regular travel agency reservation computers until you make a reservation. The airlines themselves advertise around-the-world fares, but they are expensive and can be quite inept at helping you build an itinerary.

Because consolidators have wholesale contracts with the airlines, they can give adventure travelers the advantage of utilizing the multiple stops along airline routes. You are entitled to your confirmed seat like any full-paying passenger. You cannot be denied boarding if a flight is oversold.

Shop around: bargaining exists! Research your options by bidding for a price quote on the same itinerary to several different consolidators. To get an idea of how low an around-the-world consolidator's unpublished fare is, price an airline or travel agent on a round-trip ticket to any country on your eventual itinerary. Normally, round-trip flights between North America and *one* Asian city cost at least $1,200. Also, consolidators usually sell one-way tickets for slightly more than half the lowest round-trip fare, whereas the airlines' one-way fares tend to cost as much as the round-trip fare!

most of these pet dogs are illegal in the eyes of municipal officials, unlicensed dogs can be either carried away in cages for medical experimentation or they are killed on the spot by "dog-beating teams."

The Communist leaders have always gone easier on cats, mostly because they are less of a drain on the food supply—and, like dogs, are often used as food themselves. But dogs have never fared well anywhere in modern China. After the Communists took control of the country in 1949, pet dogs were banned as a symbol of decadence, a criminal extravagance at a time of food shortages. If they were good for anything, it was dinner. Dog meat remains a common dish in China and in a number of other Asian countries, including South Korea and Vietnam. (Foreign tourists are seldom served dog meat by mistake, because the Chinese regard it as a delicacy.)

• Throughout Asia the hand motion for signifying "come here" seems like "go away."

• *Tuk-tuks* are golf carts with steel roofs used for overland travel.

• Markets in third-world countries are groups of vendors sitting atop their goods.

In most cases, tickets purchased from consolidators are good for one year. Advance purchase minimum is thirty days; the maximum is six months. A consolidator can accommodate the traveler leaving on short notice, but they may need to pick up some of their forwarded tickets from travel agents en route. You generally proceed in one general direction along the Pacific Rim (or east or west on a circle-the-globe tour, which is covered in the next part). I recommend booking advanced reservations for the entire trip and changing your itinerary, if necessary, as you proceed. You may not be aware of holidays or political events in a foreign country that could make securing a spontaneous reservation difficult.

Separate round-trip flights to destinations branching off of your basic routing can also be booked by your consolidator. Airline tickets for side trips that may be recommended by other travelers can also be purchased as you go. You never know who you'll meet! Chances are also good that you'll decide to travel overland within and between countries.

Some nomads guarantee flexibility by purchasing only spur-of-the-moment one-way flight segments on a whim. Moving with a continuously evolving itinerary is the ultimate freedom. However, as this type of travel becomes more popular, and if the dollar loses ground abroad, purchasing airline tickets as you go can add up quickly. Travel agents in London, Amsterdam, Hong Kong, Bangkok and Penang, Malaysia, who were once famous for their great airfare deals, are becoming more competitive.

Check out the consolidator of your choice with their local Better Business Bureau to see if there have been any complaints levied against them. Pay with a credit card to simplify any ticket reissues or refunds. If you lose your airline tickets en route and did not purchase the tickets with a credit card or purchase insurance covering ticket loss, you must deal directly with the individual airlines for reissues (and possibly a $50-per-ticket reissue fee).

Often, "non-refundable" is stated on consolidator tickets if the regular fare is printed, as opposed to what you paid. This airline safeguard prevents you from turning in a ticket for profit. If you cancel a flight and want a refund, you must go through the consolidator or their agent. Always understand your refund policy with each airline you fly (if you carry a U.S. passport, avoid Iraqi airlines for obvious reasons). Ask your consolidator for a copy of the refund policy in writing before you buy.

Some consolidators are strictly wholesale, distributing discount tickets only to retail travel agencies. The consolidators featured in this book are either combination wholesaler-retailers or strictly retailers. Consolidators are usually not "full-service" travel agents, so you may feel rushed. Hang in there! It takes time to design your ultimate planet-circling odyssey.

Possible Disadvantages of Using a Consolidator

Discounted tickets sometimes do not qualify for advanced seating arrangements.

Tickets are only good for the issuing airline. So if you miss your flight or it is delayed or canceled, your ticket may not be honored by another airline. However, a bit of pleading with airline personnel can often produce results.

Some airlines do not accept frequent flyer miles from tickets purchased through consolidators. However, with a little persistence, you can accumulate frequent flyer miles with tickets purchased from a consolidator. Try submitting your boarding passes to various reservation agents in the terminal or city office until your miles are credited. If this fails, mail boarding passes to the airline's frequent flyer club.

Normally, you can't upgrade a discounted ticket by paying a surcharge. But, if the regular fare is printed on the ticket, upgrading is worth a try.

Occasionally there are crowded flights with inconvenient departure or arrival times.

Destinations That Don't Overextend Your ATM Card

Anywhere in Asia, especially in China and India, with the exception of Japan and Singapore. Turkey and Pakistan are safe and cheap Muslim countries. Generally the cheaper the country, the more mind-blowing the experience. Africa is a one-year trip itself. The Soviet Republic can be cheap, but there can be major logistical and bureaucratic hassles. Traveling in South America can also be a bargain, but airfare is expensive. Here is an example of a mid-pricey trip to Nepal:

> Exchange rate: $1 = 51 rupees
> Tea houses (along the trekking routes): $.50–$2 (double)
> Meals: $.50–$2
> Quart of San Miguel beer (in festive Kathmandu): $.90–$1.40
> Trekking equipment rental (down jacket/sleeping bag): $1.50 a day
> Porter or guide: $5 per day divided by three people
> Total trekking expenses (3 weeks): $210

Here are some side-trip suggestions:
- After trekking in Nepal, hit the beaches of Thailand. There's great contrast in terrain between Nepal's Himalayas and southern Thailand's exotic island beaches. (Like a cheap Club Med if you're so inclined.)
- From Taiwan fly China Airlines (not CACC) into Tokyo (Hameda) instead of facing the hassles of Narita.
- Fly from Darwin, Australia, to Kupang, Indonesia, for approximately $120.

Student Travel Organizations

You are entitled to student discounts if you are under 25 or under 35 within three years of graduation You can get discount cards from nonprofit organizations dedicated to the pursuit of work, study and travel abroad: International Student Identity Card (ISIC), International Tourist Card (ITC), International Youth Card (IYC) and Hostelling International (HI) cards. Charter flights, discount rail passes, accommodations and guidebooks. See the index. For specific, local information contact your university registrar office.

Routing Suggestions

General Rules Concerning Possible Routings

Routing directions can sometimes be reversed for the same or slightly higher fare. Seasonality is one reason for *reversing direction* of a routing.

It is assumed in most routing that you would prefer *changeable* itineraries. *This term applies to dates or times of travel only,* not routing or airline changes; any routing changes after tickets have been issued are considered refunds and rebookings, and applicable penalties will be charged. In many cases, however, you may bypass a city on an itinerary without penalty if the airline offers such a segment. In some cases, it may even be possible to obtain a lower fare if you can positively fix your dates and times of travel.

If you do not live in a major coastal North American city, your fare will be adjusted from or to your city. You can start one of these journeys from ANYWHERE in the listed routings or anywhere in the world! If you are originating on the U.S. West Coast, your trans-Pacific fare will be lower, but your trans-Atlantic portion will make up for it, so the cost will be close to the proposed routing.

Combining different routings is possible if you like part of one itinerary and part of another. Fares will be adjusted.

Airlines used in each routing are on carriers providing the lowest economy- or coach-class fares. Substitutions may be made, but will most likely increase the cost—some nominally, some drastically. Tickets are usually non-endorsable to other carriers unless otherwise stated.

It must be stressed that *the fare designated to each routing can and will change without notice.* Be sure to verify the price before sending in payment. Furthermore, because of the strict advance purchase requirements of some fares and possible delays in obtaining tickets, the consolidators request as much advance notice as possible.

The following routings are the most frequently traveled, using the least expensive airlines. The consolidators use only major domestic and international carriers. If you prefer to use different airlines, it may affect the airfare. The departure cities featured here are New York, San Francisco and Los Angeles (West Coast departure: San Francisco or Los Angeles). Departure from any domestic city is possible and typically won't increase the airfare much.

As you study the different routings, keep in mind that these itineraries are samples of unlimited routing combinations. You may customize your own routing or request different airlines. Almost any itinerary is possible. Most routings are subject to seasonality. Children's fares are usually 67 percent of the cost of an adult fare. Also available are business class and group fares. All fares are subject to change without prior notice.

Circle-the-Pacific-Rim Routing Suggestions

West Coast Departures

$1,099	West Coast–Hong Kong–Bangkok–Jakarta–Yogyakarta–Bali–Biak–Hawaii–Los Angeles
$1,499	West Coast–Hawaii–Biak–Bali–Yogyakarta–Jakarta–Singapore–Bangkok–Hong Kong–West Coast
$1,599	West Coast–Hawaii–Auckland–Sydney–surface–Perth–Kuala Lumpur–Tokyo–Los Angeles
$1,599	West Coast–Tokyo or Taipei or Hong Kong–Bangkok–Singapore–Auckland–Figi–Cook Islands–Tahiti–Los Angeles
$1,599	West Coast–Tokyo or Taipei or Hong Kong–Bangkok–Sydney–Auckland–Hawaii–West Coast (Bali + $100)
$1,599	West Coast–Tokyo–Hong Kong–Bangkok–Brunei–Darwin–surface–Sydney–Auckland–Hawaii–West Coast

$1,599	West Coast–Tahiti–Cook Islands–Figi–Auckland–surface–Christchurch–Melbourne–Sydney–Hawaii–West Coast
$1,699	Los Angeles–Tahiti–Figi–Auckland–Singapore–surface–Bangkok–Manila–Hawaii–West Coast
$1,699	West Coast–Tokyo–Hong Kong–Bangkok–Singapore–Jakarta–Yogyakarta–Bali–Perth or Darwin–surface–Sydney–Auckland–Hawaii–West Coast
$1,799	West Coast–Tokyo or Taipei–Hong Kong–Bangkok–Singapore–Port Moresby–Cairns–surface–Sydney–Auckland–Hawaii–West Coast
$1,799	West Coast–Bali–Jakarta–Singapore–Australia (3 stops)–West Coast

East Coast Departures (New York)

$1,099–$1,799	New York–West Coast–any West Coast routing
$1,499	New York–Hong Kong–Bangkok–surface–Singapore–Jakarta–Bali–Hawaii–Los Angeles–New York
$1,749	New York–Los Angeles–Hawaii–Bali–Singapore–Bangkok–Hong Kong–Taipei–Anchorage–New York
$1,850	New York–Hong Kong–Bangkok–surface–Singapore–Bali or Brunei–Darwin–surface–Sydney–Auckland–Hawaii–West Coast–New York
$1,899	New York–Hong Kong or Taipei–Bangkok–Sydney–Auckland–Hawaii–West Coast–New York (Bali + $100)
$1,999	New York–Hong Kong–Bangkok–Singapore–Darwin–Cairns–Brisbane–Sydney–Christchurch–surface–Auckland–Hawaii–West Coast–New York
$2,199	New York–Beijing–surface–Hong Kong–Saigon–Bangkok–Bali–Cairns–Melbourne–Auckland–San Francisco–New York

Reservations

Tickets are valid for six months to one year from the date of issue. Certain tickets may have limited validity. Most sectors of your trip can either be reserved or left open, depending upon your itinerary, season of travel or length of stay. It is best to reserve your entire trip in advance when traveling in high season within time limits. This ensures both individual departures on specific dates and the completion of your trip on time. With the exception of your first international flight, almost all other flights can be left open dated. A change of your first international reservation can result in a penalty. Your remaining confirmed flights can be changed free of charge by contacting the airlines involved while you are en route.

It is essential that you reconfirm all your onward or return international flights at least seventy-two hours prior to departure by contacting the airline concerned. Failure to do so may result in the cancellation of your reservations. Always cancel any reservations you don't plan to use. Your length of stay in any one country is up to you, visa time requirements and the availability of flights per week on the particular airline.

One-month advance purchase is usually required, however, I've seen ticket brokers pull routings together in a few days. It is best to purchase tickets as soon as your plans are set. Once you are ticketed, you are protected against price increases. Some travelers prefer to pick up pre-paid tickets from the local agents of their consolidator while they are en route.

Cancellation and Refund

Paying with a credit card is highly recommended, as it simplifies refunds (certain gold credit cards offer full replacement protection against lost airline tickets). Traditionally there is a 30-percent cancellation penalty on the refundable amount of the tickets. Refunds are only given on unused tickets; partially used tickets are nonrefundable. Refunds can take up to six months or more. In the case of lost tickets not purchased on a gold credit card, you must deal with the individual airlines. Some airlines charge ticket-reissue fees or even require a completely new ticket purchase (China Airlines), and refunds are dealt with once the lost ticket expires. Travel insurance is worth considering.

Travel Insurance

Inexpensive, comprehensive programs provide refunds if you cancel your trip for any reason. Lost tickets and other scenarios are covered as well. Trip insurance companies are suggested in Appendix 1.

Important: Quoted fares don't always correspond with availability. Always call for a specific fare quote for your specific dates and destinations.

Locally, look under "Airline Ticket Consolidators" in the *Yellow Pages* of major cities. If a consolidator does not list a toll-free number, call toll-free information at (800) 555-1212 and get it. Always check the Sunday paper travel sections for new or discounted routings. Beware: Not all consolidators are legitimate. Do not buy a stolen or unauthorized ticket. One way to ensure legitimacy is to hold full payment until tickets are in your possession. Again, remember to inquire with the Better Business Bureau about any company's reputation. (See Appendix 1 for consolidator listings.)

Climate Concerns

These extended trips are obviously not for the weekend warrior, nor are they likely for anyone convinced they are entitled only to two or three weeks of holiday per year. The best time to embrace a mega-adventure is before college, during a year off from college, after graduation, "gaps" in employment (induced or voluntary), between geographic relocations, retirement or whenever you're committed. Climate is also something to consider when planning your adventure. Actually, the best time to go is whenever you want to go.

One of the most important factors in determining whether you choose to circle the globe or the Pacific should be the time of year you will be touring. At certain times of the year, certain destinations are popular, and advance reservations are recommended. Europe, for example, has its high season from June through September, whereas Australia and New Zealand have their high season from November until April. December is the month requiring the most advance booking for all destinations.

Here are a few general world weather rules:
- More rainfall and lower temperatures in mountain regions.
- Greater extremes in temperatures in inland regions.
- Most rainfall and more temperate climates in coastal areas.
- Don't expect to hear weather reports in non-Western countries.
- The farther away a region is located from the equator, the bigger the difference there is between the length of days. In the Northern Hemisphere the days become longer from January through June (the higher the altitude the longer the days). Also, the twilight periods last longer. The Southern Hemisphere mirrors these factors during these months, with the shortest days in June. Along the equator the length of days are always

the same, with a very short twilight period lasting about fifteen minutes.

Asia

Most of Turkey has a Mediterranean climate. Inland can be wet year-round and cold in the winter. In northern Asia, Siberia has an arctic climate, which extends to northern Russia and Scandinavia. The weather is severely cold and dry in the northern and northeastern areas. Central Asia, Mongolia and western China are mostly dry with cool summers and cold winters. Southwest Asia has a relatively dry climate with hot, dry summers and cold winters (colder in the mountainous areas). The Himalaya regions and foothills are wet except for mid-fall and mid-spring. India has a dry northwestern area characterized by the hot Rajasthan Desert. India's northeast is the wettest and most fertile zone. India's monsoon season starts in late May in southern India with southwesterly winds and abundant rainfall, which reaches northern India about six weeks later. Monsoon season tapers off in October, bringing cool and dry weather until March when the heat returns.

Most of China, except western China, experiences monsoon rain in the summer. Southern, central, eastern China and Taiwan share a tropical climate with mild winters. Northern China and Manchuria have severely cold, dry winters.

Southeast Asia

Hot, humid summers. Southwestern monsoon winds determine most of Southeast Asia's climate: wet and warm to hot summers and mostly dry winters, with cooler temperatures in the higher elevations.

Thailand and Malaysia

The Thai and Malay peninsulas are subject to the southwestern monsoon rains on the west coasts from May through September. The eastern coasts experience northeastern monsoon rains originating from the Pacific from October to March. Temperatures are hot year-round with high humidity. Similar monsoon scenarios influence the weather in the Malaysian, Indonesian and southern Philippine Islands. Regions facing or occupying the northeastern coastlines receive more rain from October through March. Regions on the southwestern coastline have more rain from May through October. There's bounteous rainfall year-round with hot temperatures and high humidity. The central and northern Philippine Islands experience heavy monsoons and typhoons from May through October. The dry season is from December through May, and it is hot year-round.

↟ *Japan and Korea*

These countries have moderate climates with moist, warm summers and cold, relatively dry winters. Both countries enjoy wintertime snow in the northern regions and balmy, beach weather in the southern regions.

Australia and the South Pacific

The northernmost parts of western Australia, the Northern Territories, Queensland and New Guinea have tropical climates with warm to hot temperatures year-round. There is plentiful rainfall from November through March (summer in the Southern Hemisphere). Very little rainfall occurs in the other months. Southern Queensland and the northern part of New South Wales also have the most rain from November through March, with moderate rainfall and mild temperatures during the remaining months. Sydney and its surrounding areas receive the most rainfall from February through July, with moderate rainfall in the other months. Expect warm temperatures from October through April with mild weather the rest of the year.

The Canberra Territory, Victoria and the Adelaide regions experience moderate rainfall throughout the year, with mild to warm temperatures from October through April and cooler temperatures in the remaining months. The Perth region receives most of its rainfall from May through September, with little rain in the other months. Expect warm to hot temperatures from November through April, otherwise expect mild temperatures. The interior portions of Australia receive very little rain. Temperatures are hot in their summertime and are mild in their wintertime. A key factor here is the big difference between daytime and nighttime temperatures (as is typical in all desert regions).

New Zealand

The northern island has a mild, almost Mediterranean climate with most rainfall during their winter from May through October. All months are somewhat wet. The southern island has milder summers and cooler winters, with modest rainfall on the east of the mountains and ample rain west of this region. Snow is possible year-round in all of the upper mountain regions, with heavy snowfall in the highest mountains.

Note: Check on world climates close to your departure date— *U.S.A. Today,* the *New York Times* and your local paper provide temperature and conditions in foreign cities.

PART 5

PLACES ON THE EBB: ENDANGERED PARADISES

Seems we're nearing the end of the hippie backpacker trail; most of the lost world has been found. A few places hang in the balance as anonymous Valhallas, where you can still take a walk on the wild side. But you better get moving before our globe is linked together by one continuous strip-mall. These spots, renowned for their bizarre magnificence or hedonistic profusions, still won't overextend your ATM card either.

The adventure travel business has exploded, introducing throngs of corporate thrillseekers and outward-bounders to the corners of the earth that were formerly the domain of nomadic wanderers. For instance, five years ago, two U.S. outfitters introduced fewer than fifty Americans per year to Irian Jaya, Indonesia's Stone Age region. This year, more than 20 outfitters will deliver over 3,000 trekkers there. A decade ago, an abandoned mine ghost town in Alaska welcomed a few hundred visitors per year. Last year that number swelled to over 25,000. While eco-tour companies promote treading lightly in undeveloped regions, package tourists descending upon these places on the ebb are bringing a new tackiness along with them, including suitcases, bulky comfort requirements, polyester and their volume dials twirled all the way up.

Tribal people around the world are being *contaminated* or relocated by deforestation and new highway or bridge construction. On U.S. soil, resort politics have a way of commercializing our best-kept secrets. None of the remote outposts in the world seem safe; the adventure travel business expects to double its receipts *again* in the next five years.

The paradise-to-tourist trap drill: Private Idahos are difficult secrets to keep: Ethnic food is replaced by banana pancakes, is replaced by fast food, is joined by establishments that accept American Express!

Sad but true, modern folk are prisoners of time who have been seduced into abandoning their inmost nomadic callings. We live in a world where nothing stays the same for very long. Hopefully, your taste of discovery will be sweet. Unlike the rat-race existence many of us live today, human warmth is still synonymous with these destinations. Jump in ahead of the tourist wave—the following places (like every place you have never been) will be quite different by the year 2000.

Irian Jaya, Indonesia

Irian Jaya, a land of startling contrasts that makes up the western half of equatorial New Guinea Island, is Indonesia's least populated territory. Inland inhabitants remain primitive, hunting and gathering in Stone Age tradition, providing visitors a rare opportunity to trek back in time. Irianese have little in common with western Indonesia and the rest of the world. Although tourism is increasing, it remains to be one of the last remaining primeval jungle and mountain frontiers. The awe-inspiring mountain ranges in the central part of the island are permanently covered in snow and ice, while the low-lying areas in the North and South maintain great tropical jungles. Torrential rivers plunge from the mountains into gorges, lush lowland rainforests and coastal plains. Palm tree–lined, white sand beaches rim the province.

The area was initially claimed by the Dutch in the mid-1800s as part of their Spice Island Empire, but by 1940, they had not explored further inland than the coastal plains as it was considered only empty wilderness, too rugged for habitation. In 1938, an expedition plane flew into the 5,000-foot-high Grand Baliem Valley and landed in a densely populated area inhabited by agrarian Dani tribes. These people, clothed in only penis gourds and skimpy reed skirts, were engaged in constant tribal fighting. Time remained irrelevant until the first outsider, a Dutch missionary, settled in the Baliem in 1953. Although Indonesia annexed the area in 1963, the process has not been universally accepted by native Papuans, and discontent still prevails in certain areas.

All in all it's just another brick in the wall …
—Pink Floyd, The Wall

To document this "stone age" culture before changes occurred, in 1961 the Harvard Peabody Museum sponsored a major expedition to the Grand Baliem Valley. Extremely well documented in Peter Matthiessen's book *Under the Mountain Wall,* this is the expedition after which Michael Rockefeller disappeared after he chose to stay an extra season. As a visitor today, you may receive a rousing welcome from a Dani chief, who's likely to invite ("adopt") you to spend the night in the village as an honored guest.

Beyond the Grand Valley of the Baliem River there are many other tribal groups living in smaller valleys. These people were not contacted until the 1960s and 1970s, when the missionaries began penetrating. Having less contact with western civilization are the highland Yali and lowland Kumbay tribes. Like the Dani, the Yali are recognized by the rattan hoops and penis gourds worn by the men and the simple grass or tuber skirts worn by the women. The isolated Kumbay, who have seen only a handful of outsiders, live in tree houses. The men wear hornbill hats or penis gourds, while the women don the bark of trees as their garb. Both the Yali and Kumbay were fierce headhunters and cannibals until just twenty years ago when they were first contacted by outsiders. While these practices have "stopped," little else of their customs have changed.

Tree house people. Deep in the rainforest, between the Asmat tribe of the swamps and the Dani people of the mountains, live the astonishing tree house people. Their remarkable houses are built on stilts 30–60 feet above the ground for protection from warlike neighboring tribes. You may see a native using a stone axe to cut down trees. Here, ageless tribal conflicts still dominate everyday life; headhunting and cannibalism remain part of the culture. In this region, each village has a different language, and often tribespeople cannot communicate with clans living just a few miles away! They are great bow-and-arrow hunters.

The Baliem River exits the highlands through an extensive and spectacular gorge system emerging in the coastal lowlands. First traversed in 1962 by Heinrich Harrer, the lowlands are inhabited by various tribes of the Asmat ethnological grouping. This was, and is in most cases, a lowland "stone age" culture that varied greatly from the highland tribes that survive in a totally different environment. They too are great bow-and-arrow hunters, and their jungle flora harvest revolves principally around the sago palm. Also wearing very little clothing, they live communally in small isolated locations. Sophisticated Asmat art is represented by carved shields, canoes and miniature figurines. While on their soil, you might get the chance to participate in a mask feast, an adoption ceremony or the ritual of inaugurating a shield or canoe. In the evenings, the men, some sporting huge nose decorations of shell or carved wood, gather to sing and tell stories.

Nature also provides for a spectacular showcase of old-world tropical species in Irian Jaya. Many species of birds and mammals are common to both Australia and New Guinea but absent in Southeast Asia because of the presence of the land bridge joining the former two during the Ice Age. The birds of New Guinea, however, having developed for millennia in isolation, have many unique and spectacular forms. About 90 percent of the floral species are endemic to the island. Its floral contributions have come from the long-isolated Australian region and from Southeast Asia, the richest biomass on the planet.

Endangered because: The voices of those interested in preserving any ancient culture are similar to an actor in New York or to a tree falling in the forest—you're never sure if somebody's going to hear you. Fortunately, some tribes continue to resist any contact with the outside world, maintaining a stone age existence where so-called "literacy" is nonexistent. Western visitors to tribal regions simultaneously fascinate and frighten the natives, especially in regions where the traditional penis gourd (akin to wearing only a curved whiffle-ball bat sheath to cover one's genitalia) has not yet given way to clothes. Indonesian officials, who view the wearing of clothes as a measure of progress, have failed in getting all of the inhabitants of Irian Jaya to support "Operation Penis Gourd." Local officials now claim that only 5 percent of people in the territory prefer to walk around semi-naked. Western-attired Javanese is the future.

Further endangering the indigenous culture is the Indonesian government's opinion that the Irianese haven't a right to lay claim to land that's not being "used." Evidently, hunting and gathering don't count. While Irian Jaya's mineral and oil resources are being exploited, the bleaching of native tradition is underway. Many of the valley villages can now be accessed by road. This development, along with a great influx of Indonesians coming from other islands as part of the massive *transmigration project,* is bringing many changes to the Dani and other tribal people.

Visitors to Irian Jaya usually land in Jayapura or Biak, where new construction is the heaviest. Go there now, because the trekking routes (which are actually the natives prolific trade trail system) that link the twentieth century towns with the Baliem Valley are giving into western influences. The trails are being widened and lined with brick and corrugated steel tourist guest houses (providing running water) that are unlike anything you'd find in a Dani village. Count on the less-contacted Asmat rainforest region in southern Irian Jaya (where Rockefeller disappeared in 1961) to be capitalized next. For now, Asmat is still culturally wild, so visitors must be mentally and physically fit and ready to deal with the unexpected. Arranging for a bilingual guide to lead your trek is recommended.

Note: There's recently been a "temporary" reversal in the bleaching of Irian Jaya. Garuda Airlines (Indonesia's national carrier) stopped flying there directly from the United States because their new larger planes can't land on the airfield in Biak. There are also reciprocal government regulations coming into play, i.e., one port of call per country. It's now more expensive to fly into Irian Jaya on the required domestic flight. This will eventually change.

Note: Proponents of ecotourism believe that linking adventure travelers directly with the remote tribal people, thereby "employing" them (instead of capitalists from an outlying area), gives younger tribal people an economic reason not to flee into the larger towns and cities.

PLACE: Irian Jaya, Indonesia.
HISTORICAL FUNCTION: Conversion of carbon dioxide to oxygen.
FIRST OUT-OF-TOWNER: Dutch ship captain, William Janz, who was eaten by tribespeople in 1605.

Hot Tips

The Baliem Valley in the central highlands is a fabulous checkerboard of complex Dani villages, apportioned by stone-fenced sweet potato gardens, canals and terraced mountainsides. It's possible to organize a trek into the Baliem Valley either with a U.S. adventure travel company or by locating a native guide in a local village upon arriving. Get recommendations from locals and make sure your guide speaks the Dani dialect spoken in the outlying settlements.

ENDANGERED BECAUSE: Mining, deforestation, government insensitivity and tourism.

MODERN TOURIST PURPOSE: Museum of natural history for trekking and sea kayaking.

NATURAL RESOURCES: Ranging from stone age tools to mining and oil drilling.

THE GOOD: Converting carbon dioxide to oxygen; a journey into the Stone Age; unguarded awe: flora, fauna and culture found no place else.

THE BAD: Not easily accessible; there's tribal warfare.

TRAVELER'S ESSENCE: Hopefully, ecotourists.

TOURIST MIX: Life without an alarm clock.

TRANSPORTATION: Feet, dugout canoes, prop planes.

ECONOMIC INDICATOR: A safety pin can be swapped for a shrunken head.

NIGHTLIFE: Tribal pig-trading festivals.

AFTER 2000: 501 jeans; package tour extravaganzas.

SEASON: Little seasonal variation in the mountain regions, similar to summertime in the Rocky Mountains.

COST OF ACCOMMODATION: Negligible.

Yangzhou, China

Heading up to Northeast Asia, Yangzhou, China, is an optic mind-blower where enormous totem-pole-like limestone karst peaks tower hundreds of feet into the mist, rising from a completely level horizon. The flat land below supports a bustling village, remnants of an ancient civilization that has recently keyed into adventure-travelers' cravings, allowing you to kick back in bohemian cafes with the international vagabond jetset. Yangzhou's culture shock comes in waves: browsing the gray, surreal, communist-flavored markets, riding your bike on the flat roads among the limestone peaks (climb Green Lotus or Moon Peak), boating or tubing the Li River to the stone house villages of Fuli and Xingping, where they have market days every third day (and where peering into a schoolhouse window during class is naughty, but you must do it once).

Travel in China can be harsh, but there are many affordable indulgences available in Yangzhou. Consider having silk suit jackets or happenin', draw-string pants tailor-made. Enjoy amenities such as straight-razor shaves capped off with a neck massage or browsing silk boutiques and art galleries for a distinguished local landscape scroll-painting. Cormorant fishing is an interesting option: a bird with a *leash* around its neck dives under water and catches a fish in its mouth "for you." There's

Hot Tips

- Good souvenirs to bring are safety pins, which have become the Dani's all-in-one toolbox: surgical implement, fishhook, ornament, wood etcher and much more. Velcro is also making a splash.
- Overnighting in village huts is possible, but a backup tent is advised. Police posts and missionary homes are other accommodation options.
- Cooked sweet potatoes are a Dani staple. It becomes the staple of trekkers who don't carry in enough canned or dried foods.

also the option for acupuncture treatments, all of the aforementioned activities cost next to nothing. Many of the travelers' food hangouts have outdoor seating.

What does it feel like to be there? Chic yet cheap. Although China certainly has "primitive" elements, you can rent a bike in Yangzhou and mingle with people in the countryside. It's simply the best way to feel the place. Pedal one of the large, sturdy bicycles a few miles outside of Yangzhou; veer off any dirt road that will likely turn into a dirt path. Roll on over gradual hills through farming villages. Get yourself lost. If you're into winging it, ride north toward Guilin as far you can, then find a random community on the Li River and bargain for a boat ride back to Yangzhou. As usual, the price depends on your bargaining ability.

From Hong Kong fly to Guilin, China, and take a two-hour bus ride or train south into Canton and take the overnight ferry-bus combination through Wuzhou into Yangzhou. Hovercrafts also operate between Hong Kong and Wuzhou. From Guilin, the breathtaking four-hour cruise on an "African Queen" style boat to Yangzhou winds down the Li River and passes many fantastic limestone peaks.

U.S. greenbacks go a long way in China. Have notes of "survival questions" (where is the bathroom?, etc.) written for you in Chinese by someone who is bilingual, especially to simplify overland transportation ticket purchases.

Endangered because: Considering Yangzhou's proximity to Hong Kong, capitalistic fallout from the reunification of Hong Kong with China in 1997 will have a definite impact on tourism. Modernized rail links and a likely airport will boost both Chinese and foreign tourism to this spectacular, bizarre, brain-twisting place. Cormorant fishing and the pleasantries of Li River cruising are jeopardized by upstream polluters.

PLACE: Yangzhou, China.

HISTORICAL FUNCTION: Li River port.

FIRST OUT-OF-TOWNER: China "reopened" its doors to independent travelers in 1986. President Nixon climbed Yangzhou's Moon Peak in 1972.

ENDANGERED BECAUSE: Li River pollution and Hong Kong's pending reunification with China.

MODERN TOURIST PURPOSE: Kathmandu of China.

NATURAL RESOURCE: Li River and the ungodly, bluish, cloud-wreathed limestone karst peaks.

THE GOOD: Regrouping and eating creative Western dishes after surviving other parts of China; frying your previously civilized mental circuit board. "Downtown" tourist feces, used to fertilize outlying crops, is transported by elders who carry buckets of the waste balanced on a pole laid across their backs.

THE BAD: Dog lovers (they're Chinese hors d'oeuvres). The Hard Rock Cafe franchise is a lawless one there.

TOURIST MIX: Europeans, Aussies, Kiwis, Canadians and a few Uncle Sammies.

TRANSPORTATION: Boats, buses and bikes.

ECONOMIC INDICATOR: Meals for $1–$2.

HANG-UP: Schoolteachers get angry when travelers peer into schoolyard windows.

NIGHTLIFE: Full moonlit bike rides around limestone karst peak silhouettes, riverboat rides, ping-pong in the town center hall or secretive hash-den deliberation.

CULTURAL RESOURCES: Farming villages tilled with peaceful tact.

AFTER 2000: Kathmandu of mainland China. Mass transit from Hong Kong?

COST OF ACCOMMODATION: $1–$2 rooms (cement cells); $5–$12 for upgrade to hot water, private toilet.

SEASON: They have cold, wet winters.

Northern Thailand

A step closer to civilization in Southeast Asia is northern Thailand. For centuries, the remote mountains of northern Thailand have provided a sanctuary for nomadic, shifting agriculturalists. Some 400,000 non-Thai-speaking minorities, including the Lisu and Karen people, live in small scattered villages. Venturing to some of their enclaves on foot can take days. (You also have the option to ride an elephant.) Some tribal folk still wear their marvelous, traditional embroidered costumes and massive silver jewelry. The women smoke pipes.

Trekking between rarely visited tribal villages, traveling the way the inhabitants themselves do, you'll visit or stay overnight as a guest of local families in their traditional teakwood houses. What distinguishes these tribal people from tribal people elsewhere is their incredibly peaceful nature. Even urban Thai people can seem to be relaxed to the point of *collapse*. Thai people are known for their warmth and great sense of humor.

When travelers first descended on Thailand, the southern beach scene overshadowed the mysterious northern mountains. Up north, the Mae Hong Son Loop is a windy mountain road visiting Chiang Mai, Pai, Mae Hong Son and returning to Chiang

Mai. Cruising the loop that bisects various hill-tribe areas on a motorbike safari is the 7- to 10-day cultural odyssey of a lifetime. Remote villages accessible along the loop offer a rare glimpse of the Thailand of old. Be considerate. Roaring offroad into a remote village is rude; there are times when you're better off afoot. The scenic terrain changes along the loop as often as the fascinating jumble of tribes and cultures thriving in the valleys. The landscape is replete with ancient temples, luxuriant massage retreats and exotic foodstops. The air in Thai villages is usually fat with the smell of spicy delights. The smell of burning stoves, the din of playful children and the silent bliss of shopkeepers stay with you.

Chiang Mai

Chiang Mai is the common launch point for foot treks and motorcycle safaris that visit the remarkable villages of Pai and Mae Hong Son (the Golden Triangle is also an option). Chiang Mai is abundantly equipped with dozens of theme bars, trekking outfitters and motorcycle rental shops. The Beer Bar is a medley of twenty personalized, around-the-clock watering holes linked beneath a mammoth palm-leaf thatched roof. Travelers from around the world gather there, strategizing or sharing stories about their hill-tribe treks or motorcycle safaris. Find yourself an informed guide to lead your group, or rent a motorbike and cruise the trail on your own. Adventure travel opportunities include elephant safaris or floating down the Pai River on a bamboo raft. Consider a silent meditation retreat or a course in ancient Thai massage.

Although Chiang Mai, Thailand's second largest city is "gone," in purist terminology, there are other parts of Thailand where you can hike into the "real thing." Acknowledging that most people are lazy, if you have to walk more than a day (or five) to reach a place, then it's probably worth it. Those who make the "investment" to trek far into a region assure a certain eco-quality about the trekker. The suitcasers are filtered out.

Pai, surrounded by smoky mountains, is the most remote of these three largest settlements along the loop. Although Chiang Mai is the popular launch point for treks to points north, Pai is a sleepier, more relaxed village with open spaces on all sides. It stays twenty years behind Chiang Mai, although sightseer spillover from Chiang Mai continues putting Pai on the map. Also primed with dozens of "cafes," trekking outfitters and motorcycle rental shops, Pai is actually the optimum site to initiate a less commercialized hill-tribe trek. At $2–$6 per hour, you can afford a daily massage in any of Pai's retreats. Befriend an informed guide to lead your group into the hill-tribe areas, or rent a motorbike and cruise the trail on your own. Nearby Cave Lod is your chance to go underground for spectacular spelunking. Visit the area hot springs.

Mae Hong Son

Closer to the Burmese border, marvelous Mae Hong Son is a buzzing town encompassed by hills. A convenient place to visit Buddhist monks is in the monastery located by the lake in the town center. When the monks aren't studying, praying or chanting, you may find one willing to take you on in a ping-pong match. Because Mae Hong Son is close to the Burmese border, there are opportunities to visit the increasingly exploited, curious long-neck tribes or Burmese refuge camps. The loop continues, paralleling the Mekong River along the Burmese border. This is some of most beautiful scenery in all of Thailand, and the highlight of the loop journey.

Although some Thais living in large cities speak English, English skills are quite slim in hill-tribe country. A local guide is necessary if you want communication to extend beyond hand signals, smiles and other facial expressions.

Endangered because: Beaten trekking routes are commercializing many of the hill tribes, who are also burdened by the *assimilation* efforts of the Thai government. Children and adults are learning to beg for money. Trying to convince tourists that giving money to "beggars" only perpetuates this pushy, destructive behavior is like trying to convince a tenth-grader that pimples are not the end of the world. There are numerous nonprofit organizations constructively assisting the hill tribes that could make a beneficial impact with your donation.

Hotel development.

There's a modern highway under construction connecting Chiang Mai, Mae Hong Son and other towns. This and other road projects will increase commerce, decrease native authenticity and replace the drowsy peacefulness of Thailand's tree-shaded mountain backroads.

PLACE: Northern Thailand (Mae Hong Son Loop).
HISTORICAL FUNCTION: Golden Triangle trade route annex.
FIRST OUT-OF-TOWNER: U.S. vets, Jim Thompson.
ENDANGERED BECAUSE: Overtrekked routes commercializing hill-tribe life. Modern highways.
MODERN TOURIST PURPOSE: Hill-tribe treks, meditation retreats, partying.
NATURAL RESOURCE: Pai River (river trips to Mae Hong Son).

↑ BAD FOR: Blow-dryer zealots.
TRANSPORTATION: Bus, car or motorbike.
ECONOMIC INDICATOR: Thai massage for $2–$10 per hour.
NIGHTLIFE: Weary travelers wearing reeking boots or Tevas.
CULTURAL RESOURCES: Classical Thai music, monasteries.
AFTER 2000: Exxon stations.
COST OF ACCOMMODATIONS: $3–$25.

Note: Bangkok is an intersection where around-the-world and circle-the-Pacific trips are distinguished. Eastbound voyagers head on to Burma, Delhi or Kathmandu, whereas Pacific Rimmers migrate south into Malaysia, Indonesia and *Down Under.*

The Darien Gap

There's only one place in the world where you can walk between the Atlantic and Pacific ocean without crossing a road. Back in the Americas, the Darien Gap is that narrow swath of jungle below Panama City, above Columbia, squeezed between two vast continents and two huge oceans. It's the no-man's land between Central and South America. There's no road or railway there, so the only way across is by foot (although there is a car sitting in the middle of this jungle—how it got there no one is quite sure). The region is Central America's largest and least visited national park preserve. Panama is a land of modern comforts and technology (Panama City) and also a land of pristine wilderness and ancient cultures.

Mostly uninhabited except for local Indians living by the rivers, this area bound by the Caribbean Sea (Atlantic Ocean) and the Pacific Ocean is the only road transport gap between the continents. Even before the U.S. invasion gave Panama bad publicity, suitcase tourists avoided the gap because of its reputation for being a hot and humid, swampy wasteland of a jungle packed with incredibly dense vegetation. Well, that may be true for Luis Vitton demigods, but a trans-Darien expedition is a thrillseeker's fantasy. The one- to two-week trek requires jungle combat boots, canoe skills, a machete, a compass and an aching to traverse the Continental Divide.

Panama is barely fifty miles wide at its narrowest point. For thousands of years the tiny isthmus of Panama has served as the land bridge between the North and South American continents. The existence of this link has had a profound effect on the distribution of plants, animals and our own species. It is over this land bridge that the opossums, primates and armadillos of South America and the camels, raccoon and deer of North America traveled to spread and populate both continents. Nearly 400,000 years ago people first traveled south over this land bridge to colonize, spread and develop all of the various cultures and linguistic groups of South America.

The beautiful indigenous Kuna Indians living in Darien may be camera shy, but they love to show off their gold jewelry. Kuna don't speak English, so if you want to retrace Balboa's 1513 itinerary, a professional guide is recommended. The gap is paradise for birdwatchers. Another option to traverse the gap are the cargo boats that skirt the coast. These boats move everything between Panama and Columbia that would otherwise travel on the completed highway. Boats visit the chain of islands along the Caribbean Coast. Charter a boat or hitchhike onto a cargo boat. Boat traffickers obviously see no reason for completing the Pan American Highway.

Threatened because: The Darien's status as the sole road break between the continents is jeopardized by the proposed completion of the Pan American Highway. Its construction would overrun the habitat of Kuna Indians, who live by the rivers, and malign the biosphere's delicate ecological balance. Environmentalists will fight the road to the end, but some say it's inevitable.

PLACE: Darien Gap, Panama.

HISTORICAL FUNCTION: Land bridge (isthmus) for ancient Aztec and Mayan wanderers.

FIRST OUT-OF-TOWNER: Balboa in 1513.

ENDANGERED BECAUSE: Pan American Highway.

MODERN TOURIST PURPOSE: U.S. dollars (it's their currency also).

NATURAL RESOURCE: Biosphere reserve.

THE GOOD: Beholding the Atlantic and Pacific simultaneously; undaunted travelers, Columbian guerrillas and Scarfaces heading north from Peru; slogging through uncharted territory.

THE BAD: People who thought the gluelike mud at Woodstock II was a problem; Luis Vitton demigods; people who are afraid of snakes and bats.

TOURIST MIX: Indiana Jones, Columbian guerrillas, scarfaces heading north from Peru and isolators.

TRANSPORTATION: Feet, canoes and river boats. History is changed by people who build roads.

NIGHTLIFE: Mudsliding.

AFTER 2000: Another "south-of the-border" auto rest stop; another Battery Park City landfill.

↑ COST OF ACCOMMODATION: Jungle huts are cheap.
SEASON: December to March.

Dewey Beach, Delaware

Returning to familiar U.S. soil, nod farewell to wild summer nights in Dewey Beach, Delaware, as the Venice Beach of the East swiftly crosses the capitalist line that separates unrehearsed rock-and-roll bar lunacy from a calculated resort. Comparatively, Dewey Beach is still hard to beat on the East Coast for carefree seaside partying because cars are totally unnecessary.

What makes this mile-long beach strip of bars, hotels, restaurants and shops special is its New York Hampton's tumult without the snobbery, fashion show, cover charges, police roadblocks or civil unrest. This raw, uncomplicated hedon hamlet is where you'll be invited to all-night open-house parties. Dolphins (just like on TV!) surface often 100 yards off the wide, clean beaches that are well known in the skimboarding community. Frisbees and volleyballs fly while sunbathers reflect on the night before. For those requiring a bit of solitude, the nearby Delaware State Park beach is barren. One mile north of Dewey Beach is cosmopolitan Rehoboth Beach.

Noteworthy landmarks are the Bottle and Cork and Starboard Restaurant. The Cork, a prohibition-era swoon joint, features live bands nightly plus the Saturday afternoon jam session. Jam sessions reenact spring breaks, where live DJs wheedle the mob until a band converts the indoor-outdoor beer circus into the American Bandstand, all the while, fresh faces, sometimes free of comprehension, dance their way to the bathroom.

Up the block, the Starboard's claim to fame is their Sunday morning Bloody Mary bar, a self-serve buffet line offering a baffling inventory of horseradish, spices, hot sauces and garnishes imported from around the world. The Dewey Beach Elvis, who roams and sings in the image of the King, frequently calls on the Bloody Mary bar.

Dewey is a small town of twenty-one blocks where 30,000 nonviolent weekend warriors throw caution to the wind from Memorial Day until Labor Day. It has the legal capacity to entertain 7,000 barflies at one time.

Endangered because: The police surveillance belt is tightening. Sometimes a bumper sticker says it all: DEWEY BEACH—A POLICE STATE. The message is surfacing—an ominous allusion to the massive crackdown on summer visitors and other allegedly rowdy vacationers who have been renting summer-share houses there since the sixties. As if the global sex virus, the highway

... the open road is a beckoning, a strangeness, a place where a man can lose himself.
—William Least Heat Moon

speeding-ticket circus and pre-depression inflation hadn't slaughtered enough human wildlife, now Washington's adored "Sin City by the Sea" seems to be biting the hand that feeds it by writing tickets *for everything under the sun*. Approximately 75 percent of the homes in Dewey Beach accept renters. There is increasing discord between year-round residents, cops, Dewey's city council and the faithful renters of more than 300 summer homes. Only local politicians know if Dewey Beach will become a resort for eunuchs, a strict family retreat or Delaware's "Atlantic City" in the next century.

Dewey Beach commissioners claim that the reason for the major crackdown on house parties is that the police are enforcing the 0-tolerance-for-unruly-behavior laws that were part of the platform that prompted Dewey's year-round residents to elect them into office. Depending upon who you talk to, year-round resident population in Dewey is quoted between 450 and 850. The perennial D.C. summer renters are buzzing with police harassment horror stories, wondering why their constitutional rights seem to have been blown away by the ocean breeze.

Regarding the huge increase in fines for seemingly every "beach activity," town officials insist that the ticket revenue base is equal to expenditure base of wages for additional cops and lifeguards. They also note that not a dime of the weekender's money expenditure goes into town coffers; instead it's all spent in the bars. Opponents believe that the new noise ordinance is written to allow the police force total autonomy, and as such, renters are held hostage by the subjective judgment of a summer police officer. Group houses are being blamed for most of the town's troubles when in reality, they are the force that built the town, and renters don't appreciate when their cars are swiftly towed away to the tune of $113.

The rewriting of Dewey's charter and ordinances must have spun Thomas Jefferson a few times in his grave. It seems that Dewey Beach thinks that the public is not even entitled to know *what* laws are being enforced. On the other hand, locals find it ironic that a group of inside-the-beltway Washingtonians are trying to dictate policy to a town that's 120 miles away. The motives for the town's commissioners will soon will be clear to the entire town, when opponents to the new laws participate in a class action suit against Dewey's elected officials under section 1983 of title 42 of the U.S. Code.

PLACE: Dewey Beach, Delaware.
HISTORICAL FUNCTION: Low-rent area south of Rehoboth
    Beach, Delaware.

↑ ENDANGERED BECAUSE: Inside political development plans.
MODERN TOURIST PURPOSE: East Coast hedon-hamlet. Setting fire to your feral instincts.
NATURAL RESOURCE: Atlantic Ocean; free rock bands.
THE GOOD: Human wildlife, fuzzy logic.
THE BAD: Police harassment.
TRAVELER'S ESSENCE: Cutting loose nine-to-five vines.
TOURIST MIX: 18- to 45-year-old professionals with a naughty streak.
TRANSPORTATION: Not necessary once you arrive.
ECONOMIC INDICATOR: Can of beer for $2.75.
HANG-UP: Increasing number of unnecessary noise violation tickets.
CULTURAL RESOURCES: Car towing, parking tickets, neo-vegetables.
AFTER 2000: A resort for eunuchs.
RANGE OF ACCOMMODATIONS: Average cost for a full summer-share is $800. Hotel, "double occupancy," is $79 per night.
SEASON: Early May through late September.

Kennicott, Alaska

Alaska's interior is seldom seen. Three hundred miles northeast of Anchorage, Kennicott, Alaska, is a copper mine ghost town located in the heart of Wrangell–St. Elias National Park, our largest U.S. national park (it's the same size as West Virginia). Glaciers spill out from the surrounding rugged peaks. The region is rich in mining history. Kennicott enjoyed its heyday in the 1920s and 1930s until it was abandoned in 1938 when the Kennicott Copper Corporation couldn't compete with the falling prices of copper (cheaper copper ore was discovered in Chile). The town stands now exactly as it did in 1938, when the last train rode out, carrying the population with it.

Immediately you're struck by the differences in technology that were available then and now. Built by hand using 18-inch-diameter timber supports, the colorful, red and white buildings are in great shape despite the unforgiving weather and rooftop snowloads. You get the sense of the very rugged people who made their living in the 100-plus miles of mine corridors below. The self-sustaining town, once served by rail, has (had) a hospital, a grade school, a dental office, a dairy, tennis courts, a recreation center and bachelor quarters. One lodge has been renovated for tourists (closed in winter).

Access into the 13.2-million-acre park is through two unpaved roads. The McCarthy Road, a former railroad track bed, dead ends at the Kennicott River (after a windy, bumpy 60-mile ride at 20 mph). The only way into Kennicott from there is to cross the 100-foot-wide river using the hand-operated tram, a two-seat metal cart running on a 200-foot pulley cable. A one-way trip takes about 5 minutes.

The Kennicott Glacier Lodge offers deluxe accommodations and guided tours of the area. The Kennicott area enjoys some of the nicest weather in the state of Alaska being shielded by the Wrangell Mountains to the north and the Chugach Range to the south.

Endangered because: The park was established in 1980 both for the sake of conservation and promoting tourism. Since the region is part of the state "right of way," the State Department of Transportation is planning to build a wheelchair-accessible footbridge over the Kennicott River. The bridge would allow far more people to visit the region. Presently, any motorized vehicles are driven into the area when the river freezes over each winter. The majority of the thirty people living in the region accessed by the hand-pulley cable car are opposed to a bridge allowing motor vehicles. The footbridge idea is receiving mixed reactions.

The ghost town is a private inholding within the park. If increased tourism also brings on pillage or vandalism, or if other aspects of maintaining the site get out of control, it could be closed down by its owners. The entire national park is policed by only two state troopers who would have difficulty properly monitoring Kennicott. The infrastructure dilemmas of parking, camping, toilets and trash disposal have not yet been tackled.

What is the feeling when you're driving away from people and they recede on the plane till you see their specks dispersing?
—Jack Kerouac

PLACE: Kennicott, Alaska.

HISTORICAL FUNCTION: Mining.

FIRST OUT-OF-TOWNER: Gold prospectors.

ENDANGERED BECAUSE: Footbridge will outmode hand-pulled cable tram across the Kennicott River, increasing tourist capacity.

NATURAL RESOURCE: Wildlife—moose, buffalo, black and brown bear, Dall sheep, mountain goats, wolves, wolverines, beavers and herds of caribou.

THE GOOD: A Wild West pioneer, mine town hallucination. Glacial flightseeing. Wildlife.

THE BAD: You have to bring your own toilet paper. Local residents uninterested in civilizing.

TRANSPORTATION: Shuttle service to Kennicott from neighboring town of McCarthy (year-round resident population: 35).

⬆ ECONOMIC INDICATOR: Dinner $20, double room $130.

I AFTER 2000: A new breed of gold prospectors and pinball wizards.

I COST OF ACCOMMODATION: Double room at the Kennicott Glacier Lodge is $130. Manhattan-style pricing for most goods and services in neighboring town, McCarthy. Camping is allowed in specified areas.

Hot Tips

Dhow trips—ad hoc proprietors will invite you for a dhow ride along with a barbecue on the beach. Gather a group and charter a dhow. The simplicity of Swahili sailing is delightful.

The beach—If you walk away from the local area you can dispense with your swimming costume. A number of fine old houses have been purchased by foreigners and converted into impressive holiday homes. Some are rentable. At the surfs edge, you might even bump into someone from Lamu's transvestite community.

Lamu Island, Kenya, Africa

Get a jump on the jet skiers, making a beeline for Lamu Island, Kenya, Africa. Lamu, a 12-by-5-km island off the coast of Kenya, Africa, is the oldest town in East Africa. Accessed by boat, this step back in time offers travelers a place to escape the twentieth century. Originally a Swahili port settlement, Lamu became Africa's Haight-Ashbury District in the early 1970s when Nomadic western hippies "discovered" this mellow, enchanting paradise.

A considerable amount of tourist money goes toward restoration of the Old World architecture lining the windy, narrow streets. The Arabic influence is more apparent than the African influence. The 2- to 3-story, side-by-side row houses are separated by narrow streets that barely allow a pedestrian to bypass a donkey loaded down with baskets.

The Swahili way of life emerged from a blending of African tribes and Arabic traders. In contrast to most of Africa, Lamu has a flavor that is more like the back streets of Egypt or Morocco. Children are looking for pen pals and locals sailing in *dhows* still ply their trade in the Indian Ocean. You'll have no problem communicating, because English is the second or third language of many proprietors.

Lamu's timeless character and Arab flavor have an irresistible appeal. Strolling about the ancient villages, you'll get sucked in by the pleasantly sluggish Swahili manner. Your rhythm will slow as you sit on ancient home rooftops or verandas, watching the town go by. The cacophony of donkey traffic, mosque calls and alley cats add to the serendipity.

The old stone houses are open, roofless cubes enclosing large courtyards. In some areas these old homes are built so close together you can step across the street from one roof to another. Electricity arrived twenty years ago and there are still no motor vehicles.

Endangered because: Today's largely Muslim population is very easygoing, but tourism bears a double-edged sword. The centuries-old way of life is being overrun by a population explosion—

expected to double to 30,000 by the year 2000, officially declaring war on the brittle infrastructure. Mainland Kenya's population growth rate is among the highest on the planet. As Lamu is not totally sheltered, there will be residual effects. The mainland's re-settlement program is inflating the population and low-budget adventurers could give in to airborne safari groups.

Some time ago, the local newspaper ran articles encouraging the banning of hippies from the island.

PLACE: Lamu Island, Africa.
HISTORICAL FUNCTION: Late fourteenth-century Swahili settlement.
FIRST OUT-OF-TOWNER: Portuguese pirates.
ENDANGERED BECAUSE: Pending overpopulation.
MODERN TOURIST PURPOSE: Being fairly lazy, or fishing, snorkeling and visiting other nearby islands.
NATURAL RESOURCE: Beaches, colorful people.
THE GOOD: Seafood; being fairly lazy; Swahili swooning. The self contained, mellow island life is great for winding down from your visit to other parts of Africa.
THE BAD: People lost without a car. Running water 24 hours a day.
TRAVELER'S ESSENCE: Expat homeowners, hippies, globetrotters.
TOURIST MIX: Cultural feast.
TRANSPORTATION: Dhows (traditional boats holding five people). Only car on the island is government owned.
HANG-UP: Expat takeover.
NIGHTLIFE: Local festivals.
CULTURAL RESOURCES: Lamu Museum, general medieval romance and coconut plantations.
AFTER 2000: String of obnoxious contemporary hotels along the beach. Bridge to mainland?
COST OF ACCOMMODATION: $3 (double occupancy dungeon). $10 (clean room with a veranda). Prices vary during peak seasons: December–January and July–August.

Dominica

Pronounced DAAM-MIN-EEKA and having nothing to do with the Dominican Republic, Dominica is an active volcanic 29-by-16-mile island located between Martinique and Guadeloupe in the eastern Caribbean. The landscape is far more rugged than its neighboring islands. Because it's one of the least visited or developed islands in the Caribbean, most of its natural beauty and unique charm remain intact. Dominica, a giant plant labo-

The Donkey Sanctuary

A nursing home for old and lame donkeys who have retired from Lamu's inventory of over 3,000 of the sallow beasts. The charity funded asylum keeps donkey's off the local dinner tables. It's not an official tourist attraction. That's why you should go. There's also a donkey racetrack. Take one step at a time.

ratory, is geographically staggering. Three hundred sixy-five clear freshwater rivers criss-cross the giant plant laboratory. It has some of the highest mountains in the Caribbean, peaking at 4,700 feet with trails and waterfalls descending into lush tropical rainforests, and there's a worthwhile hike to a boiling lake that's forever burping up sulfurous fumes. A 70-foot-wide bowl of aqua-gray gurgling mud-soup arise from underworld molten lava gas. The depth of the lake is unknown. There are no beaches to sunbathe on the island.

The last outpost for the Carib Indians, Dominica is still home to its earliest inhabitants (for whom the Caribbean Sea was named). The Afro-Caribbean Creole culture remains very friendly today. There's a strong British heritage, and English is widely spoken. Caribs engage in farming, fishing, basket weaving and the carving of dugout canoes. Walking among the enormous insects, beneath the towering tree ferns, you tend to re-evaluate your circumstances.

There are no poisonous plants or insects, and many of the island's 160 species of birds, like the Sisserou Parrot, are unique to the island. Steep road climbs give way to trails and waterfalls. The diving and snorkeling is first-rate.

Endangered because: For now, the gushing rivers still drown out the sounds of traffic. Although the capitol, Roseau, retains its colonial character with old wood buildings and tile roofs, space for further development is becoming a problem. Without beaches or further habitable ground, the charming villages are experiencing increasing auto gridlock. New roads continue to access formerly inaccessible areas.

A large percentage of the 8,000 visitors per year are eco-tourists. However, a few Asian luxury hotels are on the cards. The limited access to the island would be changed forever by a larger airport (which, of course, will eventually be built).

On a lighter note, one reaction of the visiting tourist, who adore beaches and shopping, might be setting fire to the town upon discovering that there isn't a beach and there's nothing to *buy*.

PLACE: Dominica.

HISTORICAL FUNCTION: Last outpost for the fierce Carib Indians, who held off European settlers for years.

FIRST OUT-OF-TOWNER: Sighted by Columbus in 1493. Eventually settled by the English.

ENDANGERED BECAUSE: Limited space for development.

MODERN TOURIST PURPOSE: Rugged, wet, ecotourism.

NATURAL RESOURCE: Liquid sunshine (sunlit mist), banana plantations, hurricanes and waterfalls.

THE GOOD: Botanists. Adventure-loving souls. Liquid sun-shine (sunlit mist). Enormous insects and towering tree ferns. Sisserou Parrots, who are unique to the island.

THE BAD: The Carib Indians, who consider this to be their last outpost. People who thought they'd find grand hotels, sandy beaches or a casino.

TRAVELER'S ESSENCE: Disappointed American Express card holders.

TOURIST MIX: Those with botanic interests.

TRANSPORTATION: Limited access.

ECONOMIC INDICATOR: Poor conditions contribute to young people's migration away from the island.

HANG-UP: Cruise ship day tourists.

NIGHTLIFE: Hmmm?

CULTURAL RESOURCES: Forts converted to lodges. Hiking and getting sweaty.

AFTER 2000: Larger airport, bigger hotels, traffic jams.

COST OF ACCOMMODATION: Low end: $20. High end: $60 and up. Camping available.

Sipadan Island, Malaysia

Twelve miles from the northeastern part of Borneo lies this holy grail for scuba divers who like to dive from shore. Thirty feet from the beach under 6 to 10 feet of water begins a coral wall that drops nearly 3,000 feet into the abyss. The wall teems with marine life, including a bounty of green and hawksbill sea turtles, white-tip reef sharks, fields of giant clams and electric-blue parrot fish.

The 30-acre island of dense jungle is entirely surrounded by powdery white sand beach. Less than a mile in circumference, the spit of sand and jungle sits atop an underwater volcanic pinnacle rising from the ocean floor. Three dive resorts provide "upscale camping" in thatched huts built on stilts. Some huts are electrified.

Divers from all over the world discuss their unforgettable underwater adventure at meal times in the main building, or mess hall. The undersea mountain with the mushroom top is still rated as one of the five best dive sites in the world. Albeit gorgeous, if you're not into diving, it may not be worth the expense and hassle of getting there.

Endangered because: The word is out. The relatively few rooms on the island fill up as much as a year in advance. Three dive "resorts" on the island are too many. Large-scale diving operators are coming to accommodate a tourist explosion. Development is clouding the water, already reducing undersea visibility from 100 feet to about 50 feet. Helicopters began flying to the island two years ago. To make things worse, Indonesia is contesting Malaysia's ownership of the island, making any government conservation efforts opposing overdevelopment less effective. Once the ownership issue is resolved, Sipadan is slated to become part of a marine park.

PLACE: Sipadan Island.
HISTORICAL FUNCTION: God's aquarium.
FIRST OUT-OF-TOWNER: Jacques Cousteau.
ENDANGERED BECAUSE: Word-of-mouth.
MODERN TOURIST PURPOSE: Upscale camping.
NATURAL RESOURCE: The coral wall.
THE GOOD: Mating and nesting (for sea turtles, that is); the coral wall; an infinite underwater Eden.
THE BAD: Non-divers looking for land action.
TRAVELER'S ESSENCE: Those searching for the infinite Eden.
TOURIST MIX: Hardcore divers.
TRANSPORTATION: Getting there involves 3 days of traveling with several plane changes, a drive and a boat ride.
HANG-UP: Rats, who were there before the dive scene. Expensive to get there.
NIGHTLIFE: Turtle and fish mantras.
CULTURAL RESOURCES: Dive shop.
AFTER 2000: Tahiti, Cancun, Hedonism III, or maybe a Swiss Family Robinson frat house? Unless the island is designated as a marine park, large-scale diving operators are coming to accommodate the tourist explosion.
COST OF ACCOMMODATION: Upscale camping fee included as part of pricey dive expeditions. Comfy in a Gilligan's Island sort of way: thatched huts built on stilts.
SEASON: Diving conditions are best July–October.

Puerto Escondido, Mexico

South of Oaxaca (pronounced Wa-HA-ka), this small-scale, easy-going, Pacific surfing magnet teeters on the tourist trapdoor. Closer to Guatemala than California, the unpretentious beach village lures surfers from around the globe seeking Hawaii-standard waves and a ride in the famous Mexican Pipeline. Puerto Escondido hosts two championship surfing contests a year (August and November). Both are followed by major pachangas (blowout parties). The ultimate fusion of Mexican-gringo partying (annual November 4 bash) is Noviembre en Puerto

Escondido, featuring polo "burro" matches—polo played on burros using brooms as mallets.

Hippies, surfers and offbeat wanderers commune here, tuning into Mother Nature or bowing to King Cannabis. You won't feel guilty if doing *anything* there is a problem. When you tire of swinging lazily in a hammock slung between palm trees, go watch the local anglers unload and sell their catch along the beach. After watching the sunset on an uncrowded beach, the bars and discos launch happy hours that segue into all-night live-music celebrations.

Sadly, the region is targeted for tourist development by the Mexican government. Its main street wasn't paved until the 1980s, yet Puerto Escondido is showing signs of pollution. For now, an unsophisticated air lingers, but it won't be long before "Fontaur," the Mexican government's resort bulldozer, roars into town. The increasing number of flights and road improvements will botch this "hidden port."

COST OF ACCOMMODATION: Low season: under $8 for dorm-style room with shared bathrooms. High season (surf championships and Christmas holidays): $25–$55.

THE GOOD: The Cheech and Chong life. What me worry? Sun kings.

THE BAD: "Decoys" (non-surfers) bobbing in the deadly riptides. People with bellies may feel insecure around surfers with cut abdomens. Those who can't adapt to the continuous warm-climate, mañana attitude (slow service) may go nuts.

AFTER 2000: Ricardo Montalban smiling with outstretched palms. Aging hippies heading east for Zipolite Beach, a lazy fishing village where you can offer your naked body to the sun. Increased crime against tourists. Puerto Escondido T-shirts.

Istanbul, Turkey

The skyline of the legendary city where East meets West is beginning to look more like Dallas. Foreign-funded, modern skyscrapers are starting to overshadow ancient mosques. However, Turkish health traditions are still very much alive within Istanbul's historic bathhouses. The bathhouse experience is a peculiar series of events: Inside a steamy, domed chamber, you lie naked on a large fire-heated stone platform until you're visited by a grumbling figure who "washes" you from head to toe with a coarse, foaming sponge that's bigger than a file cabinet.

Hot and cold rinses are followed by a massage, with the option to return to the hot stone. Afterwards, tea is served in miniature cups.

In the confusion of the unmanaged urban growth, you can still find old-style shopping bazaars, ancient ruins and cheap gourmet food. Another reason to get going is the influx of desperate refugees from the former Soviet Union who will do anything to survive, including prostituting themselves. Add the refugees to a growing list of new-world urban problems confronting Istanbul.

The Basilica of Hagia Sophia, a towering mosque, is the best place to answer one of the five haunting calls of prayer a day.

COST OF ACCOMMODATION: Low end: $6–$20 (expect to be woken by a rooster early in the morning). High end: $60–$150 (five-star hotel).

THE GOOD: A gentle introduction into Muslim culture.

THE BAD: Chatty male chauvinists.

AFTER 2000: Another sterile Singapore?

A smile loosens stiff hearts, melts angry icebergs.
—Basil Northam, Jr.

Final Thoughts

Here's what Tony Wheeler, founder of Lonely Planet Publications, had to say about other places on the ebb that will be "gone" in 10 years or so: "People always want to be able to say 'I was the first one there,' so there's always a race to be first in the door when the door re-opens. Places in that category right now include Mongolia, Syria, Eritrea, Ethiopia, the Lebanon and Cambodia. I'd say Vietnam has already had its front-of-the-line day; already everybody you meet has been to Vietnam. Cambodia may be almost too hot a destination; you want to come back as well. I'd guess the Lebanon is going to be the next to inspire ho-hums, been there, done that." Good luck escaping the reality of tourism.

PART 6

Circling the Globe

Around the World in 80 Days for $3,000

I went AROUND THE WORLD IN 80 DAYS FOR UNDER $3,000—total cost (seven countries and three U.S. states: New York, Ireland, Turkey, Pakistan, Nepal, Thailand, the Philippines, Hawaii, San Francisco).

I'm sure I wasn't the only one pounding the pavement, searching for a meaning in life beyond earning and spending. We all sometimes wonder if our career paths are steering us hopelessly away from any Ernest Hemingway–type adventures. If it's not limited vacation time, then it's limited funds preventing us from exploring the world. Decide right now not to wait until retirement for another "long" holiday and circle the globe: broaden your persepctive. Thanks to a cunning mixture of bargains involving an airline ticket consolidator and inexpensive guest houses, the month-to-month budget for this trip turned out to be less than what I *had* been paying in rent.

After parting with my odious sales job, I purchased $1,000 in traveler's checks, overpaid my credit card $300 and dusted off my backpack. I left Manhattan's taxi-driver "demolition derby" behind for twelve weeks. And, instead of battling oncoming pedestrians for passage on the sidewalks, I experienced this:

The heartfelt kindness of Irish people sipping Guiness, gathered in small coastal communities amongst lofty limestone cliffs.

Southern Turkey's stunning Roman ruin cities, hidden in the mountains, and the ancient health traditions, which are very much alive inside Istanbul's bath-houses.

The bizarre smells, sights and sounds of Pakistan, where a luxurious four-star hotel afforded me a dual cultural perspective: white tablecloth room service and the massive open markets providing everything from curry to snake charmers.

A three-week trek, away from electricity (and the media), high into the jaw-drop-ping scenery of Nepal's Himalayas.

Daily massages and other hedonistic pleasures on the palm-lined beaches of Thailand's outer islands.

Singing "Gloria" at a Christmas Eve mass in the Philippines.

Driving to the windy, snowy summit of a 13,800-foot volcanic mountain, then descending to the tropical black-sand beaches for a swim on Hawaii's "Big Island."

Walking San Francisco's diverse neighborhoods plus a mud bath in Napa Valley's wine country.

Because I decided to relocate into a rural setting upon returning to the United States, I was able to give up my apartment, which limited my domestic expenses to my long-distance phone card. Geographic relocation and gaps in employment or education are excellent opportunities for extended travel. (Although it is a good idea to get vaccinations before visiting third-world countries, I've never had a problem traveling "unvaccinated.")

It always amazes me when people who spend big bucks on bullshit are skeptical about the financial feasibility of independent, worldwide exploration. On an "off-the-beaten-path" adventure such as this, clean, safe accommodations range between $3–$12 per night, and excellent meals usually cost less than $3. Obviously, Ireland and Hawaii were more expensive than Pakistan and Thailand, and there were frequent splurges on luxurious hotels and finer restaurants. I'm also stocked on nifty gifts for the next year!

My itinerary provided fantastic dichotomies. Culturally, Ireland and the Philippines are worlds apart, and Turkey and Hawaii ain't exactly cousins either.

Two Highlights from a Circle-the-Globe Tour

Nepal

They say Nepal is there to change you, not for you to change Nepal. Wise words. While seated on a stone couch in the 15,000-foot basin near the Annapurna Sanctuary Base Camp, surrounded by rocky monoliths, I was reminded of our millisecond existence—a flash between Ice Ages. Being in the middle of those eight 25,000-foot mountains with their staggering glaciers all under a clear, warm sunny sky is one of my most intoxicating and impressionable memories.

Annapurna I (26,545-foot elevation) and her icy, jagged rock-peak sisters form a rimmed bowl where groaning glaciers bulldoze "stadiums full" of rubble. This combination of avalanches and melting snow cut a seemingly fresh-cut canyon, giving birth to a mighty river, the Modi Khola. The Modi Khola defined the route for our trekking ascent into the Annapurna Sanctuary.

I trekked with two friends I had met in Kathmandu, the capital city resembling nowhere else. Although besieged by capitalism, Kathmandu is still no place for the unadventurous. The three of us hired Nepali porters for $5 a day to ease our individual loads. Their gentle interpreting abilities gave us an inside look into the families hosting the "tea houses" where we ate and slept each night. Camping out is an option, but the tea houses,

Trekking—The ultimate in rugged hiking scenery and Nepalese cultural exploration. A dazzling combination of ridge-walking amongst the terraced terrains supporting magical Nepali communities and mountain climbing above the tree line, amid the awesome Himalayas. There are no words to express the feeling of being surrounded by the loftiest mountains on Earth (26,000 feet and up). At night the moon casts a dreamy, blue light everywhere.

which conveniently line the various trekking routes, are also great places to meet locals and fellow travelers.

Nepal (25 days)

> Pakistan International Airlines; Karachi–Kathmandu
> Exchange rate: $1 = 51 rupees
> Tea houses (along the trekking routes): $.50 (dorm)–$5 (double)
> Meals: $.50–$2
> Quart of San Miguel beer: $.90–$1.40
> Trekking equipment rental (down jacket or a sleeping bag): $1.50 per day
> Total trekking expenses (3 weeks): $210

Ireland

Ireland was an undemanding, relaxing place to begin the journey. With the exception of Hawaii, it was the only place where renting a car made sense. Following a night of Dublin pub hopping, I began a leisurely loop tour concentrating on the west coast between Limerick and Galway. It's impossible to miss the quaint, small-town warmth because the "highways" don't bypass the population centers. The major thoroughfares slow down for local "main-street" traffic before continuing on as highways. The stone-walled roads wind past towering limestone cliffs, the Atlantic Ocean sprays mist into the air. I enjoyed delicious seafood chowder in casual, living room–style pubs. In the evening, the same pubs fill with stories, small talk and smoke. The background music was provided by traditional acoustic folk bands playing enthusiastically in exchange for free pints from the bar.

Hostels abound in Ireland. I chose to upgrade to bed & breakfast accommodations. Since this was an off-season wintertime trip, I never needed a reservation and always ended up in spacious rooms with ocean views. The hosts were always cordial and eager to recommend attractions along the way.

One morning in Galway, a radio report cited local obituaries, lost pet alerts and the plight of a stolen bicycle owner who now had no means of commuting the 12 miles to his job site. This humanistic tone is typical of the Irish who seem to have unlimited smiling and conversation resources.

Ireland (10 days)

> Virgin Atlantic or Aer Lingus; N.Y.–Dublin (via London)
> Exchange rate: $1 = 1.46 Irish pounds
> Auto rental: 1 week for $175
> Bed & breakfast: $25–$35 average (double)

Alone we are born
And die alone;
Yet see the red-gold
cirrus
Over the snow-
mountain shine.
Upon the upland
road
Ride easy, stranger:
Surrender to the sky
Your heart of anger.
—Painted on a rock
wall in the
Himalayas

Meals: $3–$7 average

Pint of Guiness in pubs: $2.50 average

European Countries

The first destination for most Americans exiting the country is Europe, the genesis of our western ways. Europe is, of course, a must for everyone. However, I recommend visiting the more physically challenging parts of the globe first, benefiting from your maximum reserves of health and energy. Do Europe later, when you're bursting at the seams with cash, or when you're too fragile to undertake a month-long trek into the Amazon.

On most circle-the-globe routings you should take full advantage of your choice to stop over in one or several European cities. Here are some European highlights.

Andorra. A secluded mountain retreat with duty-free shopping.

Austria. "Hutte-to-hutte" camping in the Alps. In Vienna see the Hofburg (free on Sunday), the Spanish Riding School, the Boy's Chorus, the Imperial Treasury, Schoenbrunn Palace and the Museum of Fine Arts.

Climb Grossglockner Mountain or cruise the Grossglockner Mountain drive between Lienz and Zell-am-See.

In Salzburg, visit the Hellbrunn Palace and underground through the Hallein Salt Mine. Enjoy wearing a hard hat.

Ski the Alps (a bit cramped and expensive during Christmas and Easter).

Azores. Your own private Idaho. The hydrangeas bloom in July.

Belgium. Visit the Grand Palace and Royal Palace in Brussels.

In Antwerp see the House of Rubens and the Flemish masters in the Museum of Fine Arts. Make your way to the rural inns in the Ardennes region. The castles of Beloeil and Chimay are spectacular. Culinary delights abound!

Bulgaria. Excellent bargain hunting, especially in the Rila Mountains.

Visit the towns of Veliko Turnovo, Koprivshtitsa, Melnik, Nesebur.

The find best accommodation deals are along the Black Sea coast in late spring or early fall. Check out the Bachkovo Monastery and the Baba Vida Fortress in Vidin.

Canary Islands. Best value for your money is off-season in this desert/tropical climate. The nicest weather is off-season as well. Popular with Germans and English.

Corsica. A rustic summer destination with both crowded and remote beaches.

Crete. Bohemian island which is home to the famous ruins

of Knossos. March to November off-season.

Cyprus. Listen to bouzouki (mandolinish guitar) music in a local tavern. See the mosaics at Kato Pyrgos and the Byzantine Icons Museum in Nicosia. Stay in a local monastery?

Czechoslovakia. Tremendous eastern European culture and architecture (over 3,000 castles). Don't miss Karlstejn and Cesky Krumlov Castles. Get out of Prague and explore the Tatra Mountains or some of the smaller villages (Kutna Hora, Levoca or Tábor).

Denmark. In Copenhagen behold the Erotic Museum, Rosenborgs Castle, the Royal Theatre and the Ny Carlsberg. Also see Kronborg Castle in Helsingör.

England. The only communication barriers here are the ones you invite. Pontificating in pubs is a national sport, and the police don't carry guns. Fish and chips is the finest "fast" food.

A must: Speakers Corner, Hyde Park, in central London. The best free entertainment in the United Kingdom. Speakers of all races, ages and opinions preach and argue about the issues of the world. Do you have an angle you'd like to impart? Walks in the Lake District, Wales and the Highlands.

In London visit the British National Museum, Buckingham Palace, Houses of Parliament, National Gallery, St. Paul's Cathedral, Tate Gallery, Tower of London, Westminster Abbey.

Ride the *Magic Bus* from London to Istanbul or Kathmandu overland (cheap). See Appendix 1.

Take the *Slowcoach*, a continuous bus-shuttle loop throughout the U.K. The cost is approximately 69 pounds for an open two-month ticket.

See Canterbury, Chichester, Winchester and York Cathedrals. Visit Stonehenge and Hadrian's Wall if you like ruins. Also, Peter Scott's bird sanctuary at Slimbridge, the medieval towns of Chester, Cambridge and Oxford.

Rent a car, drive into the country and talk to the people about their beautiful gardens.

Finland. Abundant fishing in the summer. Law and order year-round.

France. Loud, unmellow Americans are often snubbed in Paris. Some folks believe the French have the right to be insular, as they enjoy fine food, romantic people and fabulous scenery. Ride-sharing: Allostop.

In Paris see the Arc de Triomphe, Eiffel Tower, Invalides and Tomb of Napoleon, the Louvre, Musee d'Orsay, Notre Dame, the Pantheon, Sacre Coeur, Sainte Chapelle, Versailles. (P.S.: Learn the French pronunciations.)

Drive the wine road between Macon and Dijon and look for country inns in which to hibernate. The Riviera is crowded dur-

> *London, though handsomer than Paris, is not so handsome as Philadelphia.*
> —Thomas Jefferson

↑ ing the summer, as are the Alps during Easter and Christmas.

Germany. Beer hall extravaganza. Don't miss the Technical Museum in Munich. Oktoberfest is their Mardi Gras. Get out of the city—into the Black Forest. See the cathedral of Cologne (Koln), experience the night scene along Hamburg's Reeperbahn and hike along the Rennsteig in Thuringer Walk in eastern Germany. Ride-sharing: Mitfahrzentralc.

Gibraltar. Duty-free bargain hunting by the Rock.

Greece. Inexpensive compared to the rest of Europe, but not as economical as Turkey. In Athens, visit the Acropolis and the National Archaeological Museum.

The islands are all a guaranteed fun time from April to November. Pick one and enjoy. See the Ruins in the Peloponnes and the monasteries of Metéora.

Hungary. Very friendly folks. Conveniently connected to the rest of Europe by Eurail.

Also try the Hungarian National Museum, any boat trip in the Danube Bend, visiting the towns of Tihany and Sopron, enjoying a spa, perhaps Heviz.

Iceland. Expensive. If you fly Iceland Air between the United States and Europe, take advantage of the free stopover in Reykjavík. Bus tours make sense to experience the hot springs, rugged volcanoes, geology, glaciers and faults. Clean hostels.

Ireland. Rent a car (make reservations in the United States) and savor the scenery, convenience and common language. The village of Doolin Pt. is known for its traditional Irish music. Since most pubs offer free pints to musicians, most pubs have music. In walkable Dublin, see the Book of Kells in the Trinity Library, Merrion Square's architecture and the National Museum. Also, the James Joyce Museum in the Martello Tower in Sandycove, the Dingle Peninsula, the Cliffs of Moher in County Clare, the city of Galway and Donegal in the northwest.

Italy. In Milan, don't miss the paintings by Leonardo da Vinci in the Pinacoteca Ambrosiana or his Last Supper in Santa Maria delle Grazie.

In the Renaissance city of Florence visit Academia, The Baptistry, Duomo, Palazzo Vecchio, Uffizi Gallery.

Rome is expensive, but see the Colosseum, Forum, Pantheon, Trevi Fountain, Vatican with St. Peter's Basilica.

See The Bridge of Sighs (also a song by Robin Trower) in Venice. Skiing in the Italian Alps is relatively inexpensive. The ruins at Pompeii and Paestum are unbelievable; so are the catacombs of Naples. Consider a driving tour in the Como Lake region or the Italian Riviera.

Liechtenstein. Nice place for a sandwich.

Ios is the place. It's the inhibition-deshacklement capitol of the Greek islands. Music, dance and laughter under the stars. Stucco skidmarks imparted by the walls of homes lining the narrow alleys. Spend two days (or two weeks) in Ios and you will catch the fever.
—Commentary from Alain Bedard, Greek Tourist Board

Madeira. Enjoy the fine wine on this lush island. Rocky shores and off-shore currents.

Majorca. Touristy. The mild, off-season winter is the best time for low-cost fun.

Malta. Take side trips to Comino and Gozo Islands. Warm people. Rocky beaches. Check out the Malta Government Crafts Center in Valetta.

Netherlands. A bicycle rider's dreamscape. Home of Amsterdam's world-famous red-light district, Rembrandt's house, Anne Frank's house and the Van Gogh Museum.

In Hague, visit the Mauritshuis Museum and Gemeentemuseum.

Keep your sense of humor and your common sense intact while visiting Amsterdam, otherwise, a maligned street urchin might cut one and steal the other.

Norway. Pricey. Take a coastal trip on the Bergen Line's mail boat (reserve months in advance). See the great fjords, especially Geirangerfjorden. Spectacular train adventure between Oslo and Bergen. In Oslo, see the Munich and Viking Ship Museums. Catch the midnight sun in the Far North from late May until late July.

Poland. The Poles are very hospitable to Americans, making it easy to get off the beaten path. In Warsaw, definitely go to the Wilanow and Lazienki Palaces. Explore the Baltic Coast or take a trip into the Tatra Mountains. See Marlbork Castle and consider visiting Auschwitz. Inexpensive.

Portugal. In Lisbon, visit the Madre de Deus church, Coach Museum, Alfambra, Torre de Belem. Elsewhere see the cathedrals of Alcobaca and Batalha. Visit the ancient towns of Elvas, Estremoz, Évora and Óbidos. See the fish market in Sines and the actual fishing at Nazaré.

Rhodes. Splendid architecture.

Romania. Lower on the "convenience" scale compared to the rest of Europe, adventure here comes easily. In Bucharest, see the Museum of Natural History's collection of 90,000 butterflies. Visit the Brukenthal Museum in the medieval city of Sibiu, which is also a great starting point for hiking. Pick a coastal point on the Black Sea and make independent arrangements with local anglers for a birding excursion. (The tour operator boats scare the birds away.)

Sardinia. Expensive resorts. Maybe a place to earn money?

Scotland. If you ask a regular tourist where to begin an adventure in Scotland, they recommend Edinburgh over Glasgow because it has more tourist attractions. Don't overlook Glasgow's new look and its down-to-earth people, who may be a bit difficult to understand even before a few lagers. The damp climate takes nothing away from many great walls.

Sicily. Ancient Greek temples and a fabulous off-season climate. Beware of motor-scooter drive-by purse and chain snatchers.

Spain. Madrid is a great walking city, and the Prado is a jaw-dropper. The coastal cities of Santander and San Sebastian are exciting, yet uncommercialized. Find a bullfight?

Sweden. In Stockholm, behold the Wasa Museum where a sunken ship is fully restored. In summer, take the Göta Kanal trip between Gothenburg and Stockholm (advanced reservations). Experience the midnight sun at Morrun in mid-March. Try to get a day's work on a salmon fishing boat.

Switzerland. Visit Zermatt and hike up or around the Matterhorn. Experience the medieval towns of Gottlieben or Stein-am-Rhein. Superior skiing in the Alps (gridlock during Easter and Christmas). Make a summertime excursion to the lake area known as Ticino.

Turkey. Definitely treat yourself to the Turkish bathhouse experience, a bizarre combination of steam, sauna, massage and bathing. Get yourself lost in the shopping labyrinth of Istanbul's Grand Bazaar and witness the magic of Muslim prayer in a mosque, especially the Basilica of Hagia Sophia (also in Istanbul). Do not miss the ancient ruins of Ephesus.

Middle Eastern Countries and Northern Africa

In spite of the gloomy media stories, the Middle East and parts of neighboring North Africa continue to be undiscovered destinations for global adventurers. If you've previously enjoyed the non-Western world and its inefficient airlines, social upheavals, despotic governments and religious wars of biblical intensity, then these regions may also interest you. Always get a report from the U.S. State Department first. State Department Travel Advisory Hotline is (202) 647-5225 or (202) 647-5226. Call for updated travel advisories.

Here are some Middle East and northern African highlights.

Egypt. The Pyramids, the Valley of the Kings, the Sphinx and King Tut's tomb make Egypt the primary destination in the East. That was true until Muslim fundamentalists began taking target practice at cruise ships on the Nile. Terrorism has devastated Egypt's tourist industry opening the door for bargain hunters. Statistically, you are in less danger of being shot in Egypt than if you were visiting a major U.S. city. Go for a camel trek across the Sinai Peninsula.

Israel. Traditionally isolated by its Arab neighbors, Israeli tourism expects to benefit from the Middle East peace process. Most of Israel is safe and accessible, except for the West Bank and Gaza Strip. Yet, even in Jerusalem, soldiers and citizens carry guns in the wake of ongoing troubles with Palestine.

Travel restrictions into neighboring Jordan have eased. Definitely consider a trip to Petra, a rose-red city carved into a canyon by the ancient Nabateans.

Lebanon. Although Lebanon is recovering from its ongoing civil anarchy, Beirut still looks like a war zone. The Mediterranean beaches and nearby ski resorts invite the same "sea and ski in the same day" opportunity as Hawaii's Big Island.

Unfortunately, the U.S. State Department puts Lebanon off-limits to American citizens. Theoretically, penalties can be expensive, but in reality penalties are rare. Many Lebanese embassies and consulates will issue you a visa on a piece of paper instead of stamping it in your passport. There is no standard policy on this practice.

Westerners, no longer appealing to kidnappers, enjoy Lebanon's excellent restaurants.

Morocco and Tunisia. Along with Egypt, Morocco and Tunisia are North African countries inviting tourism. Adventure bargains exist! Morocco's Riff Mountains are fabulous.

Oman. Oman is an exception from the other Gulf states and welcomes tourists, especially rich ones. Each year more westerners discover Oman's pristine beaches and untamed wilderness.

Saudi Arabia. A place to make money. Proud home of the two holiest Islamic sites, Mecca and Medina, and an incredible expanse of desert wilderness. For those with a taste for gore, it has public beheadings.

However, Saudi Arabia is not keen on western tourists and in the interest of screening out western decadence, they have banned tourists and even satellite dishes. The only way to enter is to have business in the kingdom and a Saudi sponsor.

Syria. Damascus, the capital and home of magnificent mosques can resemble a police state. Syrian embassies frequently reject tourist visa applications for no obvious reason. One definite reason for rejection is having an Israeli stamp in your passport (or even if you have a "Jewish-sounding" name).

Expect to be regarded with suspicion when applying for a tourist visa. Tourists are rare, and Syrians, involved in the supposed hospitality business, possess the customer service skills of a Chinese train station ticket clerk. Also similar to China in the past, is the special tourist money you must use to pay your bills. The tourist money rate is about half the official bank rate.

Yemen. The once easygoing Yemen recently erupted into civil war.

I don't recommend travel to Algeria, Libya, Iran and Iraq for obvious reasons.

Ten Rules of Behavior in Arab-Speaking Countries

The dos and don'ts in Arabic-speaking countries can often be traced to Islamic teachings, which are unfamiliar to many of us. Hospitality holds a very important place in the Arab world, and every effort will be made to treat visitors cordially, but since many common customs—even courtesies—in the West may offend or embarrass Arab hosts, the following basic guidelines should be followed. (The degree to which these rules of behavior are followed varies from country to country, but it never hurts to err on the conservative side.)

1. Never give a gift of an alcoholic beverage or a representation of women (photos, sculpture, etc.). Cologne makes a nice present.
2. Don't point or use your hands to signal someone.
3. Compliment in a general sense ("You have a beautiful house."), but avoid specifics ("What a nice vase!"). Your host may feel obliged to give you what you admire.
4. Don't refuse a gift; to do so is very offensive. Accept (and give) gifts with your right hand only.
5. Don't wear shoes when walking on carpets.
6. If you're a man and another man invites you to his home, don't assume your wife or girlfriend is included in the invitation. If she is invited, she may end up eating with the women of the household—separately from the men.
7. Men shouldn't bring a hostess a gift or inquire about a host's wife if she's not present during a meal. If she's introduced, shake hands only if she offers her hand first.
8. Dress modestly if you're a woman: keep shoulders and upper arms covered, and don't wear short dresses or skirts above the knee.
9. Offer refreshments such as coffee or tea if you're acting as host.
10. Don't walk in front of someone who is praying.

Routing Suggestions

West Coast Departures (San Francisco or Los Angeles)

$1,249 West Coast–Hong Kong or Tokyo or Taipei–Bangkok–Bombay–Delhi–Europe–surface–London–New York

$1,349 West Coast–Hong Kong or Tokyo or Taipei–Bangkok–Cairo–Istanbul–surface–London–New York

$1,549 West Coast–Hong Kong or Tokyo or Taipei–Bangkok–surface–Kuala Lumpur–Europe–West Coast

$1,549 West Coast–Manila–Brunei–surface–Bangkok–Madrid–surface–Paris–West Coast

$1,549 West Coast–London–surface–Rome–Seychelles–Singapore–surface–Bangkok–Tokyo–Los Angeles

$1,549 West Coast–Amsterdam–surface–Athens–Bangkok–Hong Kong–Tokyo–West Coast

$1,699 West Coast–Hong Kong–Bangkok–Calcutta–surface–Delhi–Amman–Casablanca–surface–Paris–West Coast

$1,699 West Coast–Europe–Moscow–Delhi–Bangkok–surface–Singapore–Jakarta–Bali–Hawaii–Los Angeles

$2,099 West Coast–London or Europe–surface–Athens–Bombay–surface–Delhi–Kathmandu–Bangkok–surface–Singapore–Hong Kong–Taipei–West Coast

$2,199 West Coast–London or Europe–surface–Athens–Cairo–Nairobi–Bombay–Delhi–Kathmandu–Bangkok–Jakarta–Bali–West Coast

East Coast Departures (New York)

$1,349 New York–Hong Kong–Singapore–surface–Bangkok–Bombay–Delhi–Europe–surface–London–New York

$1,449 New York–Hong Kong–Bangkok–Cairo–Paris–New York

$1,549 New York–Hong Kong–Bangkok–surface–Kuala Lumpur–Europe–surface–London–New York

$1,599 New York–Hong Kong–Bangkok–Kathmandu–Delhi–surface–Bombay–Cairo–Athens–surface–Paris–New York

$1,649 New York–London–Kathmandu–Bangkok–Seoul–New York

$1,699 New York–London–surface–Rome–Bangkok–

Manila–Sydney–surface–Melbourne–Auckland–Los Angeles–New York

$1,749   New York–Amsterdam–Bangkok–Vietnam–Cambodia–Hong Kong–Taipei–New York

$1,799   New York–Tokyo–Kuala Lumpur–Madras–Colombo–Frankfurt–Iceland–New York

$1,999   New York–London or Europe–surface–Athens–Pakistan–Delhi–Kathmandu–Bangkok–Tokyo–Hawaii–San Francisco–New York

$2,299   New York–Paris–surface–London–Namibia–Capetown–surface–Johannesburg–Mauritius–Singapore–Hong Kong–New York

Typical airline ticket cost for circle-the-globe flights? $1,700!, using one airline ticket consolidator. Circle-the-globe expense approximations are similar to Circle-the-Pacific-Rim expenses. This particular routing: New York, Dublin, London, Istanbul, Karachi, Kathmandu, Bangkok, Manila, Honolulu, San Francisco for $1,700. Not bad, huh? (All prices are approximations. Contact a consolidator for latest deals.)

Note: When renting a car overseas, make all arrangements (including LDW/CDW via a gold card) with a U.S.-based agency.

Most travelers content themselves with what they may chance to see from car windows, hotel verandas, or the deck of a steamer … clinging to the battered highways like drowning sailors to a life raft.
—John Muir

Eurail Passes and Air Passes

A Eurail Pass allows you to travel on any train in most European countries and in North Africa. The United Kingdom has an independent system, but the channel links the systems. Prices range from $500 for a two-week pass to $1,400 for a three-month pass for first-class accommodations. Special second-class passes are available for travelers under twenty six years of age.

An Air Pass is a "multiflight coupon book" of discount airline tickets within a country which are sold outside of the country you wish to travel in. If you plan to be in a specific country for an extended period and want to minimize long train and bus rides, take advantage of the airlines' answer to a Eurail Pass. For example, an Australian air pass allowing four flights within Australia costs $445. These passes cannot be purchased within the country of travel.

Usually, you must purchase the pass before you arrive in the country. Most often an air pass must be purchased in conjunction with an international flight you purchase from the same airline. You can book these passes on your own by contacting the airlines directly. Usually starting and ending dates must be set, but intermediate dates can be left open.

Climate Concerns

Seasonal concerns are even more valid for circle-the-world tours than for circle-Pacific tours. The Weather Channel provides worldwide forecasts.

Europe

There are three basic climate zones in Europe. Northwestern Europe has a wet, temperate climate. Rain occurs at any time, and it can be especially heavy in Ireland and the British Isles. There are rarely great extremes in hot or cold weather. Central and eastern Europe have wet climates with cold winters and warm, dry summers. Southern Europe has a Mediterranean climate with mild, wet winters and warm to hot, dry summers.

Africa

Northern Africa has a predominantly dry, desert climate. Most of the rain falls in the wintertime in the northern coastal regions. Sharp drops in temperature occur in the evenings in the inland desert areas. A similar climate can be found on the Arabian Peninsula. Middle Africa has a hot tropical climate—hot and very wet in countries on or near the equator. Elsewhere, there is a distinct pattern of wet and dry seasons. Southern Africa has a desert climate inland, with a cold winter season. The southwest coast has a hot and dry climate. The southeast coast has a warm and wet climate. The southernmost part of South Africa resembles a Mediterranean climate.

The Middle East

The Middle East has a predominantly dry, desert climate.

TRAVELING ACROSS NORTH AMERICA

See and feel the real America. Sample the regional cuisine instead of eating plastic-roof franchise burgers. Buy a road atlas and use your imagination. Stay off the interstates when you can. They hide the landscape and the people. Life doesn't happen along interstates. It's against the law. You needn't leave the country to set your gypsy blood on fire. There are many bells to sound and whistles to blow right in your own backyard.

Audrey's Story

Audrey graduated from college and like many other recent graduates, decided to spend that summer exploring Europe gallivanting on a Eurail Pass. It was a great experience and she met lots of people, including a surprising number of fellow Americans. Upon returning, she began a demanding career in advertising. Whenever she had vacations she made it a point to "get away from it all," visiting the Caribbean, taking African safaris or revisiting her beloved Europe. One evening she met a couple who had just moved from Washington, D.C., to San Francisco and were raving about their recent drive across America. Their eyes glowed as they described their visits to the Grand Canyon, Zion National Park and Great Sand Dunes National Monument.

It dawned on Audrey that even though she was internationally well-traveled she had never explored her own country. Soon after using a domestic charter company offering one-way, coast-to-coast flights ($129) and an auto driveaway (no charge to transport car between cities), she and a friend set out on a mission for manifest destiny. She learned more about her country in two weeks than in her entire previous lifetime and made friends in every state. Every time she looks at a U.S. map she smiles. This was truly an adventure to remember.

To the Coast and Back for Peanuts

This adventure involves flying to either U.S. coast on an air charter or low-cost commercial flight, and then leisurely driving back across the country using a free auto driveaway car, renting an inexpensive car, truck or van, or joining a road-adventure travel excursion.

Driving a round-trip national loop from your hometown could result in too much driving time. You can always take another cross-country tour in the other direction another time. If you don't live in a city with air charters, look into other low-fare flight options. Fly one-way to either coast: New York; Boston; Portland, Maine; San Francisco; Seattle; Portland, Oregon or Miami in summer; Norfolk; Washington, D.C.; San Diego or Los Angeles in winter. Since the airlines aren't cost effective for one-way travel consider a domestic air charter company.

Air Charters

Charter companies rent or own airplanes that are contracted (chartered) out to businesses and group travel organizations. Charter companies resemble mini-airlines. Any ensemble of travelers can purchase blocks of seats on an air charter. Some air charter companies refer to filling empty seats as "hitching a ride." One-way and round-trip seats are often available up to the day of the flight as last-minute add-ons. In these cases, tickets can be purchased from the charter company at the airport.

Scour your local Sunday newspaper travel section for advertisements. Some travel agents can find you a seat on an air charter; however, travel agents are not usually aware of many charter flights because they're not in their computer systems. Because charter companies may only have one flight per day, their flight numbers, departure gates and times and baggage pick-up points can change, causing major confusion. Always double check all charter flight details.

American charter companies are bonded by the U.S. Government, making refunds possible. Do check on any charter company's stature by contacting the Better Business Bureau.

Locate "Discount Regional Airlines and Air Charters" in Appendix 1, your local *Yellow Pages*, or contact a travel agent.

Inexpensive Major Airline Fares

It's tough to beat the major airlines' short-term promotional fares (provided you can comply with cancellation penalties, minimum or maximum length of stay, nonrefundable or advance-purchase requirements). Keep your eye on the newspapers for their short-term promotions such as straight fare reductions, free tickets to one destination if you purchase a ticket to another, or free companion tickets. Sharp travel agents can be up on such deals before word hits the street.

When there are no promotions available, consider these cost-cutting strategies:

Hub fly through. Some cities are cheaper to fly to if you pretend that you are going to another destination. When an airline monopolizes flights in and out of its hub city, ticket prices to that city can be stiff. Often, it's cheaper to buy a ticket to a different city using your desired destination for a connection stopover. Simply disembark the aircraft during the stopover (carry-on luggage only!). This strategy of buying a ticket from point A to point C via point B to avoid the larger expense of a direct A to B flight does break the airline's rules. However, when fares are

It began in mystery, and it will end in mystery, but what a savage and beautiful country lies in between.
—Diane Ackerman

not related to the distance traveled, you might as well save a buck.

A possible problem arises when your A to C ticket is also your return-trip ticket and there is no record of your reboarding the flight in city B. Your return reservation can be canceled from the airline computer.

There are three ways around this snafu: 1. Book a return flight with another airline (but now you may have paid an atrocious one-way fare). 2. Check in at city B but never get on the plane (you need to be quite swift for this one). 3. Inform the airline of your stopover for "sudden business or personal reasons," and make sure that your return flight will not be affected. This way the reservation agent can bypass the automatic reservation-dump command.

Conversely, because most airlines operate on a hub-and-spoke system, you will occasionally find one offering double frequent-flyer miles to passengers foregoing direct flights by flying via the hub (possibly changing planes) between the two spoke cities.

Split tickets. If you take advantage of promotional specials or fare wars, a split ticket can save you big bucks on certain routes. A ticket from your home city to an intermediate point A combined with a second ticket from A to your final destination B can cost less than your best deal on a direct "home" to B flight. Got that?

The downside is that the added connections can add hours to your trip. On the other hand, just think of the connections as additional opportunities to volunteer yourself to be bumped off a oversold flight in exchange for a free domestic round-trip flight.

Back-to-back excursions. This scenario prevents you from being penalized on a round-trip ticket where you don't stay over on a Saturday night. It can also provide you with an identical, free round-trip flight. If the cheapest round-trip excursion costs less than half the unrestricted one-way fare, it then makes sense to buy two round-trip coach excursions tickets: one from your home city to your destination and one from your destination to your home city. You save money by using the first half of each round-trip ticket with the option to use the second halves of these tickets for another round-trip!

Buying frequent flyer mileage awards. There are agencies that buy and sell frequent-flyer miles. They advertise in newspapers and magazines. The best deals from these agencies are for first- and business-class service. Buying and selling frequent-flyer mileage violates airline rules. Warning: In a situation such as this, where you break the airline's rules, you run the risk of dishonoring your ticket, then having to pay the higher fare on the spot.

Also consider the smaller, low-cost airlines. These no-frill airlines, such as Kiwi and American Trans Air, offer rock-bottom fares for anyone willing to sit out a meal and put up with tighter than normal seating. Refer to the list of low-fare airlines in Appendix 1.

If you must fly without advance reservations, contact a last-minute ticket broker. As opposed to flying standby, when you don't have a confirmed reservation, last-minute programs fill charter or airline seats that would have otherwise gone empty. These agencies can also offer a 30- to 50-percent savings on last-minute bookings for tours, cruises and accommodations. Some have annual fees around $20–$50 and provide newsletters and toll-free hotlines.

Senior programs. Look into Continental Airline's Freedom Passport Senior Program: $1,999 for one trip every week of the year (26 round trips). Adds up to $38.44 per flight, which could be up to five connecting flights to cross the States (great if you enjoy "flying around"!).

You are supplied with unlimited blank vouchers, so you literally "write your own tickets"! Consider joining their VIP "President's Club" if you fly frequently. The free drinks, snacks and other amenities will offset the cost. The lounges are also a sanctuary from airport chaos.

You can add international trips at discounted prices (European cities cost only $500 more).

Continental's Passport comes in a first-class version for an additional $1,500. For a mere $67.50 you can go first class anywhere, weekly!

Usually, you only may make reservations or select seats within a week of travel, for noon on Monday through noon Thursday or all day Saturday. You must stay over for Sunday night and may visit each city only three times, but this can be circumvented by using nearby cities and renting a car, though some cities have several airports considered as one. However you can fly standby on any flight, any time, even holidays. And most rules don't seem to apply to standby.

Road Trips

Road Warrior Reflections

It wasn't hard for me to persuade myself to abandon the relative charms of hearth and home again. I hadn't one for a year (or however long it had been). Experience has since proved to me that on any sojourn, the pencil is mightier than the pen. Plans never pan out. Plan on nothing except for recurring travel imbroglios, like getting lost or a spontaneous invite for dinner with a church group.

When a strategy is necessary, trust that cops and bartenders know more about their hamlet than the chamber of commerce because they work nights as well. Street-smart folk usually enjoy consulting strangers on the whereabouts of the best meal deals, danger zones, reasonable accommodations, safe camping, worthwhile attractions, scenic hikes and noteworthy hangouts. It's also vital to discern which tavern is the cornerstone for the old-timers, who speak loudly, making it easier to eavesdrop on local gossip. Tactics as such were used by Steinbeck, Kerouac and Moon.

And what about the classic road-trip authors? Steinbeck's insightful masterpiece is nearly forty years old. Kerouac ended up living with his mother. Kesey's legacy took a major blow with the passing of Jerry Garcia. Heat Moon never misbehaved or even tactfully roused his environs. Pirsig (*Zen and the Art of Motorcycle Maintenance*) progressed ever-so-slowly into another mental excursion book, *Lila*. Hunter S. Thompson has taken to ripping apart the polo world.

Go write your own book.

Then he was told: Remember what you have seen, because everything forgotten returns to the circling winds.
—lines from a Navajo wind chant

Buy a road atlas (11-inch-by-18-inch) and begin creating. Depending upon the season, plan a northern or southern route. Avoid interstates whenever possible (it's not a race). Adventure Cycling (formerly Bike Centennial), an evolution of the Bicycle Travel Association, provides informative maps highlighting the optimum routes for cyclists pedaling cross-country. They are ideal for routing motorcycle and auto crusades as well. Adventure Cycling, P.O. Box 8308, Missoula, MT 59807; (406) 721-1776.

A northern route itinerary might include (from west to east) exploration along California's coastal Highway 1, camping in Washington's Cascade Mountain Range; a night on the town in Missoula, Montana; Wyoming's Grand Tetons; Mount Rushmore; Badlands National Park; a bit of disco dancing in Rapid City, South Dakota; a swim in the Missouri River; a draft beer in Milwaukee; a ball game in Chicago; a glimpse of Niagara Falls; New York's Adirondack Mountains and down to New York City's Central Park for a frisbee toss in the sheep meadow.

Our national parks are home to some of the most incredible scenery on earth. The National Park Service and the U.S. Department of the Interior usually provide maps at park entry points. The more spectacular parks are no secret, so you may want to consider an off-season excursion. Here is a list of parks you must see:

Grand Teton	Hawaii Volcanoes, Big Island
North Cascades	Glacier Park
Yellowstone	Smoky Mountains
Great Sand Dunes National Monument, Colorado	Joshua Tree National Monument
San Juan National Forest	South Padre Island, Texas
Arches National Park	Craters of the Moon, Idaho
Bryce Canyon	Black Hills, South Dakota
Zion National Park	Baxter State Park, Maine
Grand Canyon	Wrangell–St. Elias, Alaska
Badlands, South Dakota	The Appalachian Trail
Canyonlands	White Mountains, New Hampshire
Yosemite	
Blue Ridge Parkway	Cape Hatteras National Seashore, North Carolina
Alligator Alley, Florida	
Adirondack Mountain Park, New York	Boundary Waters, Minnesota
	Isle Royale, Minnesota

Here's a drive cross-country cost breakdown (fly one-way; return via a two-week auto tour):

$129	one-way air charter fare: San Francisco—New York or Los Angeles—New York (either way)
$0	auto driveaway vehicle
$175	gas based on a wandering 3,750-mile tour
$420	expenses at $30 per day for 14 days (2 or more persons)
$724	total

The one- to three-week time frames for these type of adventures allow an individual with limited vacation time to enjoy life "off the beaten path," even if they're not bursting at the seams with cash. Plus, you don't need a passport.

See Appendix 1 for cross-country drive circuit suggestions.

Six Classic Auto Tours

Here are brief descriptions of six dazzling North American driving tours.

Blue Ridge Mountain Dirt Road Dream. Hunters Creek near Big Island, Virginia. This state-maintained dirt road winds along the Appalachian Trail (AT) within Jefferson National Forest. This region is rarely visited by myopic vacationers busying themselves along the nearby Blue Ridge Parkway. The heavily trafficked parkway is best utilized as a shortcut to backroads. Although Big Island is home to a paper mill, the town and surrounding community is genuine Appalachia. Lynchburg, Virginia, is the nearest met-

Hot Tip

Order the Green Tortoise Cross-country Communal Bus Brochure for road-tour routing ideas (it's free!); call (800) 867-8647.

ropolitan area. No fee or permit is required for camping at Hunters Creek. They have horse trails and basic cuisine.

Off the Blue Ridge Parkway: From Route 81 S., take 64 E. to Blue Ridge Parkway S., to milepost 69. Three-tenths mile past milepost 69 at the James River Valley parking area take the dirt road on the left heading down the mountain 2.9 miles to the bridge at the intersection and make a right toward Hunters Creek and beyond to cross the ford and eventually the Appalachian Trail.

From Lynchburg, Virginia: Take 501 N. to Big Island. Go left on Route 122 for 4.4 miles. Take a right on Route 602, go .4 mile to the intersection and make a left toward Hunters Creek and beyond.

California Triangle. Los Angeles, Yosemite, San Francisco, Pacific Coast Highway (PCH), Los Angeles. (You can also start from San Francisco.) Drive, air charter or take the magic bus (Green Tortoise) to the West Coast and rent a car. Yosemite is less crowed during the week. PCH vistas are more spectacular southbound. Don't pay to enter Big Sur Redwood Forest: park across the street.

Off-the-beaten-path on PCH: San Carpoforo Beach. Clever motorists often take up temporary residence parking off the PCH. Even more curious are the surfers taking up residence in driftwood huts on the beach. San Carpoforo is a locals' surf beach accessed via a 10-minute climb down into a green valley with a cove 7 miles south of Gorda and 15 miles north of the Hearst Castle (6.5 miles north of the Texaco Mini-mart/Motel). Ask a local where camping is free. It's .2 mile north of San Carpoforo Creek.

Adirondack *Mountain-Bushwhacking Beaver Dam Extravaganza.* The rugged Adirondacks, teeming with mountains and lakes, also present trail-less hikes for the bold thrillseeker. This particular hike offers views into a complex beaver colony in a pristine wilderness.

Take 87 N. from Albany, New York (Adirondack Northway), to Exit 25–Chestertown. Take Route 8 W. toward Riparius. After crossing Hudson River in Riparius, make a right .2 mile after the bridge onto River Road Cutoff (alternate route to North Creek). Join River Road and drive approximately 4 miles, park on the left side after crossing the bridge and follow the river upstream on the left into the beaver colony. Be careful—no trails. Eat and sleep in North Creek or Chestertown.

Colorado's San Juan Loop. From Durango, Colorado, head north on Route 550 through Silverton and visit Ouray, an artists' hamlet surrounded by crisp, jagged peaks. Continue clockwise onto Route 62 or Route 145 and experience Telluride (win-

Dreams take up a lot of space? All you'll give them.

William Least Heat Moon, Blue Highways

ter or summer). This resort town is nestled at the end of a U-shaped valley of staggering mountainscapes. Great restaurants, pubs, street-craft vending and an abundance of earthy inhabitants.

Hawaii's Big Island. Rent a car at the airport in either Hilo or Kailua Kona and proceed in a loop using Routes 200, 190 and 19. By bisecting the island using Route 200 (the saddle road), it's possible to drive atop the summit of Mauna Kea, which is the highest point in Hawaii at 13,796 feet. There is an astronomical observatory on the summit, where hail and snow are common. A downhill, thrilling ride through black lava fields leads you to black-sand beaches and warm surf. On the loop drive, definitely hike down into the Waipio Valley and spend at least two days in Hawaii Volcanoes National Park.

Be careful—driving atop Mauna Kea is dangerous, and the car rental agencies are not at all keen on the idea. Rental contracts may be voided by driving on the saddle road. Ask questions, and no matter what, find a way to drive the full length of Route 200 (Saddle Road).

Driving to Mexico and Central America. You and a few friends convene in Austin, Texas, or another southern Texas town. Buy a station wagon or van (check insurance details). Drive as far south as you wish, sell the car and go home. It's definitely been done.

Road Adventure Travel Companies

A multiple of on-the-road adventure companies offer one 1- to 31-day tours for the pampered and the bohemian. Some venture into Canada and Mexico. Appendix 1 lists companies with trip explanations and prices for these assorted "auto-pilot" junkets.

Suggestion: Link together your domestic options: air charters, auto driveaways, auto rentals, road adventure companies. Here's an example: From Washington, D.C., take the East Coast Explorer to New York City. Charter a flight to San Francisco. Return to Washington, D.C., via the Green Tortoise cross-country tour. Here's the cost breakdown:

$32	East Coast Explorer to New York City (full day)
$129	air charter to San Francisco (or Los Angeles)
$279	Green Tortoise cross-country tour (2 weeks) return to D.C.
$440	

Car Rental

Once you fly into a coastal city, the simplest option is renting a car (hatchbacks are not recommended since they limit the amount of luggage you can conceal). Request a quality radio and tape

A man travels the world in search of what he needs and returns home to find it.
—George Moore

Hot Tips

- Cops and Bartenders know everything about their districts: best meal deal, perilous parts of town, reasonable accommodations, safe camping, worthwhile attractions, hikes, hangouts and probably a lot more.
- If America interests you, take the backroads.
- While road touring, college and university cafeterias are fun places to eat (and they are happy to take your cash). The scholarly populace-watching and the all-you-can-eat plan are a splendid blend. Student-union bulletin boards are usually overflowing with information on local entertainment possibilities. In the summer, some schools rent out their dormitory rooms.

deck and bring some of your own music. Always inspect the vehicle for pre-existing damage. Always verify that the rental company offers unlimited mileage. Unlimited mileage is becoming a standard in the industry, but one-way drop-off charges can be stiff. Agencies claiming no drop-off charge usually raise the daily rate accordingly.

Car rental agencies sometimes have directional imbalances, where they need additional cars in a particular city. In these cases they may be willing to waive one-way drop-off charges. You'd be surprised what you can save by probing for drop-charge exceptions. The largest agencies (Avis, Budget, Hertz and National) are most likely to have patterns conducive to low one-way rates. There may be restrictions on model type for inexpensive one-way rentals.

A credit card is necessary to rent a car. Most gold credit card holders are automatically entitled to free insurance coverage and may waive the expensive rental agency's collision damage agreement.

Comparison shopping, persistence and watching out for the rental company hidden charges will save you money. The best deals are in Florida and California. Some rental agencies try to bait and switch from their advertised promotions. Suddenly there are charges for extra insurance, mileage, taxes, additional drivers and one-way rental drop-off. Ask questions and fight back. These specials can also be limited to customers holding airline tickets. Another ploy is the upgrading of your vehicle class because of limited availability. (You should not pay more for an upgrade you didn't request.) Stand firm on the car you reserved and don't let an agent sway you into a more expensive car. In case of a breakdown, the larger agencies will repair or replace your vehicle quickly.

When you call a rental company's toll-free number, the reservation agent does not automatically volunteer their best bargains. You must probe for them. Make direct reference to their advertisements and cite the discount code in the fine print of their coupons. If you are renting a car for a cross-country tour, you will obviously satisfy all weekend and minimal-keep requirements. Search for companies that lower the per-day rate as rental time increases. You do need to be sure that you will be covered by their insurance in every state you visit. Also, be aware of your extra-day charges in case you miss your return deadline.

Keep an eye out for these auto rental bill inflaters:
- CDW/LDW (collision-damage waiver/loss-damage waiver). Surprise! At the rental processing counter the

agent attempts to scare you into paying an extra $7–$18 per day to clear you of responsibility if the car is damaged or stolen. Keep in mind that rental agencies and their employees are rewarded for CDW/LDW "sales." One false scare is stating that the renter cannot leave the state without coverage until a claim is settled. That's against the law.

- Each contract is different so read the fine print. The risk supposedly covered by CDW/LDW is often covered by your personal auto policy (find out before renting). Be careful, an increasing number of auto insurance companies are eliminating this coverage.

As I discussed in Part 2—Before You Hit the Road, the majority of gold status credit cards provide CDW/LDW coverage. Gold card coverage has time limitations. Standard Visa and MasterCard cover rentals for 15 days (time limitations vary by issuing banks). In the case of cross-country rentals, you may need to re-rent a car to maintain credit card insurance coverage. Do not drive without coverage. In case of a claim, you will deal directly with the credit card issuer.

Beware: Some CDW/LDW fine print can be arranged to hold you responsible for nearly any damage.

Other Things to Know about Renting a Car

If you are ever denied a car overseas for refusing this coverage, accept the coverage making a notation on the contract that you were coerced to do so. Demand a full refund when you return.

Purchasing CDW/LDW coverage does not provide liability insurance. The rules on liability insurance are changing fast. Find out if your personal auto insurance will cover your rental. If not, buy extra liability coverage in case the rental agencies policy is insufficient.

Always let the rental agency know the states you plan to visit and be sure all coverages apply.

Renting a car in New York City is insanely expensive.

Some agencies offer discounts to seniors (AARP membership is a good option).

Couples may want to consider renting a mini-van or station wagon. Equipping either one with an inflatable air mattress provides an ideal napping area.

For Canadian excursions it is cheaper to rent a car in the United States. Your auto insurance usually provides the same coverage as it does in the United States (check the policy).

Car Rental Companies

Alamo (800) 327-9633
Avis (800) 331-1212
Budget (800) 527-0700
Dollar (800) 800-4000
Hertz (800) 654-3131
National Rent-A-Car (800) 227-7368
For toll-free information, call (800) 555-1212.

Additional Drivers

Agencies can tack on charges for additional cross-country drivers. Some allow spouses to drive at no additional charge. It is absolutely necessary to list additional drivers. Breaking a rental contract and having an accident will turn your trip and your bank account into a nightmare. Hunt for a rental agency that doesn't charge for additional drivers.

Breakdowns

Avis, Budget, Hertz and National have far more offices than the smaller agencies. In case of an accident or breakdown the larger agencies are the safest bet for a rapid repair or vehicle replacement. Call collect or use their specified toll-free numbers for instructions.

The Gas Deal

When a car is rented with a full tank you are required to return it full. If they have to fill it up you will be stung by extremely high gas prices. Make sure the tank is full (beyond F) when you receive the car and return it full (on the F!). Now you're getting crafty!

Local Car Rental Agencies

A less expensive way to rent a vehicle upon flight arrival is to check the local *Yellow Pages* (and even the local chamber of commerce) for a local car rental agency. Airport general information desks and tourist literature stands also advertise the smaller rental agencies. Inquire about any geographical limits. The downside may be slow service in case of an emergency.

Auto Driveaways

The least expensive option is an auto driveaway company. You (and your pals?) provide one-way transportation for a company and your only expense is gas. As opposed to "Rent a Wrecks" (see your local *Yellow Pages*), driveaways are usually nice cars. A refundable deposit is required (returned upon delivery), and a reasonable destination date is arranged (often negotiable). If the initial destinations that are available at your time of travel are not ideal, the driveaway company can often link you to a second driveaway terminating closer to your final destination. Occasionally, they can arrange return cars following flight arrivals.

Questions and Answers about Auto Driveaways

Q: What is it?
A: Auto driveaway services, with offices throughout the United States and Canada, are basically matchmakers. Travelers need transportation between two geographic points. Clients pay driveaway services to transport vehicles between the same two points. An office places a traveler into a car and the match is made—both traveler and car arrive at their destination.

Q: How much does it cost?
A: There is no charge to drive one of these late-model autos. The cash deposit you place (usually $250) is refunded when you reach your destination. You even receive your first tank of gasoline free. Your expenses include part of the fuel and your normal food and lodging costs. There are no hidden expenses. There is no limit on the number of passengers.

Q: What about stopovers?
A: You and the driveaway agent agree on a routing and time of arrival. They recommend that you drive no more than eight hours a day (experience has shown that with pit stops and meals along the way, it averages out to 400 miles per day). This permits time for en route sightseeing or off-the-road excursions— just don't overdo it. Remember that you have signed an agreement signifying your intent to abide by the necessary requirements.

Q: What are those requirements?
A: Very simple—you're qualified if you are at least 21 and have a driver's license. You'll be fingerprinted, and along with a cash deposit, they'll need a verifiable destination address. ("All of this is for our protection as well as yours.") Auto driveaway rates for auto-owner customers and the regulations governing your rules of the road are the under the jurisdiction of the Interstate Commerce Commission. This is to your benefit.

Q: Who owns these cars?
A: A corporation who transfers an executive to another part of the country. A vacationer who wants their auto moved south for winter or north for summer. A "fleet car" is reassigned to another salesperson in a different part of the country. A dealer pur-

chases a car at an auction and wants it moved to their show-room. (Vacations, emergencies, transfers, relocations and resales represent only some of the stories behind auto driveaways.)

Q: Sell me—auto driveaway vs. air travel.
A: No contest, particularly if you want to *see* the United States or Canada as opposed to airline terminals. Give a driveaway company a few weeks to plan and you will nearly always have a choice of late-model cars, pickup trucks or vans. From Banff to Key West to the Grand Canyon, all it takes is a few extra days, and that allows for enterprising along the way. You can begin or continue your travel with an auto driveaway from almost anywhere.

Q: How do I sign up?
A: Hunt for auto driveaways in Appendix 1 or in your *Yellow Pages* under "Auto Transporters and Driveaway Companies."

Buying a Car?

Groups of Europeans and Australasians (people who live in New Zealand or Australia) visiting America often buy a car when they arrive and sell it when they leave. The idea is equally sensible for Americans visiting other Western countries (seems popular in Africa as well).

With a limited budget, you increase your chances of buying a lemon. A compression test is worth the money. Here are a few anti-lemon safeguards:

1. Sellers can often be convinced to drive their car to where you are. Run the engine for a least 15 minutes, listen for odd noises and keep an eye on the thermostat.
2. Drive the car to a speed of at least 65 miles per hour; be aware of hesitation or shaking.
3. Drive the car 10 miles per hour on a flat surface (preferably a parking lot) and depress the brake pedal quickly: the car should stop without pulling to one side. If it pulls to one side, there may be an alignment problem.
4. Match the mileage on the title with the odometer; look for a reversal of the odometer.
5. Check oil level (color), other fluid levels, tires (uneven wear?), belts (cracked or worn?), spare tire and jack.
6. Bargain till the cows come home.
7. Join AAA.
8. Pray.

Trains and Buses

Some travelers opt for bus or train travel. Buses are cheap and they go everywhere. However, they can be musty and claustrophobic. It's tough to sleep or move around and socialize on a bus like you can on a train.

On a train, the cheapest standard coach accommodation often resembles a semi-reclining Laz-E-Boy chair. For longer trips a sleeper berth is worth considering (ask about the old SlumberCoaches). All sleeper accommodations are first class. First-class customers are entitled to use Amtrak's Metropolitan Lounges (New York, Chicago, D.C., Philadelphia and Los Angeles). These lounges provide free soft drinks, coffee and tea in a civilized environment. Lounge cars are fine places for storytellers. The older coaches creak and moan as they gently rock from side to side. Trains can be mysterious and romantic.

The further in advance you purchase your ticket, the less you'll pay. Train fares, similar to airfares, vary depending upon peak status and holiday blackouts.

Amtrak

Amtrak is America's nationalized passenger rail service, also serving Toronto and Montreal (four trains making eight border crossings per day). Unlike plane travel, train passengers are eager to open up to strangers. Taking a train is an adventure in itself, providing great opportunities to interact with travelers from all over the world.

All Aboard America. A regional coach fare ($259–$339) reserving a specific itinerary for up to forty-five days of transit. Restrictions include date and route availability and having to set your itinerary prior to travel (date changes can be made only prior to travel). You are permitted three stopovers en route (not including your final destination). All Aboard America is a choice option for cross-country adventurers since you can disembark in America's western, central and eastern regions. Amtrak's cross-country trips are timed so that most of the dazzling scenery is experienced in sunlight.

Great American Vacations (a transcontinental package tour). Combinations of scenic Amtrak travel with air and hotel deals. Amtrak tours link air travel (United Airlines) in one direction with train travel in the other. These promotion rates are similar to typical transcontinental round-trip airfares ($459–$549). For more information on Great American Vacations, call Amtrak's toll-free number and request a complimentary copy of Amtrak's America. Shorter loop excursions are available. (Children and seniors receive discounts on Amtrak. See Appendix 1 under "Railway Services" for more information.)

Via Rail

The Canadian system is called Via Rail. To complete a Canadian cross-country tour you have to take three trains. In the Atlantic and western regions domed sightseeing cars are available. A fixed-price Can-railpass allows travelers unlimited coach travel for twelve days within a thirty-day period. Reserve early. Passengers on cross-country excursions can save 25 percent of coach fare by traveling during off-peak seasons (early January to late April) and up to 40 percent with a seven-day advance purchase (*Super Saver Rate*). Travelers under 25 and seniors over 60 receive additional discounts on Via Rail. (See also "Railway Services" in Appendix 1 for more information.)

Hitchhiking

The effigy of a stranded figure holding out their thumb on an American roadside is nearly a relic of the past. People don't trust much anymore. The West is more trusting than the East. If hitching is required, catching a ride along the side of a road should be your last resort (it's also usually illegal). You are better off gently approaching possible drivers outside of gas stations, truck stops and convenience stores. By explaining your situation and volunteering some identification you will increase your chances of getting a lift and making a friend. It's a good idea to get permission from the store manager first.

University ride-boards and newspapers advertise ride-shares for riders willing to split expenses. The ride-boards also provide resources for folks seeking rides. A cardboard sign stating your destination, or simply "Please," helps. Drivers make their decisions in 3 seconds. Dress neatly and smile.

Where to Stay

Selecting your nightly accommodations can provide boatloads of spontaneous fun. Every state has hostels and campgrounds. My travel philosophy discourages predictability, i.e., advanced registration for lodging. Of course, there are exceptions, but if you have an open itinerary and tent for backup, you should have smooth sailing. If you are prepared to camp often, there are private and public campgrounds everywhere: contact Kampers of America (KOA) and the National Campers and Hikers Association. Using discretion, consider camping free. The Bureau of Land Management offers free camping (most common on the

... I think about all the different ways we leave people in this world. Cheerily waving good-bye to some at airports, knowing we'll never see each other again. Leaving others on the road, hoping that we will.
—Amy Tan

For my part, I travel not to go anywhere, but to go. I travel for travel's sake. The great affair is to move.
—Robert Louis Stevenson

West Coast). The back country of national forest land is usually free for camping.

With the exception of camping, hostels and YMCA/YWCAs are the cheapest way to go. There are hundreds of hostels in the United States charging an average of $7–$25 per night. These are great places to meet people and gather information on special places to visit. Both organizations have complete listings. Call local information in any city for either organization (see Appendix 1 for general information). See also Appendix 2— Hostel Guide for a listing of many U.S. and Canada hostels.

Hotel and motel charges can add up, yet some travelers prefer convenience and have concrete hygiene ideologies. Shop around and bargain; it's not always critical to mention additional guests, and checkout times are always flexible. If the town or city feels right, splurging on a fancy hotel can be memorable (check for weekend specials).

Recommended Reading Geared to Inspire the Aspiring Road Warrior

> *Blue Highways—A Journey into America*, by William Least Heat Moon. Fawcett Crest Books/Ballantine Books.
>
> *Travels With Charley*, by John Steinbeck.
>
> *Zen and the Art of Motorcycle Maintenance*, by Robert M. Pirsig.
>
> *Fear and Loathing in Las Vegas*, by Hunter S. Thompson.
>
> *On the Road*, by Jack Kerouac.
>
> *Illusions*, by Richard Bach.

U.S. Tourist Board Event Information

State divisions of travel and tourism: Many states have hotlines providing information on vacation ideas, information on local fairs, festivals and even updated information on the dates for peak leaf-color changing. These bureaus will mail out free tourism catalogs.

See also "Domestic Tourist Boards" in Appendix 1 for more information.

Hot Tip

Camping gear—Be careful of overpriced sporting goods stores. K-Mart and Wal-Mart often have similar equipment for 50 percent less. Don't forget second-hand stores.

GLOBAL ADVENTURE RESOURCES:
A Thorough Guide to the Budget-Adventure Subculture

The following is a listing of reputable courier services, around-the-world airline ticket brokers, air charter companies, auto driveaway companies, shoestring tactic miscellany, adventure travel companies, offbeat travel-related publications, newsletters and more. Although there was great effort to provide accurate information, organizations close or can change their address or focus. My apology for any inconvenience.

Railway Services

AMTRAK: (800) 872-7245; Amtrak's *Great American Vacations*: (800) 321-8684. Write for Amtrak's America rail-travel planner: Amtrak Distribution Center, P.O. Box 7717, Itasca, IL 60143.

VIA RAIL CANADA: (514) 871-1331, or contact your local travel agent.

EURAIL: RAIL EUROPE INC., 226-230 West Avenue, White Plains, NY 10604; (800) 438-7245/(800) 848-7245.

RAIL VENTURES PUBLISHING: P.O. Box 1877, Ouray, CO 81427. Detailed itinerary suggestions of train routes in the United States, Canada and Mexico. Mail-order for *Rail Ventures: The Comprehensive Guide to Train Travel in North America*, by Jack Swanson. $14.95 (add $2 for postage).

The Official Railway Guide. Schedules and tariffs for AMTRAK and VIA RAIL. K-III DIRECTORY CORP.: 424 W. 33rd Street, New York, NY 10001; (212) 714-3100.

GRAY LINE OF ALASKA: (800) 544-2206. Luxurious, domed rail cars explore Alaskan wilderness. Narrated tours include meal and beverage services.

PRINCESS TOURS: (800) 835-8907. Similar to Gray Line (above) with better food.

Air Courier Companies

NOW VOYAGER: 74 Varick Street, Suite 307, New York, NY 10013; (212) 431-1616. *Air Courier Broker* services most European cities, plus South America, the Caribbean, Mexico and Asia. $50 registration fee good for one year. Excellent pre-recorded information for first-time couriers. Call at 9:30 A.M. for updates and last-minute specials.

DISCOUNT TRAVEL INTERNATIONAL (DTI): 169 W. 81st Street, New York, NY 10024; (212) 362-3636/fax (212) 362-3236. Call for daily update of last-minute specials. Offers flights to west Europe, Asia, Puerto Rico, Mexico and South America. No registration fee. Also has domestic and international "space-available" program.

COURIER TRAVEL SERVICE: (516) 763-6898. Services a wide range of European cities, as well as Hong Kong, Tel Aviv, Central and South America. No fee.

HALBART EXPRESS: 147-05 176th Street, Jamaica, NY 11434; (718) 656-8189/8379/8279. *Wholesale Courier* has flights to most European hubs, including those in central and eastern Europe. It also has flights from D.C., Chicago, Miami, Boston, Atlanta, Houston and Los Angeles. All processing is done through the N.Y. office. Call at 9:30 A.M. for last-minute specials.

AIR FACILITY: 153-40 Rockaway Boulevard, Jamaica, NY 10017; (718) 712-1769/0630. Services only South America (Brazil, Uruguay, Argentina, Venezuela and Chile). No registration fee. Flexible return.

EAST WEST EXPRESS: 507-535 Rockaway Avenue, Valley Stream, NY 11581; (718) 656-6246. Pacific Rim hub cities and Johannesburg.

JUPITER AIR: 160-23 Rockaway Boulevard, Jamaica, NY 11434; (718) 656-6050/(718) 656-6041. West Imperial Highway, Building 4, Section E, Los Angeles, CA 90045; (310) 670-5123. Flights to Hong Kong, London and Singapore. $35 registration fee good for one year.

JOHNNY AIR CARGO: (718) 397-5163/(800) 227-6182 The Philippines. Security deposit required.

WORLD COURIER: (800) 221-6600/(718) 978-9408. Milan, Mexico City. Possible hand-carries.

POLO EXPRESS: (415) 742-6692/(310) 410-6827. London and Europe from San Francisco and New York

INTERNATIONAL BONDED COURIERS (IBC): Pacific-1595 East El, Segundo Boulevard, El Segundo, CA 90245; (415) 697-5985 (recorded information). Flights **South America, Mexico City, Pacific Rim hubs** and **Sydney.**

RUSH COURIER: (718) 439-9043/8181. Only flies to **Puerto Rico.** Flights Tuesday through Saturday. No registration fee.

COURIER TRAVEL: 3011 S. Wolf Road, Westchester, IL 60154; (708) 409-1600. Chicago agent for *Halbart Express.* Services **London** and **Mexico City.**

MIDNITE EXPRESS INTERNATIONAL COURIERS: 930 West Hyde Park Boulevard, Inglewood, CA 90302; (310) 672-1100. Flights to **London.**

TNT EXPRESS WORLDWIDE: 4309 Transworld Drive, Schiller Park, IL 60176; (708) 671-9400.

EXCALIBUR INTERNATIONAL COURIERS: 6310 West 89th Street, Los Angeles, CA 90045; (310) 568-1000. Flights to **Asian hubs.**

1ST WORLD TRAVEL/SILVERFLIGHT: 11952 Wilshire Boulevard, Los Angeles, CA 90025; (310) 207-6353/(818) 881-5117. Los Angeles to **New York** and Los Angeles to **Hong Kong.**

IMS COURIER SERVICE: 2821 E. Commercial Boulevard, Suite 203, Fort Lauderdale, FL 33308-3459. Flights to **Jamaica.**

UTL TRAVEL: 320 Corey Way, South San Francisco, CA 94080; (415) 583-5074. Flights to **Hong Kong, Singapore, Manila** and **London.**

WAY TO GO TRAVEL: 1850 Union Street, Suite 6, San Francisco, CA 94123; (415) 292-7801. **Southeast Asia, Australia, London** and **Mexico City.**

LINE HAUL SERVICES: 7859 NW 15th Street, Miami, FL 33126; (305) 477-0651. Flights to **Argentina, Caracas, Lima, Brazil, Rio, Guayaquil, Quito.**

Newsletter: INTERNATIONAL ASSOCIATION OF AIR TRAVEL COURIERS: P.O. Box 1349, Lake Worth, FL 33460; (407) 582-8320. Membership includes courier update newsletter and a shoestring traveler newsletter. Registration fee is $35 a year. Write for a sample copy.

TRAVEL UNLIMITED: P.O. Box 1058, Allston, MA 02134. Twelve issues a year for $25.

AIR COURIER ASSOCIATION (club): 191 University Boulevard, Suite 300, Denver, CO 80206; (303) 279-3600. $30 lifetime membership fee; annual dues are $28. Call for a sample of impressive literature.

WORLDWIDE COURIER ASSOCIATION: 757 W. Main Street, Rochester, NY 14611-2332; (716) 464-9337/(800) 780-4359. Request newsletter: information and testimonials from happy couriers. Money-back guarantee membership ($58).

The Courier Air Travel Handbook: Field Travel Services, Department 4524, P.O. Box 45760, Seattle, WA 98145-0760. $9.95.

Around-the-World and Circle-the-Pacific-Rim Airline Ticket Consolidators

AIR BROKERS INTERNATIONAL INC.: 323 Geary Street, Suite 411, San Francisco, CA 94102; (415) 397-1383/(800) 883-3273. **Around-the-world** and **circle-the-Pacific** ticket brokers since 1987. Informed, courteous staff able to provide details on all aspects of "shoestring travel." Long-standing relationship with *Garuda Airlines,* the national carrier of **Indonesia.** Free newsletter.

SUNCO TRAVEL INTERNATIONAL: 690 Market Street, Suite 1501, San Francisco, CA 94104; (800) 989-6017/(415) 291-9960. Established, full-service discount international travel specialists. Experienced providers of **around-the-world** and **circle-the-Pacific** tickets with the option for land arrangements.

DEMOCRACY TRAVEL: 4818 MacArthur Boulevard NW, Washington, D.C. 20007; (800) 536-8728/(202) 965-7200. **Around-the-world** and **circle-the-Pacific** fares. Call for highly informative routing and rate brochure. As a full-service travel agency, Democracy Travel can also assist you in securing hotel reservations, car rental and escorted or independent tours. It also offers invaluable travel tips and details on how to obtain a visa.

TRAVEL TIME: 1 Hallidie Plaza, Suite 406, San Francisco, CA 94102; (415) 677-0799/(800) 956-9327. Customized, discount **around-the-world** itineraries. Strong in **Africa.**

GLOBAL ACCESS: 595 Market Street, Suite 2810, San Francisco, CA 94105; (415) 896-5333/(800) 938-5355.

The Frugal Globetrotter

Circle-the-globe and circle-the-Pacific ticket brokers with the ability to dip into South America economically. Groundbreaking consolidator to offer economic Circle–South America fares. (Bargain around-the-world fares dipping into the Southern Hemisphere. Visit Africa or Australia, bypassing the pricey South American airfares.)

PAN EXPRESS TRAVEL: 25 West 39th Street, Suite 705, New York, NY 10018; (212) 719-9292. For journeys originating in Canada, call (800) 363-3273.

High Adventure Travel, Inc.: 353 Sacramento Street, San Francisco, CA 94111; (415) 912-5600/(800) 428-8735. E-mail: airtrek@highadv.com. WWWeb:http://www.highadv.com. Personable, reliable. Call for free catalog.

Additional Consolidators

AIRFARE BUSTERS: Houston (713) 961-5109.

CHEAP TICKETS: (800) 377-1000.

CONSUMER WHOLESALE TRAVEL: New York (800) 223-6862.

DER TOURS: Los Angeles (800) 782-2424.

EURAM TOURS: Washington, D.C. (800) 848-6789.

THE FRENCH EXPERIENCE: (Europe only) New York (212) 986-3800.

GLOBE TRAVEL SPECIALISTS: New York (800) 969-4562.

INTERWORLD: Florida (800) 468-3796.

INTRAC: Boston (800) 873-4687.

OVERSEAS EXPRESS: Chicago (800) 343-4873.

STA TRAVEL: Los Angeles (213) 934-8722.

TRAVAC: New York (800) TRAV-800.

TRAVEL NETWORK: Bellevue, WA (800) 933-5963.

REBEL: (800) 227-3235, US to Europe.

EXPRESS DISCOUNT TRAVEL: (800) 228-0513 U.S. West Coast and Alaska to Mexico.

SUPERTRIP TRAVEL: (800) 338-1898 Around-the-world.

STERLING WORLDWIDE: 9841 Airport Boulevard, Suite 1126, Los Angeles, CA 90045; (310) 641-3138.

ACCESS: (800) TAKE OFF/(800) 825-3633.

UNITRAVEL: (800) 325-2222.

P & D TRAVEL: (213) 483-8539.

PEOPLE'S AIR TOURS, INC.: (800) 635-7184.

TRAVEL MANAGEMENT INTERNATIONAL: 39 JFK Street, 3rd Floor, Cambridge, MA 02138; (800) 245-3672/(617) 661-8187.

CUT THROAT TRAVEL/AERO TRAVEL GROUP: 731 Market Street, San Francisco, CA 94103; (415) 981-8747/(800) 642-TRIP. Around-the-world routings. Big discounts with Thai Airways. Also provides low round-trip fares to Europe and Hawaii.

Air Passes

ARGENTINA
Visit Argentina Air Pass on Aerolineas Argentinas (800) 333-0276.
The Visit Argentina Air Pass allows 4 flights within Argentina for $450. You can add up to four additional flights for $120 each. The pass is valid for 30 days and must be bought outside Argentina in conjunction with an international ticket to Argentina on any airline.

ASIA
Discover Asia Airpass on SilkAir (800) 745-5247.
Good for travel to or from Singapore and cities served in Cambodia, China, Indonesia, Malaysia, Myanmar (Burma), the Philippines, Taiwan and Thailand. Each flight costs $119 and is available to U.S. residents only. There is no minimum or maximum number of flights. Date and time changes may be made without penalty. Other changes cost $25. Nonrefundable.

AUSTRALIA and NEW ZEALAND
Australian Explorer Pass on Qantas (800) 227-4500.
Good for domestic travel within Australia and New Zealand. Does not permit international flights between Australia and New Zealand. Basic pass is $554, which includes four flight coupons. You can purchase up to 4 additional coupons for $146 each. If you don't plan on flying to Alice Springs, Ayers Rock, Dunk Island, Great Keppel Island, Lizard Island, Perth, Ramson Island or Queenstown, New Zealand, the pass drops to $484 and $121 for additional flights. The pass is valid as long as your international ticket to or from Australia is valid. It is fully changeable and refundable if not used at all. See also Qantas's South Pacific pass

(under "South Pacific") if you want to travel within and between Australia, Fiji and New Zealand.

Visit Australia Air Pass on Ansett Australia (800) 366-1300.
Ansett Australia has a Visit Australia Air Pass which is good for domestic travel within **Australia** and **New Zealand**. It is similar in price and destinations to Qantas's Australian Explorer Pass.

BALTIC STATES and SCANDINAVIA
SAS Visit Baltic Pass (800) 221-2350.
Buy 2–4 coupons; 2 for $210, 3 for $290, 4 for $370. Flights valid between **Copenhagen, Helsinki, Oslo, Stockholm, Scandinavia, Kaliningrad, Kiev, Moscow, Riga, St. Petersburg, Tallinn and Vilnius.** Coupons are valid for three months. Must be purchased in conjunction with a round-trip airfare from North America on SAS.

BOLIVIA
VIBOL Pass on Lloyd Aereo Boliviano (800) 327-7407.
The VIBOL Pass allows travel to any 5 cities in **Bolivia** excluding Potifi and Pando for $135. The pass must be bought in conjunction with an international ticket to **Bolivia** from Miami on Lloyd Aereo Boliviano.

BRAZIL
Brazil Air Pass on Varig (800) 468-2744.
Pass costs $440 for five flight coupons which are good for 21 days after the first flight. Fly anywhere in **Brazil**. The only restriction is that you can't repeat the same segment in the same direction. Must be purchased outside of Brazil.

CARIBBEAN
Super Caribbean Explorer on LIAT (800) 253-5011/ (Solidus) (212) 251-1717.
The Caribbean Explorer allows you 3 stops anywhere in the Caribbean where LIAT flies except Georgetown and Caracas, Venezuela during a 21-day period for $199. LIAT also offers a Super Caribbean Explorer Pass, which includes unlimited stops in the Caribbean in one direction during a one-month period for $357. These passes are nonrefundable. Changes are permitted for $25. Travelers cannot visit the same island twice except for making a connecting flight.

BWIA Caribbean Butterfly Fare (800) 327-7401.
BWIA has a pass which allows you to travel to **Antigua, Barbados, Grenada, Jamaica, St. Lucia** and **Trinidad** during a one-month period for $356. No backtracking is permitted; however, you may fly to the same airport twice for connecting flights.

CHILE
Visit Chile Pass on Lan Chile Airli[...]
The Visit Chile Pass is a regional [...] ther the northern or southern regi[...] ther north or south of Santiago. Ei[...] or you can combine both for $55[...] many flights as you want within a 21-day period, but you can't backtrack or fly the same route twice. The pass must be issued in conjunction with an international ticket to **Chile** on any airline. Advance reservations are recommended as space is limited. Flight and date changes are allowed at no charge. Routing changes cost $30. If you want to add **Easter Island** the pass costs $1,080 for one region or $1,290 for both regions and Easter Island.

COLOMBIA
Discover Colombia Air Passes on Avianca (800) 284-2622.
Avianca has several different air passes for visiting Colombia, depending on when you travel, where you want to go and which airline you fly to **Colombia**. The pass allows 5 flights within **Colombia** during a 21-day period. High season prices (June, July, August, December) are $20–$30 higher. Fly Avianca to Colombia, bypassing Laticia and San Andres and you can save quite a bit. Passes must be purchased in the United States for travel originating outside of Colombia.

Non-Avianca to Colombia $399, $429 (high season).
Avianca to Colombia $220, $250 (high season).
Non-Avianca and no Laticia, San Andres $289, $309 (high season).
Avianca and no Laticia, San Andres $142, $162 (high season).

EUROPE
Europe Air Pass on British Airways (800) 247-9297.
The Europe Air Pass is good for travel on British Airways, TAT, Deutsche BA and GTAir in **Europe**, the **Middle East** and **North Africa**. The pass is valid for 7–90 days, and you must buy a minimum of three and a maximum of twelve flight coupons. Pricing per flight varies from $75–$150 depending on which of the four regional zones you wish to travel in. Many intra-Europe destinations will require two coupons and backtracking through a major hub such as **London**, but you will still save considerable money. Itineraries need to be planned at least 7 days prior to international departure. Routing changes are not permitted; however, dates and flights may be changed for a $40 penalty providing the change is made prior to the flight date. This pass is available only to U.S. residents and must be purchased in conjunction with a transatlantic flight

don, Birmingham, **Manchester** or **Glasgow**
ny airline using any published fare. Discounted rates
re available for children and infants.

Discover Europe with British Midlands Air Pass (800)
788-0555.
British Midland Airlines which flies from London to
points throughout **Great Britain** and **Europe** has a
new flexible air pass program. Buy as many flights as
you want for only $109 per flight. You will need to
purchase the pass before you leave and it is valid for 90
days. You must be a U.S. resident to purchase this pass,
and you must buy it from a travel agent.

Euroflyer Pass with Air France (800) 237-2747.
If you buy a round-trip ticket from the United States
to **Paris** on Air France, or to **Brussels** on Sabena, or to
Prague on CSA-Czechoslovak Airlines, you can then
purchase coupons for air travel within Europe on any of
these airlines plus Air Inter for $120 each. Each cou-
pon entitles you to a one-way flight in Europe to over
100 European cities. You must purchase a minimum
of 3 coupons and a maximum of 9 coupons and use the
coupons within 2 months after the first one. The coupons may be purchased in conjunction with any published fare, which means consolidator tickets are probably out. You must purchase the pass in the United
States.

Passport to Europe on Northwest and KLM (800) 374-
7747.
Buy a ticket to Europe on Northwest or KLM and you
can buy a Passport to Europe ticket including 3 flights
within Europe for only $330. Price increases to $405
during high season (April 1–10; June–September; December 11–January 2). Additional flights can be purchased as well. The only drawback to this ticket is that
all KLM flights go through Amsterdam, which will
require two coupons for most intra-Europe flights. The
pass is valid for as long as your international ticket.

SAS Visit Europe Pass (800) 221-2350.
Purchase a minimum of 3 flight coupons for $327 and
$109 for each additional flight up to 8. Valid between
Scandinavia and all European destinations on SAS and
within the U.K. and between the **U.K.** and **Europe** on
British Midland. Must be purchased in conjunction
with a round-trip airfare from North America on SAS.
Pass is valid for 3 months.

Austrian Airlines (800) 843-0002.
Buy a ticket to **Austria** or **Switzerland** from the United
States on any airline and you can buy a minimum of 3
and a maximum of 8 European flights on Austrian Air-

lines, SwissAir, Tyrolean or Crossair for $130 each. Dates
may be changed without penalty. Routing changes in-
cur a $50 penalty. No changes permitted on the first
flight. Coupons are valid for 2 months or as long as
your international ticket (whichever is shorter).

Malev Hungarian Airlines (800) 223-6884.
Buy a transatlantic ticket to **Budapest** on Malev, the
Hungarian airline, and you can buy 3 flight coupons
for flights within Europe on Malev for $299. Price in-
creases to $379 for flights during June, July and Au-
gust. Additional coupons may be purchased. All of
Malev's flights go through Budapest, and connecting
flights will require 2 coupons.

FIJI
See South Pacific Pass on Qantas (under "South Pacific").

FINLAND
Finnair Holiday Ticket (800) 950-5000.
The Finnair Holiday Ticket includes 10 flight coupons
and costs $377. It is valid for as long as your interna-
tional ticket.

FRANCE
Le France Pass on Air France and Air Inter (800) 237-
2747.
Air France and Air Inter have teamed up to offer 3 passes
allowing air travel anywhere within **France**. The basic
Le France Pass is $279 and allows unlimited air travel
on any 7 days in a 1-month period. There's also a Le
France Air-Car Pass for $299, which allows for 2 days
of air travel and a 1-week car rental with unlimited
mileage. For students there's also a Le France Youth
and Student Pass for $189, which is the same as the
basic pass for anyone under 25 or students under 27.
All passes are valid for one year after purchase and must
be bought in the United States.

INDIA
Discover India Pass on Indian Airlines.
The Discover India Pass costs $400 and is good for 21
days. You are allowed unlimited flights as long as you
don't backtrack. Indian Airlines doesn't have an office
in the United States, but you can contact Air India at
(800) 223-2250 for more information on the pass, and
you can purchase the pass from your travel agent.

INDONESIA
Visit Indonesia Decade Pass on Garuda Indonesia (800)
342-7832.
The Visit Indonesia Decade Pass costs $300 for 3 flights
anywhere within **Indonesia**. Additional flights may
be purchased for $100 each, up to a maximum of 10
flights. The pass is valid for a minimum of 10 days and

a maximum of 60 days. You must enter Indonesia through a "valid" gateway city on Garuda. In the United States, the pass must be bought from Garuda or a Garuda consolidator. You can buy the pass in Indonesia as long as you do it within 14 days of arrival and present your Garuda ticket. All flight segments must be ticketed and confirmed 3 days prior to departure from the United States. Flight dates on segments after the first one may be left open.

MALAYSIA
Visit Malaysia Pass on Malaysia Airlines (800) 421-8641.
The basic Visit Malaysia Pass is good for 5 flights within the Malaysia Peninsula for $94. The pass is valid for 21 days. If you want to travel to **Sabah** and **Sarawak**, the pass increases to $194. You must combine the pass with one international sector to or from **Malaysia** on Malaysia Airlines. Pass is available only from Malaysia Airlines and only to non-Malaysia passport holders.

MEXICO
Visit Mexico with Aero Mexico (800) 237-6639.
The Visit Mexico pass includes 2 flights and costs $70–$175, depending on where you want to travel. The pass is good for 2–45 days. A $20 charge applies to changes once ticketed.

NEW ZEALAND
Air New Zealand Explorer Pass (800) 262-1234.
The Air New Zealand Explorer Pass is a flexible pass that includes a minimum of 3 flights and a maximum of 8 flights. The basic pass includes 3 flights and costs approximately $240. Additional flights cost approximately $75 each. The pass is valid for one year. Routing must be confirmed ahead of time and cannot be changed. Dates can remain open and may be changed without penalty.

See also Ansett's Visit Australia Pass and Qantas's Australia Rover and South Pacific Passes, which also include New Zealand travel.

NORWAY
Visit Norway Pass with Braathens Safe.
Each coupon costs $70 (within **North Norway** or **South Norway**) or $140 between North and South Norway. Must be purchased in conjunction with a round-trip airfare from North America on SAS. Call Five Stars of Scandinavia at (800) 722-4126.

PERU
Visit Peru with Faucett (800) 334-3356.
The Visit Peru Pass on Faucett costs $200 if purchased in conjunction with a Faucett ticket from the United States and $250 if you arrive on another carrier. You are allowed unlimited trips within **Peru** during a 90-day period; however, you cannot go to the same city more than once, except for unlimited connections as necessary through Lima. Date changes can be made, but routing changes may not be made once you purchase the ticket.

SCANDINAVIA
SAS Visit Scandinavia Pass (800) 221-2350.
The Visit Scandinavia Pass costs $80–$420 for a maximum of 6 flight coupons. Must be purchased in conjunction with a round-trip airfare from North America on British Midland, SAS or Varig. Fly between **Denmark, Norway** and **Sweden**; between Finland and Sweden; and within Norway and Sweden. Pass is valid for 3 months.

SOUTH PACIFIC (Australia, Fiji, New Zealand)
South Pacific Pass with Qantas (800) 227-4500.
Qantas's South Pacific Pass allows travel both domestically within and internationally between Australia, Fiji and New Zealand. The basic pass costs AUS$220 (about USD$160) per flight for a minimum of 4 and maximum of 8 flights. If you don't plan on flying to Alice Springs, Ayers Rock, Dunk Island, Great Keppel Island, Lizard Island, Perth, Ramson Island or Queenstown, New Zealand, the pass drops to AUS$170 (about USD$124) per flight. The pass is valid as long as your international ticket to or from Australia is valid. It is fully changeable and refundable if not used at all. This pass must be bought outside Australia or New Zealand at a Qantas office or travel agent.

THAILAND
Discover Thailand Air Pass with Thai Airways (800) 426-5204.
The Thailand pass costs $239 for 4 flight coupons. Additional flights may be purchased for $50 each, up to a maximum of 8. Must be issued in conjunction with a round-trip international ticket to **Thailand** on any airline. If you must take a connecting flight through Bangkok, it will count as 2 flight segments. Member WFrankJ says that he bought one in conjunction with a free frequent-flyer ticket. Pass is valid for 60 days.

NORTH AMERICA
Several of the U.S. and Canadian airlines have visit U.S.A. or North America passes. These are only available for purchase by non-U.S. and non-Canadian passport holders outside the United States. Most also require that the passes are purchased in conjunction with a ticket on the participating airline to the United States

or Canada. Here is information about a couple of these passes:

Visit North America on Continental and Air Canada (800) 776-3000.
Valid for travel anywhere in **North America** that Air Canada and Continental airlines fly. Available only to non-U.S., non-Canadian passport holders. Must be bought outside the United States in conjunction with an international fare to the United States or Canada. For high-season travel in July and August, buy a minimum of 3 flight coupons for $389. Additional coupons are available up to a maximum of 8 for $679. Slightly lower fares are available for low-season travel.

Canadian Airlines Pass (800) 426-7000.
Valid for travel anywhere in **North America** that Canadian Airlines flies except Hawaii. Available only to non-U.S., non-Canadian passport holders. A minimum of 3 flight coupons costs $475 and increases to $560 during July and August. Additional flights up to 8 may be purchased for $40 or $60 each during July and August. For Hawaii travel there's a special pass costing $700 for 4 flight coupons.

Small Airlines

Air South (800) 247-7688	Columbia based; serving Atlanta, Baltimore, Columbia, Jacksonville, Miami, Myrtle Beach, Raleigh-Durham, Tampa or St. Petersburg, Tallahassee
AirTran (800) 247-8726	Orlando based; flying from Albany, Cincinnati, Hartford-Springfield, Huntsville, Islip (Long Island), Knoxville, Newburgh (Westchester, NY), Providence, Syracuse to Orlando and Ft. Lauderdale
Air 21 (209) 348-2700	Fresno based; flying to Las Vegas, Los Angeles, Palm Springs, San Francisco
American Trans Air (800) 225-2995	Chicago to Bahamas, Florida, Hawaii, Las Vegas, Los Angeles, Phoenix, Salt Lake City, San Francisco, Seattle; Indianapolis to Bahamas, Caribbean, Cancun, Florida, Las Vegas, Phoenix; Milwaukee to Florida, Phoenix; Boston or Philadelphia to Orlando, St. Petersburg, Ft. Lauderdale; New York to Riga, Latvia and Belfast; North Ireland to San Francisco; Los Angeles to Hawaii; St. Louis to Ft. Lauderdale, Ft. Myers, Las Vegas, Orlando, St. Petersburg; Salt Lake City to Hawaii
Carnival (800) 8-AIR FUN	Miami based; flying from Islip, Newark, New York, Newburgh, Philadelphia, White Plains to several Florida destinations, Nassau, San Juan and also Miami and Ft. Lauderdale to Los Angeles
Grand Airways (800) 634-6616	Dallas–Ft. Worth, Las Vegas, Oakland
Kiwi (800) JET-KIWI	Newark based; serving Atlanta, Chicago, Newark, Orlando, Puerto Rico, Tampa, West Palm Beach
Mahalo Air (800) 4-Mahalo	Hawaii inter-island
MarkAir (800) 627-5247	Denver hub; Atlanta, Chicago (Midway Field), Dallas–Ft. Worth, Kansas City, Las Vegas, Los Angeles, Minneapolis–St. Paul, New York (LaGuardia), Phoenix, San Diego, Seattle
Midway (800) 446-4392	Raleigh-Durham hub; Boston, Chicago (Midway), New York (LaGuardia), Newark, Orlando, Raleigh-Durham, Tampa, Washington, D.C. (National) West Palm Beach
Nation's Air (800) CITY JET	Boston, Myrtle Beach, Philadelphia, Pittsburgh
Reno Air (800) 736-6247	Reno, Lake Tahoe, Las Vegas and San Jose hubs flying to Arcadia, Burbank, Chicago, Chico, Colorado Springs, Eureka, Klamath Falls, Laughlin, Los Angeles, Medford, Monterey, Newark, Ontario,

	Orange County, Phoenix, Portland, Redding, San Diego, Santa Rosa, Seattle, Tucson
Spirit Airlines (800) 772-7117	Philadelphia to Orlando; Atlantic City to Ft. Lauderdale, Ft. Myers, Orlando, Tampa
Southwest Airlines (800) I-FLY-SWA	Phoenix and Baltimore hubs flying to Albuquerque, Amarillo, Austin, Baltimore, Birmingham, Boise, Burbank, Chicago, Cleveland, Columbus, Corpus Christi, Dallas, Detroit, El Paso, Harlingen, Houston, Indianapolis, Kansas City, Las Vegas, Little Rock, Los Angeles, Louisville, Lubbock, Midland-Odessa, Nashville, New Orleans, Oakland, Oklahoma City, Omaha, Ontario, Orange County, Phoenix, Reno, Tahoe, Sacramento, Salt Lake City, San Antonio, San Diego, San Francisco, San Jose, Seattle, Spokane, St. Louis, Tucson, Tulsa
Sunbird (800) 786-2473	Orlando based; flying to Dallas–Ft. Worth, Detroit, Minneapolis, New York (LaGuardia)
Tower Air (800) 221-2500	New York to Amsterdam, Bombay, Las Vegas, Los Angeles, Miami, New Delhi, Paris, San Francisco, São Paulo, Tel Aviv, Los Angeles to Miami
ValuJet (800) 825-8538	Atlanta and Washington (Dulles) hubs flying to Chicago, Columbus, Dallas, Detroit, Ft. Lauderdale, Ft. Myers, Hartford, Springfield, Indianapolis, Jackson, Jacksonville, Kansas City, Louisville, Memphis, Miami, Nashville, New Orleans, Newport News, Norfolk, Orlando, Philadelphia, Raleigh, Durham, Savannah, Tampa, West Palm Beach; connecting flights available between most of these cities as well

Vanguard (800) VANGUARD	Dallas, Denver, Kansas City, Milwaukee, Salt Lake City
Western Pacific (800) 930-3030	Colorado Springs hub flying to Kansas City, Las Vegas, Los Angeles, Oklahoma City, Phoenix, San Francisco

Space-Available Flight Companies

AIRTECH: 584 Broadway, Suite 1007, New York, NY 10012; (212) 219-7000. A space-available service for flexible travelers. One-way and round-trip flights on commercial aircraft between the following:

U.S. East and West Coasts for $129 one-way (New York City, Boston, Baltimore or D.C. to Los Angeles or San Francisco).

United States and **Europe** for $169 one-way from the East Coast, $229 from the Midwest and Southeast, $249 from the West Coast (U.S. gateways: New York City, Boston, Baltimore, D.C., Chicago, Detroit, Miami, Tampa, Los Angeles, San Francisco, Seattle, Vancouver. European gateways: **Amsterdam, London, Paris, Frankfurt, Madrid, Rome**). Airtech also sells Eurail passes.

United States and a **Caribbean** island or coastal **Mexico** (occasionally a resort in tropical **South America**) for $189 round-trip (from New York City, Boston, Philadelphia, Baltimore, D.C., Cleveland, Pittsburgh, Detroit).

Although similar to stand-by, Airtech's service differs in that it monitors seat availability of those carriers to whom it has access and pre-positions you to take advantage of empty airplane seats before you leave home for your trip. On occasion, during certain peak periods of travel, passengers may have to stand by for a flight. In the unlikely event that no seats become available, Airtech will redirect you to another flight. If, after any five-day period Airtech is unable to secure transportation, your money will be promptly refunded. *Note:* This happens to a very small percentage of passengers.

Planning your trip: You need to be flexible both in terms of time and destination by providing a five-day travel window during which you can fly and by listing a destination preference. Airtech does its best to satisfy all preferred destinations. However, should a given destination be unavailable during your travel window, you will be offered a flight to another city. In such instances you will be expected to accept whatever is available.

The Frugal Globetrotter

Given that Airtech is not destination-specific, departure-point specific nor departure-date specific, Airtech cannot guarantee that you will fly directly into, or out of, any specific airport on any given date.

Airtech is a "spin off" of Airhitch (see below) and has similar services.

AIRHITCH: 2472 Broadway, Suite 200, New York, NY 10024; (800) 326-2009/(212) 864-2000/(510) 451-2366/(310) 394-0550. Has been in business longer than Airtech (above).

Discount Regional Airlines and Air Charters

EASTWINDS: (800) 644-FLYB. Trenton, NJ, hub. One-way and round-trip flights from Trenton, NJ, to Boston, Greensboro, West Palm Beach and Jacksonville.

COUNCIL CHARTER: 205 E. 42nd Street, 16th Floor, New York, NY 10017; (800) 223-7402/(800) 800-8222/(212) 661-0311. Purchases blocks of seats on commercial airlines. Specializes to western Europe from New York, Boston, Washington, Los Angeles and San Francisco.

WINGS OF THE WORLD: (800) 835-9969. Provides space-available flights.

VALU JET: (800) VALU JET/(800) 825-8538. Seven Florida destinations served through Atlanta, Philadelphia and Washington, D.C. Rates rise from $59 depending upon advance purchase.

SUN JET: (800) 4 SUNJET/(800) 478-6538. Newark, NJ, to Florida (St. Petersburg, Orlando and Ft. Lauderdale). Rates graduate by increments of $10, from $79-$129 as their planes fill. Also services Ft. Worth, TX, and Long Beach, CA.

AMERICAN TRANS AIR (domestic): (212) 686-6118.

WAY TO GO TRAVEL: 4837 Voltaire Street, San Diego, CA 92107.

JET VACATIONS, INC. (Paris): (800) JET-0999/(212) 247-0999.

MARTIN AIR HOLLAND: (800) 366-4655/(516) 627-8711.

TOURLITE INTERNATIONAL: (800) 272-7600/(212) 599-2727.

TRAVAC INTERNATIONAL: (800) 872-8800/(212) 563-3303.

TRAVELWISE: (800) FLY4FUN.

Last-Minute Ticket Agencies

As opposed to flying standby, where you have no reservation confirmation, last-minute programs exist because filling a seat on a charter or airline at any price beats flying empty. These agencies can also offer 30- to 50-percent savings on last-minute bookings for tours, cruises and accommodations. Some have annual fees of $20–$50 and provide newsletters and toll-free hotlines.

DISCOUNT TRAVEL INTERNATIONAL: (800) 332-9294.

LAST MINUTE TRAVEL CLUB: (617) 267-9800/(800) 527-8646.

Short-Notice Cruises and Vacation Packages

Cruise lines and tour operators turn to the following companies with their unsold inventory. Although cruise lines ballyhoo their early-booking discounts, plenty of deals still are available closer to departure. However, purchasing short-notice, high-cost airfare may negate your cruise savings.

CRUISES OF DISTINCTION: (800) 634-3445. Charges $39 for its "instant-notice service," which is applied to any cruise you purchase. Specializes to Caribbean, Mexico and transatlantic cruises. Monthly newsletter.

MOMENT'S NOTICE: (212) 980-9550/(212) 750-9111 (hot line). Offers air and hotel packages to Caribbean, Mexico and Europe. $25 for a one-year family membership.

SHORT NOTICE VACATION SAVINGS CARD: (800) 444-9800/(301) 731-5448. Up to 50 percent off tour packages to Caribbean and Mexican resorts. Has air-only prices from cities throughout the United States. The annual fee is $36.

SPUR OF THE MOMENT CRUISES: (800) 343-1991/(310) 521-1060. Caribbean and Mexico. Issues a free availability list.

VACATIONS TO GO: (800) 338-4962/(800) 446-6258 (hot line). 40- to 65-percent savings on cruises. No booking fee, but a club membership fee of $19.95 a year. Fee includes subscription to *Cruises and Tours* magazine and two bulletins a month on discounted cruising.

WORLDWIDE DISCOUNT TRAVEL CLUB: (305) 534-2082. $50 a year per family and issues a monthly bulletin of specials.

Auto Driveaway Companies

AUTO DRIVEAWAY: (800) 346-2277/(800) 827-9356/(800) 621-4155 for national offices. Information or New York: (212) 967-2344. Driveaway Service: (718) 762-3800. Washington, D.C.: (703) 524-7300. San Francisco: (415) 777-3740. $250 deposit returned via mail.

A-1 AUTO MOVERS: 415 S. 7th Street, Renton, WA 98055; (800) 227-2728. Seattle-based agency with over 80 satellite agents. $250 deposit with option for deposit return at point of delivery. Call or consult your local *Yellow Pages* for agents in your city.

ANTHONY'S DRIVEAWAY: E. Rutherford, NJ; (800) 659-9903.

A ECONOMY AUTO TRANSPORTERS: 1700 Worthington Road, West Palm Beach, FL 33401; (800) 466-7775.

ACROSS AMERICA DRIVEAWAY: (219) 852-0134/(310) 798-3374.

CITILINK TRAVEL SERVICES: (718) 940-6807. Ride-shares arranged from New York City. Small fee for matching you with a car and driver going in your direction. Drivers with cars list free!

RENT A WRECK: A franchise providing second-rate rentals for roughly two-thirds the late-model rental rates. Some provide cars for local travel only. Check the *Yellow Pages* for listings in your area.

Note: Also see newspaper classifieds under "Auto Transport" and check out university ride-boards.

AAA: (800) 222-4357 (national information)/(212) 757-2000. Maps, road service, towing, car rental and motel discounts. $45 a year. $15 a year for additional family members.

NATIONAL AUTO TRANSPORTERS, INC.: IL—(312) 489-3500; MN—(612) 777-7780; CA—(415) 342-9611/(818) 988-9000/(619) 562-8666/(310) 719-9915/(818) 963-9252; FL—(305) 945-4104; MO—(816) 525-3500; MT—(810) 465-5210; OH—(513) 528-1642; GA—(404) 257-0605; AZ—(602) 992-5200; OR—(503) 252-3967.

Domestic and International Road Adventure Tours

Domestic

EAST COAST EXPLORER (Wanderlusting): 245 Eighth Avenue, New York, NY 10011; (800) 610-2680/(718) 694-9667. Off-the-beaten-path day trips between New York City and D.C. ($32) and between New York City and Boston ($29) each way. Highly recommended. Take scenic backroads and see the real America with stops at places of natural, historical and cultural interest. Small groups (maximum is 14 people). Door-to-door service—pick up and drop off at most budget hotels and hostels. Run by budget travelers, for budget travelers. Excellent value—price includes transportation, tolls and highly informed guide. They stop for tasty, cheap meals, or bring your own lunch. Closed for winter.

VAGABOND TOURS INC., 2 Oxford Street, New Brunswick, NJ 08901; (800) 700-0790. Roadtrips from New York City to **Boston, D.C, Montreal** and **Quebec City**. Price includes round-trip charter bus and room: $119 quad, $145 triple, $166 double, $244 single. Optional sightseeing excursions available.

GREEN TORTOISE ADVENTURE TRAVEL: (800) TORTOIS/(800) 227-4766/(415) 834-9060. Sleeper coach "magic bus" cross-country bus tours. Imaginative fourteen-day adventures includes national parks, rafting, hot springs, camping and gourmet meals cooked on the bus. East Coast departures: New York, Boston, Hartford. Night driving while you sleep. Earthy, communal excursion. $279 and up. Many options.

THE BLUE RIDGE PARKWAY DIRECTORY: Write for a free, informative publication: Blue Ridge Parkway Association, P.O. Box 453, Asheville, NC 28802. Attractions, outdoor recreation, accommodations, restaurants and shops along the spectacular 470-mile-long recreationally oriented motor road.

TREK AMERICA: (800) 221-0596. Thirteen-passenger maxi-van camping tours throughout North America. Active and soft endurance tours for all ages. Departure cities: New York, Los Angeles, Minneapolis, San Francisco, Seattle, Anchorage, Cancun, Mexico City.

GO WEST: c/o Robert Dryden P.O. Box 674, Dauphin, PA 17018; (717) 921-0131. Cross-country tours.

DESERT ADVENTURES: 611 South Palm Canyon Drive #7-455, Palm Springs, CA 92264; (619) 864-

6530. **Indian Canyon Oases, Mystery Canyon** and the **San Andreas Fault** via jeep explorations.

SMOKE TREE STABLES: 2500 Toledo Avenue, Palm Springs, CA 92264; (619) 327-1372. Private horseback tours of the **Palm Springs Desert.**

TRAIL HEADS: (800) 884-GEAR. Mountain-bike tours of Virginia's **Blue Ridge Mountains.**

CANOE EXCURSION IN FLORIDA: Contact the Deptartment of National Resources, Division of Recreation and Parks, 3900 Commonwealth Boulevard, Tallahassee, FL 32399-3000; (904) 487-4784.

International
DRAGOMAN: Dragoman 18 Camp Green, Debenham, Suffolk IP14 6LA, England; 071 370 1930. Overland expeditions from **England** to and through **India** and **Nepal.** England to **Kathmandu** (9–15 weeks). **Indian overlands** (3–10 weeks).

BUTTERFIELD'S INDIAN RAILWAY TOURS: Burton Fleming, Driffield YO25 OPQ, England; 01262 470230. Specially converted railway carriage escorted tours (3 weeks) visiting **South and North India** and **Pakistan.**

EXODUS EXPEDITIONS LTD.: 9 Weir Road, Balham, London. Converted trucks (Bedford or Mercedes) drive and camp across the continent: **England–Belgium–Germany–Austria–Italy–Greece–Turkey–Syria–Jordan–Syria–East Turkey–Iran–Pakistan–India–Nepal.** 1,700 pounds includes camping. Roughly 150 pounds for 3 meals per day. 26 people maximum. Mucho virgin turf! Write for information.

Road Trip Miscellany

ADVENTURE CYCLING: (U.S.A. backroad maps) P.O. Box 8308, Missoula, MT 59807; (406) 721-1776.

Europe by Van and Motorhome and *New Zealand by Motorhome*: Books covering buying, renting, shipping, campers, RVs, driving, language, kids. Call Shore or Campbell at (800) 659-5222.

Going Off the Beaten Path—An Untraditional Travel Guide to the U.S., by Mary Dymond Davis; published by the Noble Press, Inc.

PER ANNUM, INC.: 114 E. 32nd St., Suite 1200, New York, NY 10016; (212) 213-8230/(800) 548-1108. Publisher of *City Diaries*—mini day-planners

with key entertainment and survival information, including maps and restaurants.

TRIPBUILDER: 1449 Lexington Avenue, Suite 3A, New York, NY 10128; (212) 410-0920. Compact maps and information helping busy people easily create personalized itineraries in **New York City, D.C., London, England, France** and **Holland.**

Trip Insurance Companies

ACCESS AMERICA
P.O. Box 90310
Richmond, VA 23230
(800) 284-8300

CAREFREE TRAVEL INSURANCE
The Berkeley Group
120 Mineola Boulevard,
P.O. Box 310
Mineola, NY 11501
(800) 645-2424

CIEE
Council on International Educational Exchange
205 East 42nd Street
New York, NY 10017
(212) 661-1450

HEALTHCARE ABROAD/HEALTH CARE GLOBAL
Wallach & Company
243 Church Street NW, Suite 100-D
Vienna, VA 22180
(800) 237-6615

INTERNATIONAL SOS ASSISTANCE
8 Neshaminy Interplex, Suite 207
Trevose, PA 19053
(800) 523-8930

TELE-TRIP
Mutual of Omaha
P.O. Box 31762
Omaha, NE 68131
(800) 228-9792

TRAVEL ASSISTANCE INTERNATIONAL
1133 15th Street NW, Suite 400
Washington, DC 20005
(800) 821-2828

TRAVEL GUARD INTERNATIONAL
1145 Clark Street
Stevens Point, WI 54481
(800) 782-5151

TRAVEL INSURED INTERNATIONAL, INC.
52-S Oakland Avenue
P.O. Box 280568
East Hartford, CT 06128-0568
(800) 243-3174

TRAVMED
P.O. Box 10623
Baltimore, MD 21385
(800) 732-5309

Adventure Travel Companies: Touring and Trekking Outfitters

ABOVE THE CLOUDS TREKKING: P.O. Box 398, Worcester, MA 01602-0398; (508) 799-4499/(800) 233-4499. Worldwide adventure for the discerning traveler.

ADVENTURE CENTER: 1311 63rd Street, Suite 200, Emeryville, CA 94608; (510) 654-1879/(800) 227-8747. Worldwide exploration. Represents many *overland expedition* outfitters, including **Guerba (Africa)**, **Dragoman (Latin America, Asia, Africa)**. *Encounter Overland* (**Latin America, Asia, Africa**) and *Explore* (worldwide including **Greece, Turkey** and the **South Pacific**).

ADVENTURE CYCLING ASSOCIATION: 150 E. Pine Street, Missoula, MT 59802; (406) 721-1776. Comprehensive association for both hard-core cyclists (**Alaska to Argentina**) and weekend *mountain-bike* warriors. U.S. bike maps highlight bike shops, hostels, campgrounds and the best offbeat roads with the best scenery. Maps are not marketed to motorcyclists of cross-country auto voyagers, but it's a valuable resource nonetheless. It also offers organized cycling tours.

ALASKA WILDLAND ADVENTURES: P.O. Box 389, Girdwood, AK 99587; (800) 334-8730/(908) 783-2928 (Alaska). 7- to 12-day trips visiting **Chugach National Forest, Kenai National Wildlife Refuge, Denali National Park** and ecological tours in **Southcentral Alaska**. Accommodation options include camping or staying in cabins and small inns along the way. Family and senior *safaris* available. *Fishing!*

AMERICAN ALPINE INSTITUTE, LTD.: 1515 12th Street, Bellingham, WA 98225; (206) 671-1505. Instructional *mountain-climbing* programs in the **United States, South America, Europe** and **Asia**.

ASIAN PACIFIC ADVENTURES: 826 South Sierra Bonita Avenue, Los Angeles, CA 90036; (213) 935-3156/(800) 825-1680. Cultural adventure tours of **Asia**.

BACKROADS: 1516 5th Street, Berkeley, CA 94710; (800) 462-2848/(510) 527-1555. *Bicycle and walking tours* throughout **Asia, Europe** and **North America**. Accommodations vary from camping to luxurious hotels.

BIVOUAC ADVENTURES: (313) 761-8777. From **Alaska** to **Asia**. Highly recommended.

ECOSUMMER EXPEDITIONS: 1516 Duranleau Street, Vancouver, B.C. V6H 354, Canada; (800) 688-8605. *Kayaking* trips in remote waters of **North and Central America** (including **Yukon**). Proper tourism: take it in, take it out.

ELK RIVER VALLEY LLAMA COMPANY: Box 674, Clark, CO 80428. *Llama treks.*

EXPLORE WORLDWIDE (RGC): 1 Frederick Street, Aldershot, GU11 1LQ, England; 01252 344161 (24 hours). 160 unique *tours, treks, safaris* and *expeditions* in eighty countries. Small escorted groups.

FITS EQUESTRIAN: 685 Lateen Road, Solvang, CA 93463; (800) 666-3487/(805) 688-9494. *Horseback-riding tours* all over the world (**Africa, Australia, the British Isles, Canada, the Caribbean, Europe, Iceland, Mexico, New Zealand**).

HIMALAYAN TRAVEL: (800) 225-2380.

INTERNATIONAL EXPEDITIONS INC.: One Environs Park, Helena, AL 35080; (205) 428-1700/(800) 633-4734. Leader in nature travel and workshops worldwide. Specialize in high-quality travel programs to the world's greatest natural history destinations.

JOURNEYS INTERNATIONAL: 4011 Jackson, Ann Arbor, MI 48103; (313) 665-4407/(800) 255-8735. **Africa, the Americas, Asia** and the **Pacific**. Strong in **Nepal** and **India**. Family plans.

LOST WORLD ADVENTURES: 1189 Autumn Ridge Drive, Marietta, GA 30066; (800) 999-0558. **Venezuelan** specialists. Regional diversity via charter flights connecting **Caracas, Amazon, Andes** and **Llanos** grasslands.

MINDFUL JOURNEYS: (800) 654-7975. **Asia** and the **Himalayas**.

MOUNTAIN TRAVELS/SOBEK: 6420 Fairmount Avenue, El Cerrito, CA 94530; (510) 527-8100/(800) 227-2384. Twenty-five years of experience in guiding *worldwide* adventure travel excursions.

OUTWARD BOUND: National Office, Route 9D, R2 Box 280, Garrison, NY 10524-9757; (914) 424-4000/ (800) 243-8520. *Wilderness adventures* designed to bring you face to face with nature and with your own abilities.

OVERSEAS ADVENTURE TRAVEL: (800) 221-0814.

PERRYGOLF: 8302 Dunwoody Pl., Suite 305, Atlanta, GA 30350; (800) 344-5257/(404) 641-9696. *Golf tours* in **Scotland** from late April through early October. Also **Ireland, England, Wales, Spain** and **Portugal.** Exotic sporting vacations on a *silk* shoestring.

REI ADVENTURES: (800) 622-2236.

SIERRA CLUB/OUTING DEPARTMENT: (415) 923-5630.

SOUTHWINDS: (800) 533-3423. **South America.**

SPUR HOTEL: P.O. Box 1047, 110 N. Center, Archer City, TX 76351; (817) 574-2501. Eleven-room restored hotel in **Texas,** the way it oughta be.

TROPICAL ADVENTURES: 111 Second North, Seattle, WA 98109. (800) 247-3483. *Diving.*

UNITED TOURING INTERNATIONAL: 400 Market Street, Suite 260, Philadelphia, PA 19106; (215) 923-8700/(800) 223-6486. **African** *safaris.*

VOYAGERS INTERNATIONAL: (800) 633-0299. **Galapagos, Ecuador,** the **Amazon.**

THE WAYFARERS: 172 Bellevue Avenue, Newport, RI 02840; (401) 849-5087. *Walking tours* through gorgeous parts of **England, France, Ireland, Scotland** and **Wales.**

WILD LAND ADVENTURES: (800) 345-4453. **Latin America** (including the **Galapagos Islands), Turkey, Alaska.**

WILDERNESS TRAVEL: 801 Allston Way, Berkeley, CA 94710; (800) 368-2794. **South America, Europe, Asia, Africa.** Exclusive, unusual trips through the back door; slice through arctic fjords, visit tree-house people in **Irian Jaya.**

WINGS OF THE WORLD TRAVEL: Seven-day *cigar-smoking* adventures in **Cuba,** and other wacky ideas. Newsletter. 1200 William Street, P.O. Box 706, Buffalo, NY 14240; (800) 465-8687.

WORLDWIDE ADVENTURE: (800) 387-1483.

Domestic Tourist Boards (United States and Canada)

United States

ALABAMA
Bureau of Tourism and Travel
P.O. Box 4927
Montgomery, AL 36103-4927l
(800) 252-2262/(334) 242-4169/(334) 242-4554 (fax)

ALASKA
Division of Tourism
P.O. Box 110801
Juneau, AK 99811
(907) 465-2010

ARIZONA
Arizona Office of Tourism
1100 West Washington Street
Phoenix, AZ 85007
(800) 842-8257/(602) 542-8687

ARKANSAS
Arkansas Tourism Office
1 Capitol Mall
Little Rock, AR 72201
(800) 628-8725/(501) 682-7777

CALIFORNIA
California Office of Tourism
(800) 462-2543/(916) 322-2881

COLORADO
Colorado Tourism Bureau
P.O. Box 1964
Englewood, CO 80150
(800) 265-6723

CONNECTICUT
Connecticut Vacation Center
865 Brook Street
Rocky Hill, CT 06067
(800) 282-6863/(203) 258-4355

DELAWARE
Delaware Tourism Office
99 Kings Highway, P.O. Box 1401
Dover, DE 19903
(800) 441-8846/(302) 739-4271

DISTRICT OF COLUMBIA
Washington Convention and Visitors Association
1212 New York Avenue NW
Washington, D.C. 20005
(202) 789-7000

FLORIDA
Florida Division of Tourism
126 West Van Buren Street
Tallahassee, FL 32399
(904) 487-1462

GEORGIA
Georgia Department of Industry and Trade
P.O. Box 1776, Department TIA
Atlanta, GA 30301
(800) 847-4842/(404) 656-3590

GUAM
Guam Visitors Bureau
1150 Marina Village Parkway, Suite 104
Alameda, CA 94501
(800) 873-4826
fax: (510) 865-5165

HAWAII
Hawaii Visitors Bureau
Waikiki Business Plaza
2270 Kalakaua Avenue #801
Honolulu, HI 96815
(808) 923-1811

IDAHO
Idaho Department of Commerce
700 West State Street
Boise, ID 83720
(800) 635-7820/(208) 334-2470

ILLINOIS
Illinois Bureau of Tourism
100 West Randolph #3-400
Chicago, IL 60601
(800) 223-0121/(312) 814-4732

INDIANA
Indiana Division of Tourism
1 North Capitol Avenue #700

Indianapolis, IN 46204
(800) 289-6646/(317) 232-8860

IOWA
Iowa Department of Tourism
200 East Grand Avenue
Des Moines, IA 50309
(800) 345-4692/(515) 242-4705

KANSAS
Kansas Travel and Tourism Division
700 SW Harrison Street, Suite 1300
Topeka, KS 66603
(800) 252-6727/(913) 296-2009

KENTUCKY
Kentucky Department of Travel Development
Visitors Information Service
500 Mero Street
Frankfort, KY 40601
(800) 225-8747/(502) 564-4930

LOUISIANA
Louisiana Office of Tourism
P.O. Box 94291
Baton Rouge, LA 70804
(800) 334-8626/(504) 342-8119

MAINE
Maine Publicity Bureau
P.O. Box 2300
Hallowell, ME 04347
(800) 533-9595/(207) 623-0363

MARYLAND
Maryland Office of Tourism Development
217 East Redwood Street, 9th Floor
Baltimore, MD 21202
(800) 543-1036/(410) 333-6611

MASSACHUSETTS
Massachusetts Office of Travel and Tourism
100 Cambridge Street, 13th Floor
Boston, MA 02202
(800) 447-6277/(617) 727-3201

MICHIGAN
Michigan Travel Bureau
P.O. Box 3393
Livonia, MI 48151
(800) 543-2937/(517) 373-0670

MINNESOTA
Minnesota Office of Tourism
121 7th Place East
St. Paul, MN 55101
(800) 657-3700/(612) 296-5029

MISSISSIPPI
Mississippi Division of Tourism Development
P.O. Box 1705
Ocean Springs, MS 39566
(800) 927-6378

MISSOURI
Missouri Division of Tourism
P.O. Box 1055
Jefferson City, MO 65102
(800) 877-1234/(314) 751-4133

MONTANA
Travel Montana
P.O. Box 200533
Helena, MT 59620
(800) 847-4868/(406) 444-2654

NEBRASKA
Nebraska Division of Tourism
P.O. Box 98913
Lincoln, NE 68509
(800) 228-4307/(402) 471-3796

NEVADA
Nevada Commission on Tourism
Capital Complex
Carson City, NV 89710
(800) 638-2328/(702) 687-4322

NEW HAMPSHIRE
Office of Travel and Tourism
P.O. Box 1856
Concord, NH 03302-1856
1-800-FUN-IN-NH, ext. 162/(603) 271-2343 ext. 162

NEW JERSEY
New Jersey Division of Travel and Tourism
20 West State Street CN 826
Trenton, NJ 08625
(800) 537-7397/(609) 292-2470

NEW MEXICO
New Mexico Department of Tourism
491 Old Santa Fe Trail
Santa Fe, NM 87503
(800) 545-2040

NEW YORK
New York Division of Tourism
1 Commerce Plaza
Albany, NY 12245
(800) 225-5697/(518) 474-4116

NORTH CAROLINA
North Carolina Division of Travel and Tourism
430 North Salisbury Street
Raleigh, NC 27603
(800) 847-4862/(919) 733-4171

NORTH DAKOTA
North Dakota Tourism
604 East Boulevard
Bismarck, ND 58505
(800) 435-5663/(701) 224-2525

OHIO
Ohio Division of Travel and Tourism
P.O. Box 1001
Columbus, OH 43266
(800) 282-5393/(614) 466-8844

OKLAHOMA
Oklahoma Tourism and Recreation Department
500 Will Rogers Building
Oklahoma City, OK 73105
(800) 652-6552/(405) 521-3981

OREGON
Oregon Tourism Division
775 Summer Street NE
Salem, OR 97310
(800) 547-7842/(503) 373-1270

PENNSYLVANIA
Pennsylvania Office of Travel Marketing
Dept of Commerce
453 Forum Building
Harrisburg, PA 17120
(800) 847-4872/(717) 787-5453

PUERTO RICO
Puerto Rican Tourism Company
575 Fifth Avenue, 23rd Floor
New York, NY 10017
(212) 599-6262

RHODE ISLAND
Rhode Island Tourism Division
7 Jackson Walkway
Providence, RI 02903
(800) 556-2484/(401) 277-2601

SOUTH CAROLINA
South Carolina Department of Parks, Recreation and Tourism
P.O. Box 71
Columbia, SC 29202
(800) 346-3634/(803) 734-0122

SOUTH DAKOTA
South Dakota Department of Tourism
711 East Wells Avenue
Pierre, SD 57501
(800) 732-5682/(605) 773-3301

TENNESSEE
Tennessee Tourism Division
P.O. Box 23170
Nashville, TN 37202
(800) 836-6200/(615) 741-2158

TEXAS
Texas Department of Commerce
P.O. Box 12728
Austin, TX 78711
(800) 888-8839/(512) 462-9191

U.S. VIRGIN ISLANDS (St. Croix, St. John, St. Thomas)
U.S. Virgin Islands Division of Tourism
3460 Wilshire Boulevard #412
Los Angeles, CA 90010
(213) 739-0138

UTAH
Utah Travel Council
Council Hall
Capitol Hill, Department TIA
Salt Lake City, UT 84114
(800) 200-1160/(801) 538-1030

VERMONT
Vermont Department of Travel and Tourism
134 State Street
Montpelier, VT 05602
(800) 837-6668/(802) 828-3239

VIRGINIA
Virginia Division of Tourism
901 E. Byrd Street
Richmond, VA 23219
(800) 847-4882/(804) 786-4484
e-mail: 75143.1111@CompuServe.Com

WASHINGTON
Washington Tourism Development Division
P.O. Box 500

Olympia, WA 98504
(800) 544-1800/(206) 586-2012

WEST VIRGINIA
Division of Tourism and Parks
2101 Washington Street East
Charleston, WV 25305
(800) 225-5982/(304) 345-2286

WISCONSIN
Wisconsin Division of Tourism
P.O. Box 7606
Madison, WI 53707
(800) 432-8747/(608) 266-2161

WYOMING
Wyoming Division of Tourism
I-25 at College Drive
Cheyenne, WY 82002
(800) 225-5996/(307) 777-7777

Canada

ALBERTA
Alberta Tourism
City Center, 3rd Floor
10155 102nd Street
Edmonton, Alberta
Canada T5J 4L6
(800) 661-8888/(403) 427-4321

BRITISH COLUMBIA
Tourism British Columbia
1117 Wharf Street
Victoria, British Columbia
Canada V8W 2X2
(800) 663-6000

MANITOBA
Travel Manitoba
Department 20
155 Carlton Street, 7th Floor
Winnipeg, Manitoba
Canada R3C 3H8
(800) 665-0040/(204) 945-3777

NEW BRUNSWICK
Tourism New Brunswick
P.O. Box 12345
Fredericton, New Brunswick
Canada E3B 5C3
(800) 561-0123

NEWFOUNDLAND and LABRADOR
Newfoundland and Labrador Tourism Branch
P.O. Box 8730
St. John's, Newfoundland
Canada A1B 4K2
(800) 563-6353/(709) 729-2830

NORTHWEST TERRITORIES
TravelArctic
P.O. Box 1320
Yellowknife, Northwest Territories
Canada X1A 2L9
(800) 661-0788

NOVA SCOTIA
Nova Scotia Department of Tourism and Culture
P.O. Box 130
Halifax, Nova Scotia
Canada B3J 2M7
(800) 341-6096

ONTARIO
Ontario Travel
Queen's Park
Toronto, Ontario
Canada M7A 2E5
(800) 668-2746/(416)-314-0944

PRINCE EDWARD ISLAND
Prince Edward Island Department of Tourism and Parks
P.O. Box 940
Charlottetown, Prince Edward Island
Canada C1A 7M5
(800) 565-0267/(902) 368-4444

QUEBEC
Tourisme Quebec
C.P. 979
Quebec
Canada 83C ZW3
(800) 363-7777

SASKATCHEWAN
Tourism Saskatchewan
1919 Saskatchewan Drive
Regina, Saskatchewan
Canada S4P 3V7
(800) 667-7191/(306) 787-2300

YUKON
Tourism Yukon
P.O. Box 2703
Whitehorse, Yukon
Canada YEA 2C6
(403) 667-5340

International Tourist Boards

ANGUILLA TOURIST INFORMATION
c/o Medhurst & Associates, Inc.
271 Main Street
Northport, NY 11768
(800) 553-4939

ANTIGUA and BARBUDA
Antigua and Barbuda Department of Tourism and Trade
610 Fifth Avenue, Suite 311
New York, NY 10020
(212) 541-4117

ARGENTINA
Consulate General Argentina
12 W. 50th Street
New York, NY 10019
(212) 603-0400

ARUBA
Aruba Tourism Authority
1000 Harbor Boulevard
Weehawken, NJ 07087
(800) 862-7822

AUSTRALIA
Australian Tourist Commission
100 Park Avenue, 25th Floor
New York, NY 10017
(800) 333-0199/(212) 687-6300

Australian Tourist Commission
2121 Avenue of the Stars #1200
Los Angeles, CA 90067
(310) 552-1988

AUSTRIA
Austrian National Tourist Office
P.O. Box 1142
New York, NY 10108
(212) 944-6880

Austrian National Tourist Office
11601 Wilshire Boulevard #2480
Los Angeles, CA 90025
(310) 477-3332

BAHAMAS
Bahamas Tourist Office
150 E. 52nd Street, 28th Floor N.
New York, NY 10022
(212) 758-2777

Bahamas Tourist Office
3450 Wilshire Boulevard #208
Los Angeles, CA 90010
(800) 422-4262

BARBADOS
Barbados Tourism Authority
800 Second Avenue
New York, NY 10017
(212) 986-6516

Barbados Board of Tourism
3440 Wilshire Boulevard, Suite 1215
Los Angeles, CA 90010
(213) 380-2198

BELGIUM
Belgian Tourist Office
780 Third Avenue #1501
New York, NY 10017
(212) 758-8130

BERMUDA
Bermuda Department of Tourism
310 Madison Avenue #201
New York, NY 10017
(212) 818-9800

Bermuda Department of Tourism
3151 Cahuenga Boulevard W. #111
Los Angeles, CA 90068
(213) 436-0744

BONAIRE
Bonaire Government Tourist Office
444 Madison Avenue, Suite 2403
New York, NY 10022
(800) 826-6247/(212) 832-0779

BRITISH VIRGIN ISLANDS
British Virgin Islands Tourist Board
370 Lexington Avenue
New York, NY 10017
(800) 835-8530

British Virgin Islands Tourist Board
1686 Union Street #305
San Francisco, CA 94123
(415) 775-0344

BULGARIA
Bulgarian Tourist Information Center
41 E. 42nd Street #508
New York, NY 10017
(212) 573-5530

CARIBBEAN
Caribbean Tourist Association
20 E. 46th Street, 4th Floor
New York, NY 10017
(212) 682-0435

CAYMAN ISLANDS
Cayman Islands Tourist Office
420 Lexington Avenue #2733
New York, NY 10170
(212) 682-5582

Cayman Islands Tourist Office
3440 Wilshire Boulevard #1202
Los Angeles, CA 90010
(213) 738-1968

CHILE
Chilean National Tourist Board
510 W. Sixth Street #1210
Los Angeles, CA 90014
(213) 627-4293

CHINA
China National Tourist Office
60 E. 42nd Street #3126
New York, NY 10165
(212) 867-0271

Republic of China Tourism Bureau
166 Geary Street #1605
San Francisco, CA 94108
(415) 989-8677

COOK ISLANDS
Cook Islands Tourist Authority
6033 West Century Boulevard #609
Los Angeles, CA 90045
(310) 216-2872

COSTA RICA
National Tourist Bureau Office
1101 Brickell Avenue
B.I.V. Tower, Suite 801
Miami, FL 33131
(800) 327-7033/(305) 358-2150

CUBA
Cubatur
Calle 23 #156
Vedado, Habana
Cuba

CURACAO
Curacao Tourist Board
475 Park Avenue South, Suite 2000

New York, NY 10016
(212) 683-7660/(800) 270-3350/(800) 332-8266
(212) 683-9337 (fax)

CYPRUS
Cyprus Tourism
13 E. 40th Street
New York, NY 10016
(212) 683-5280

CZECH AND SLOVAK REPUBLICS
Czech & Slovak Service Center
1511 K Street NW, Suite 1030
Washington, DC 20005
800-Y-PRAGUE (800) 977-2483/ (202) 638-5505/
(202) 638-5308 (fax)

DENMARK
Scandinavian National Tourist Offices
655 Third Avenue
New York, NY 10017
(212) 949-2333

EGYPT
Egyptian Tourist Office
630 Fifth Avenue #1706
New York, NY 10111
(212) 332-2570

Egyptian Tourist Authority
8383 Wilshire Boulevard #215
Beverly Hills, CA 90211
(213) 653-8815

ENGLAND (see GREAT BRITAIN)

EUROPEAN TRAVEL COMMISSION
630 Fifth Avenue #565
New York, NY 10111
(212) 307-1200

FIJI
Fiji Visitors Bureau
5777 Century Boulevard #220
Los Angeles, CA 90045
(310) 568-1616

FINLAND
Finnish Tourist Board
655 Third Avenue
New York, NY 10017
(212) 949-2333

FRANCE
French Government Tourist Office
444 Madison Avenue
New York, NY 10022
(212) 838-7800

French Government Tourist Information Line
(900) 990-0040 (50 cents per minute)

French Government Tourist Office
9454 Wilshire Boulevard #715
Los Angeles, CA 90212
(310) 271-2358

French Government Tourist Office
676 North Michigan Avenue, Suite 3360
Chicago, IL 60611-2819
(312) 751-7800/(312) 337-6339 (fax)

FRENCH WEST INDIES
French Government Tourist Information Line
(900) 990-0040 (50 cents per minute)

GERMANY
German National Tourist Office
122 E. 42nd Street, 52nd Floor
New York, NY 10168
(212) 661-7200

German National Tourist Office
11766 Wilshire Boulevard #750
Los Angeles, CA 90025
(310) 575-9799

GREAT BRITAIN
British Tourist Authority
551 Fifth Avenue #701
New York, NY 10176
(800) 462-2748/(212) 986-2200

British Tourist Authority
World Trade Center
350 South Figuroa Street #450
Los Angeles, CA 90071
(213) 628-3525

GREECE
Greek National Tourist Office
645 Fifth Avenue
New York, NY 10022
(212) 421-5777

Greek National Tourist Organization
611 W. Sixth Street #2198
Los Angeles, CA 90017
(213) 626-6696

GRENADA
Grenada Board of Tourism
820 Second Avenue, Suite 900D
New York, NY 10017
(800) 927-9554

GUADELOUPE
French Government Tourist Information Line
(900) 990-0040 (50 cents per minute)

GUAM
Guam Visitors Bureau
1150 Marina Village Parkway, Suite 104
Alameda, CA 94501
(800) 873-4826/(510) 865-5165 (fax)

GUATEMALA
Guatemalan Tourist Commission
299 Alhambra Circle #510
Coral Gables, FL 33134
(800) 742-4529

HONG KONG
Hong Kong Tourist Association
590 Fifth Avenue
New York, NY 10036
(212) 869-5008

Hong Kong Tourist Association
10940 Wilshire Boulevard #1220
Los Angeles, CA 90024
(310) 208-4582

HUNGARY
IBUSZ Hungarian Travel Company
1 Parker Plaza #1104
Fort Lee, NJ 07024
(201) 592-8585

ICELAND
Scandinavian National Tourist Offices
655 Third Avenue
New York, NY 10017
(212) 949-2333

INDIA
India Tourist Office
30 Rockefeller Plaza, North Mezzanine
New York, NY 10112
(212) 586-4901

India Tourist Office
3550 Wilshire Boulevard #204
Los Angeles, CA 90010
(213) 380-8855

INDONESIA
Indonesia Tourist Promotion Office
3457 Wilshire Boulevard #104
Los Angeles, CA 90010
(213) 387-8309/(213) 387-2078

IRELAND
Irish Tourist Board
345 Park Avenue
New York, NY 10154
(800) 223-6470
(212) 418-0800/(212) 371-9052 (fax)

Irish Tourist Board
17875 Von Karman #202
Irvine, CA 92714
(714) 251-9229

ISRAEL
Israel Government Tourist Office
350 Fifth Avenue
New York, NY 10118
(212) 560-0650 /(800) 596-1199/(212) 499-5645 (fax)

Israel Government Tourist Office
6380 Wilshire Boulevard #1700
Los Angeles, CA 90048
(213) 658-7462/(800) 596-1199

ITALY
Italian Government Travel Office
Rockefeller Center
630 Fifth Avenue
New York, NY 10111
(212) 245-4822

Italian Government Travel Office
500 North Michigan Avenue
Chicago, IL 60611
(312) 644-0990

Italian Government Travel Office
12400 Wilshire Boulevard #550
Los Angeles, CA 90025
(310) 820-0098

JAMAICA
Jamaica Tourist Board
3440 Wilshire Boulevard, Suite 1207
Los Angeles, CA 90010
(213) 384-1123

JAPAN
Japanese National Tourist Organization
630 Fifth Avenue

New York, NY 10111
(212) 757-5640

Japan National Tourist Organization
360 Post Street, Suite 601
San Francisco, CA 94108
(415) 989-7140/(415) 398-5461 (fax)
e-mail: sfjnto@aol.com

KENYA
Kenya Tourist Office
424 Madison Avenue
New York, NY 10017
(212) 486-1300

Kenya Tourist Office
9150 Wilshire Boulevard #160
Beverly Hills, CA 90212
(310) 274-6635

KOREA
Korea National Tourism Office
2 Executive Drive, 7th Floor
Fort Lee, NJ 07024
(212) 688-7543

Korea National Tourism Corporation
3435 Wilshire Boulevard #350
Los Angeles, CA 90010
(213) 382-3435

LUXEMBOURG
Luxembourg National Tourist Office
17 Beekman Place
New York, NY 10022
(212) 935-8888

MACAU
Macau Tourist Information Bureau
3133 Lake Hollywood Drive
P.O. Box 1860
Los Angeles, CA 90078
(213) 851-3402

MALAYSIA
Malaysian Tourist Information Center
818 W. Seventh Street
Los Angeles, CA 90017
(213) 689-9702

MALTA
Malta Tourist Office
249 E. 35th Street
New York, NY 10016
(212) 213-6686

MARTINIQUE
Martinique Promotion Bureau
A division of the French Government Tourist Office
444 Madison Avenue
New York, NY 10022
(800) 391-4909
e-mail: Martinique@NYO.COM

MEXICO
Mexico Government Tourist Office
405 Park Avenue
New York, NY 10022
(800) 446-3942/(212) 755-7261

Mexico Government Tourist Office
10100 Santa Monica Boulevard #224
Los Angeles, CA 90067
(310) 203-8191

MONACO
Monaco Government Tourist and Convention Bureau
845 Third Avenue, 19th Floor
New York, NY 10022
(800) 753-9696/(212) 759-5227

MOROCCO
Moroccan Tourist Office
20 E. 46th Street #1201
New York, NY 10017
(212) 557-2520

NETHERLANDS
Netherlands Board of Tourism
225 N. Michigan Avenue #326
Chicago, IL 60601
(312) 819-0300

NEW ZEALAND
New Zealand Tourism Board
501 Santa Monica Boulevard #300
Santa Monica, CA 90401
(800) 388-5494/(310) 395-7480

NORTHERN IRELAND (see GREAT BRITAIN)

NORWAY
Norwegian Tourist Board
655 Third Avenue
New York, NY 10017
(212) 949-2333

PHILIPPINES
Philippine Department of Tourism
447 Sutter Street #507

San Francisco, CA 94108
(415) 956-4060

POLAND
Polish National Tourist Office
275 Madison Avenue #1711
New York, NY 10016
(212) 338-9412

PORTUGAL
Portuguese National Tourist Office
590 Fifth Avenue
New York, NY 10036
(800) PORTUGAL/(212) 354-4403

PUERTO RICO
Puerto Rican Tourism Company
575 Fifth Avenue, 23rd Floor
New York, NY 10017
(212) 599-6262

Puerto Rico Tourism Company
3557 Cahuenga Boulevard, Suite 560
Los Angeles, CA 90068
(800) 223-6530

ROMANIA
Romanian Tourist Office
573 Third Avenue
New York, NY 10016
(212) 697-6971

RUSSIA
The Russian National Tourist Office
800 Third Avenue, Suite 3101
New York, NY 10022
(212) 758-1162/(212) 758-0933 (fax)

SABA AND ST. EUSTATIUS
Saba and St. Eustatius Tourist Office
c/o Medhurst & Associates, Inc.
271 Main Street
Northport, NY 11768
(516) 261-7474

ST. BARTS
French Government Tourist Information Line
(900) 990-0040 (50 cents per minute)

ST. CROIX (See U.S. Virgin Islands)

ST. JOHN (See U.S. Virgin Islands)

ST. KITTS AND NEVIS
St. Kitts and Nevis Tourism Office

414 E. 75th Street, 5th Floor
New York, NY 10021
(800) 582-6208

ST. LUCIA
St. Lucia Tourist Board
820 Second Avenue
New York, NY 10017
(800) 456-3984/(212) 867-2950

ST. MARTIN
French Government Tourist Information Line
(900) 990-0040 (50 cents per minute)

ST. THOMAS (See U.S. Virgin Islands)

ST. VINCENT AND THE GRENADINES
St. Vincent and the Grenadines Tourist Office
801 Second Avenue, 21st Floor
New York, NY 10017
(800) 729-1726

SCANDINAVIA (Iceland, Norway, Sweden, Denmark, Finland)
Scandinavian National Tourist Offices
655 Third Avenue
New York, NY 10017
(212) 949-2333

SCOTLAND (see GREAT BRITAIN)

SINGAPORE
Singapore Tourist Promotion Board
590 Fifth Avenue, 12th Floor
New York, NY 10036
(212) 302-4861

Singapore Tourist Promotion Board
8484 Wilshire Boulevard #510
Beverly Hills, CA 90211
(213) 852-1901

SINT MAARTEN
Sint Maarten Tourism Representative
275 Seventh Avenue, 19th Floor
New York, NY 10017
(212) 989-0000

SLOVAK REPUBLIC (See CZECH AND SLOVAK REPUBLICS)

SLOVENIA
Slovenia Tourist Office
122 E. 42nd Street
New York, NY 10168
(212) 682-5896

SOUTH AFRICA
South African Tourism Board
500 Fifth Avenue
New York, NY 10110
(212) 730-2929/(800) 822-5368

South African Tourism Board
9841 Airport Boulevard #1524
Los Angeles, CA 90045
(310) 641-8444

SPAIN
Tourist Office of Spain
665 Fifth Avenue
New York, NY 10022
(212) 759-8822

Tourist Office of Spain
8383 Wilshire Boulevard #960
Beverly Hills, CA 90211
(213) 658-7188

SWEDEN
Swedish Tourist Board
655 Third Avenue
New York, NY 10017
(212) 949-2333

SWITZERLAND
Switzerland Tourism
608 Fifth Avenue
New York, NY 10020
(212) 757-5944/(212) 262-6116 (fax)

Switzerland Tourism
150 N. Michigan Avenue, Suite 2930
Chicago, IL 60601
(312) 630-5840/(312) 630-5848 (fax)
e-mail: STChicago

Switzerland Tourism
222 N. Sepulveda Boulevard #1570
El Segundo, CA 90245
(310) 335-5980/(310) 335-5982 (fax)

SYRIA
Tourist Office of Syria
26691 Plaza #210
Mission Viejo, CA 92691
(714) 582-2905

TAHITI
Tahiti Tourist Promotion Board
300 N. Continental Boulevard #180
El Segundo, CA 90245
(310) 414-8484

Tahiti Tourism
444 Madison Avenue, 16th floor
New York, NY 10022
(212) 838-7800 (ext. 246)/(212) 838-9576 (fax)

TAIWAN
Taiwan Visitors Association
1 World Trade Center #7953
New York, NY 10018
(212) 466-0691

Taiwan Visitors Association
33 N. Michigan Avenue
Chicago, IL 60601
(312) 346-1037

Taiwan Visitors Association
166 Geary Street #1605
San Francisco, CA 94108
(415) 989-8677

THAILAND
Thailand Tourist Office
5 World Trade Center
New York, NY 10048
(212) 432-0433

Tourism Authority of Thailand
3440 Wilshire Boulevard #1100
Los Angeles, CA 90010
(213) 382-2353

TONGA
Tonga Consulate General
360 Post Street #604
San Francisco, CA 94108
(415) 781-0365

TRINIDAD AND TOBAGO
Trinidad and Tobago Tourism Development Authority
25 W. 43rd Street, Suite 1508
New York, NY 10036
(800) 232-0082

TURKEY
Turkish Tourism and Information Office
821 United Nations Plaza
New York, NY 10017
(212) 687-2194

TURKS AND CAICOS
Turks and Caicos Tourist Board
P.O. Box 594023
Miami, FL 33159
(800) 241-0824

U.S. VIRGIN ISLANDS
U.S. Virgin Islands Division of Tourism
1270 Avenue of the Americas #2108
New York, NY 10020
(212) 332-2222

U.S. Virgin Islands Division of Tourism
3460 Wilshire Boulevard #412
Los Angeles, CA 90010
(213) 739-0138

WALES (see GREAT BRITAIN)

Travel Organizations
(Student, Senior and Miscellaneous)

Student discounts: You are entitled to student discounts if you are under 25 or under 35 within 3 years of graduation.

SEMESTER AT SEA: University of Pittsburgh, 811 William Pitt Union, Pittsburgh, PA 15260; (800) 854-0195/(412) 648-7490. Earn 12 credits for a semester of world exploration. Fall and spring itineraries. Also an excellent option for 50-plus adventurers. $12,000 for a 100-day adventure covers everything except port spending money.

COUNCIL ON INTERNATIONAL EDUCATION EXCHANGE: 205 E. 42nd Street, New York, NY 10017; (212) 661-1414. Nonprofit organization dedicated to the pursuit of work, study and travel abroad. Two subagencies offering budget travel services: 1. COUNCIL TRAVEL—ISIC, ITC, IYC and HI cards. 2. COUNCIL CHARTER—charter flights, discount rail passes, accommodations and guidebooks.

GLOBAL EXCHANGE: 2017 Mission Street, #303, San Francisco, CA 94110; (415) 255-7296/(800) 497-1994. Build ties between U.S. citizens and people in the third world, advancing the internationalists citizen's movement. Many cultural exchange programs.

EDUCATIONAL HOMESTAY PROGRAM: (800) 666-4032.

EDUCATION TRAVEL CENTER (ETC): 438 N. Francis Street, Madison, WI 53703; (608) 256-5551. Low-cost domestic and international flights. Hostelling International cards. Free brochure: *Taking Off.*

STUDENT TRAVEL ASSOCIATION (STA TRAVEL): (800) 777-0112/(212) 477-7166 (212) 986-9470. Is-

sues student ID cards on the spot (or just go to Times Square). Not good for air charter travel.

INSTITUTE OF INTERNATIONAL EDUCATION (INFORMATION CENTER): 11E/809 U.N. Plaza, New York, NY 10017; (212) 984-5413. Reference books, foreign university catalogs, Study-abroad brochures. Worth a visit while in Manhattan.

STUDENT TRAVEL AUSTRALIA (STA): 7204$^{1}/_{2}$ Melrose Avenue, Los Angeles, CA 90046; International Student Identity Cards (ISIC). STA card. 120 offices worldwide.

NATIONAL REGISTRATION CENTER FOR STUDY ABROAD: 823 N. 2nd Street, Milwaukee, WI 53203; (414) 278-0631 (800) 558-9988. Call or write for list of programs nationwide.

CAMPUS TRAVEL: 52 Grosvenor Gardens, London SW1W OAG; (071) 730-8832. Student and youth fares for all transportation options. Travel insurance for students and individuals under 35.

INTERNATIONAL STUDENT EXCHANGE FLIGHTS (ISE): 5010 East Shea Boulevard, #a104,. Scottsdale, AZ 85254; (602) 951-1177. Multiple student travel discounts. Free catalog.

AMERICAN ASSOCIATION OF RETIRED PERSONS (AARP): 601 E Street NW, Washington, DC 20049; (202) 434-2277. Annual dues are $8 per household. Hotel and travel discounts for people over 50.

VISA SERVICES: Travel Agenda, 119 W. 57th Street, Suite 1008, New York, NY 10019; (212) 265-7887.

TRAVEL COMPANION EXCHANGE: P.O. Box 833, Amityville, NY 11701; (800) 392-1256/(516) 454-0880. Same-sex pairing: $36 for six months, $60 per year. Opposite-sex pairing: $66 for six months, $120 per year. Bimonthly newsletter with free profile.

UNIVERSAL ESPERANTO ASSOCIATION: (212) 687-7041/(800) 233-3475.

Travel-Related Books

LONELY PLANET PUBLICATIONS: Embarcadero West, 155 Filbert Street, Suite 251, Oakland, CA 94607. (510) 893-8555/(800) 229-0122/(800) 275-8555 (orders). Comprehensive, regionalized budget travel guides of tremendous value (once you arrive at your destinations). Free newsletter.

Wild Planet: 1,001 Extraordinary Events for the Inspired Traveler.

The Frugal Globetrotter

Moon Travel Handbooks, MOON PUBLICATIONS: P.O. Box 3040, Chico, CA 95927-3040; (800) 345-5473/ (916) 345-5473. Publishers of travel handbooks to **Asia**, the **Pacific** and the **Americas** for over 20 years. Each *Moon Handbook* begins with an in-depth essay on the land, the people, their history, arts, politics and social concerns—an entire bookshelf squeezed into a one-volume encyclopedia. The handbooks provide accurate, up-to-date coverage of all the practicalities: language, currency, transportation, accommodations, food, entertainment and services, to name a few.

Let's Go Travel, HARVARD STUDENT AGENCIES, INC.: 53a Church Street, Harvard University, Cambridge, MA 02138; (617) 495-9469/(800) 553-8746. Travel guidebooks and other budget-oriented travel services put together by Harvard students. Shaky reputation stemming from proof (*Rolling Stone* 3/7/95) that student "writers" rely on word of mouth and tourist boards for information.

Berkeley Guides, Berkeley students taking on Harvard with their own shoestring adventure guides. More liberal than *Let's Go.*

Insight Guides, Two versions: Full books focus mostly on history, culture and atmosphere. Pocket books focus on sights and neighborhoods.

Camp the U.S. for $5 or Less (eastern and midwestern states—for tent and RV campers), Mary Helen and Shuford Smith. Globe Pequot Press.

The Best Bargain Family Vacations in the U.S.A., Laura Sutherland and Valerie Wolf Deutsch. St. Martins Press.

Traveling with Children, Forsyth Travel Library, P.O. Box 2975, Shawnee Mission, KS 66201; (800) 367-7984.

Woman Traveling Alone: Handbook for Woman Travelers, by Maggie and Gemma Moss. Published by Piatkus Books/Memoir of a Woman Alone, Penguin Books. $9.

The Peace Corps and More: 114 Ways to Work, Study and Travel in the Third World.

THE COLLEGE CONNECTION: 19 Newton Turnpike, Westport, CT 06880; Write for *The Passport:* Tips on travel and study abroad.

The Ultimate Adventure Source Book, by Paul Mcmenamin, Turner Publishing, Inc., One CNN Center, P.O. Box 105366, Atlanta, GA 30348-5366. Stimulating, unbiased directory of trips including ballooning, hanggliding, safaris and snowmobiling.

Adventure Vacations, Sobek's International Explorers Association, John Muir Publications, P.O. Box 613, Santa Fe, NM 87504. A dictionary of worldwide tours and treks.

Great American Vacations for Travelers with Disabilities, softcover 600 pages, $18, published by Fodor's Travel Publications, Inc.

Note: Libraries stock guidebooks. New York Public Library, 40th Street and Fifth Avenue; (212) 930-0800.

Travel Magazines and Newsletters

Big World (Travel on-the-cheap and down-to-earth), a bimonthly journal of alternative travel and offbeat adventure for the independent world explorer. One year subscription (six issues) $12. Submissions always welcome. Request a set of writers guidelines. Highly recommended. Big World, P.O. Box 21, Coraopolis, PA 15108.

Wings-0-Gram, a newsletter for the discriminating world traveler. Previews international adventure tours. Have you visited 100 countries? If so, you are eligible for membership in their prestigious *Century Club.* To enjoy the camaraderie of those who have accomplished this amazing feat, get in touch. Wings of the World Inc., 1200 William Street, # 706, Buffalo, NY 14240.

Travelin' Magazine: Exploring the Backroads and Byways of the West, Road trip tales and game plans. Six issues per year $14.95. Travelin' Magazine, P.O. Box 23005, Eugene, OR 97402-0424; (503) 485-8533.

International Travel News (ITN), 520 Calvados Avenue, Sacramento, CA 95815; (800) 366-9192. Monthly subscription publication. Hidden, mid-price adventure travel bargains.

TNT Magazine (your guide to free-spirited travel): 52 Earls Court Road, London W8 6EJ, England; 071 244 6529. Subscribe to this immensely useful, alternative magazine. Nuts-and-bolts information, stories and travel ideas.

INTERNATIONAL TRAVEL NEWS (ITN): 520 Calvados Avenue, Sacramento, CA 95815; (800) 366-9192.

Student Travels (magazine published by Marblehead Communications, Inc.): 376 Boylston Street, Boston, MA 02116-3812; (617) 424-7700. Great way to identify student hangouts around the globe. Write for a copy or look around your university student union.

Travel Unlimited Newsletter, Steve Lantos, P.O. Box 1058, Allston, MA 02134-1058. E-mail: STEVEL25555 @AOL.COM. and Internet: HTTP://NEXUS. DATAWAVE.NET/TRAVEL/TRAVEL.HTML. Courier tips and other travel bargains. 1 year for $25.

Consumer Reports Travel Letter, Subscription Department, P.O. Box 51366, Boulder, CO 80321-1366. $37 for 12 issues of loads of air travel bargains.

ANTI-JET LAG DIET WALLET CARD: Write for one: Argonne National Labs, Public Affairs Office, 9700 S. Cass Avenue, Argonne, IL 60439.

Plane-Talk (Networking at 30,000 Feet), Don Gabor/ Conversational Arts Media, P.O. Box 150-715, Brooklyn, NY 11215-0008; (800) 423-4203. Entertaining conversation tips for frequent flyers. Free.

CONSUMER INFORMATION: Center-2C, P.O. Box 100, Pueblo, CO 81002. Informative booklets (all $1 or less), including: *Fly Rights—A Guide to Air Travel in the U.S., Your Trip Abroad, New Horizons for the Air Traveler With A Disability,* Travelers to the———— (numerous destinations).

Going Solo, P.O Box 123, Apalachicola, FL 32329. (904) 653-8848. Bimonthly publication focusing on solo travel. $29 per year. Sample copy $6.

Airfare Secrets Uncovered, Universal Information Corporation, 2812 Santa Monica Boulevard, Suite 203A, Santa Monica, CA 90404.

Book on Pubs: find one if visiting **England, Scotland** or **Ireland.**

Lee Baxandall's World Guide to Nude Beaches and Recreation, N Editions, P.O. Box 132, Oshkosh, WI 54902.

Retail Magazines focusing on "good strange" travel:

Backpacker
Conde Nast Traveler
Men's Journal
Outside Magazine
National Geographic Traveler

Note: The Sunday travel section of any major newspaper is an excellent resource for the latest travel bargains.

Wall Street Journal, "Tracking Travel," "Marketplace" (section B). Frequent column (usually Tuesdays). Business traveler tips.

Happiness-Related Publications, Organizations and Products

Joy Gazette, 12 issues for $14.95. (800) MORE-JOY. Not a travel publication. Monthly paper focusing exclusively on positive events and trends. Request a complimentary issue; it'll put you in a good mood!

PEACE RESEARCH FOUNDATION: 225 Crossroads No. 145, Carmel, CA 93923. Robert R. Tyler, Founder/ President (408) 626-3722/Fax (408) 375-6888. Encourages the widespread study of what propels worldwide peace.

UNIVERSAL ESPERANTO ASSOCIATION: (212) 687-7041/(800) 233-3475. Collection of worldly enthusiasts who speak an invented, common language (most similar to German) that is not native to any country.

BACKPACKER GUITARS BY MARTIN & CO.: (800) 633-2060. Very portable acoustic guitars.

Accommodations

CRITICAL PUBLICATION: *The Hostel Handbook,* c/o Jim Williams, 722 St. Nicholas Avenue, New York, NY 10031; (212) 926-7030. E-mail: InfoHostel@AOL. com. Invaluable guide to every hostel (independent and otherwise) in North America. Send $3 check (includes shipping) payable to Jim Williams. See Appendix 2 for more information.

HOSTELING INTERNATIONAL (HI): 733 15th Street NW, Washington, D.C.; (202) 783-6161. 6,000 locations in 70 countries, usually with kitchen facilities. Average $7–$20 per night. One year membership: $25.

U.S. Bed & Breakfast, Free Regionalized printouts of B&Bs in specific regions. (800) US-B-AND-B.

NEW YORK INTERNATIONAL HOSTEL (HI): 891 Amsterdam Avenue and 103rd Street, New York, NY 10036; (212) 932-2300.

Working Abroad

International Employment Gazette, 1525 W Wade Hampton Boulevard, Greenville, SC 29609. (800) 882-9188. 400 or more listings every 2 weeks; 6 issues for $35.

The Frugal Globetrotter

O-HAYO SENSEI: 1032 Irving Street, Suite 508, San Francisco, CA 94122; Fax (415) 731-1113. English-teaching jobs in Japan.

OVERSEAS EMPLOYMENT: (514) 739-0795.

INTERNATIONAL EMPLOYMENT NEWS: (514) 421-6831.

BUNAC: 16 Bowling Green Lane, London EC1R OBD, England; (071) 251-3472. Six-month work permits and placement in both career orientated and casual jobs. Fee. Worthwhile.

CIEE, WORK ABROAD: 205 East 42nd Street, New York, NY 10017-5706; Jobs and internships worldwide.

PEACE CORPS VOLUNTEERS: (800) 424-8580. Care (212) 686-3110.

Homestay Programs

UNITED STATES SERVAS, INC.: 11 John Street, Suite 407, New York, NY 10038; (212) 267-0252. Washington, D.C., contact: (703) 528-1119/(202) 783-6161. Pioneer homestay program opening doors for travelers into homes and hearts in over 100 countries. Minimal fee. Worthwhile.

WORLD LEARNING, INC./SCHOOL FOR INTERNATIONAL TRAINING: Kipling Road, P.O. Box 676, Brattleboro, VT 05302; (800) 451-4465/(802) 257-7751. Homestays, masters of arts in teaching programs, intercultural management, bachelor program in world issues, grassroots development and NGO management; certificate program in Zimbabwe (College Semesters Abroad).

ELDERHOSTEL: 80 Boyleston Street, Suite 400, Boston, MA 02116; (617) 426-7788. Study programs in the United States and abroad for senior citizens.

AMERICAN-SOVIET HOMESTAYS, INC.: Route 1, P.O. Box 68, Iowa City, IA 52240.

FRIENDS OVERSEAS: New York, Connecticut.

NATIONAL CAMPERS AND HIKERS ASSOCIATION: 4804 Transit Road, Building 2, Depew, NY 14043; (716) 668-6242. (KOA).

CAMPMOR: P.O. Box 700-A, Saddle River, NJ 07458-0700; (800) 226-7667. Insanely inexpensive camping supplies. Order a free catalog featuring everything from compasses to zip-off pants.

Health-Related Agencies and Publications

STATE DEPARTMENT TRAVEL ADVISORY HOTLINE: (202) 647-5225. Call for updated travel advisories.

CENTERS FOR DISEASE CONTROL AND PREVENTION HOTLINE: (404) 332-4559. Lists areas where there are outbreaks of yellow fever, plague, etc.

Suggested reading: *Health Hints for the Tropics,* American Society of Tropical Medicine and Hygiene, 60 Revere Drive, Suite 500, Northbrook, IL 60062. Send a check for $5, Attention: Secretariat.

Directory of Physicians (primarily the United States and Canada) specializes in traveler and tropical medicine. Send a stamped ($1), self-addressed envelope (9-by-11 inches) to Dr. Leonard C. Marcus, 148 Highland Avenue, Newton, MA 02165.

Find A Doctor, (716) 754-4883. A passport-sized directory of English-speaking doctors worldwide.

INTERNATIONAL SOCIAL ACTION GROUP: Burma Action Group, Collins Studios, Collins Yard, Islington Green, London N1 2XU, England; 071 359 7679/Fax: 071 354 3987/e-mail: bagp@gn.apc.org. Protesting the military dictatorship and the enslavements of prostitutes in Burma. Campaign for the withdrawal of the foreign investments that fuel this corruption.

Valuable Travel Miscellany

NATIONAL OUTDOOR LEADERSHIP SCHOOL (NOLS): (307) 332-8800.

DEFINE APEX: *Advanced Purchase Excursion* (30 percent off of virtually all major international carriers).

EXPEDITION PLANNING: *The Explorers Club,* 40 E. 70th Street, New York, NY 10021; (212) 628-8383.

S.A. EXPLORERS CLUB: 1510 York Street, #214, Denver, CO 80206.

AMERICA ON LINE: (800) 827-6364.

PATAGONIAS OUTDOOR ACTIVITIES GUIDELINE: (800) 523-9597.

Great Expeditions, A Canadian magazine offering free classified ads for subscribers; a good way to find travel partners.

FREIGHTER TRAVEL: Sea-freighter travel around the world is certainly an inexpensive transportation option for those with an open-ended adventure schedule. Contact FORD'S TRAVEL GUIDES: 19448 Londelius Street, Northridge, CA 91324; (818) 701-7414. Ask for a list of freighter companies providing transatlantic and worldwide sea travel.

ANTARCTIC POLAR FLIGHTS: Contact ADVEN-TURE NETWORK INTERNATIONAL: 200-1676 Duranleau Street, Vancouver, BC, Canada V6H 3S5; (604) 683-8633. Best choice in **Antarctica.**

AKLAK AIR LTD.: P.O Box 1190, Inuvik, NWT, Canada X0E 0T0; (403) 979-3555. **Arctic** specialists from the **Bering Sea** to the **North Pole.**

BRADLEY AIR SERVICES: Carp Airport, Carp, ONT Canada K0A 1L0; (800) 267 7331 (Canada); (613) 839-33404. **Arctic** bases, largest carrier.

DOUG GEETING AVIATION: P.O. Box 122, Talkeetna, AK 99676; (907) 733-2366. Famous in the region.

RUSTY'S FLYING SERVICE, INC.: P.O Box 190325, Anchorage, AK 99519-0325; (907) 243-1595.

WRIGHT AIR SERVICE: P.O. Box 60142, Fairbanks, AK 99706; (907) 474-0502.

TEMSCO AIRLINES: P.O. Box 8615, Ketchikan, AK 99901; (907) 225-9810.

WORLDBITS!: Country-a-day calendars that stimulate interest in the global village by teaching a small "bit" of information each day. Worldbits! Corporation, 100 E. 42nd Street, 8th Floor, New York, NY 10017; (212) 479-2337/Fax (212) 479-2510. David Meadows, Project Director.

BOGOTA TO BROOKLYN: A CD ROM capturing the photography and music of an overland adventure between **Columbia** and **New York City.**

HOSTEL GUIDE (UNITED STATES AND CANADA)

▼ This symbol indicates listings taken from *The Hostel Handbook* for the U.S.A. and Canada. These listings include both affiliated and unaffiliated (independent) hostels.

The Hostel Handbook includes well over five hundred hostels in the United States and Canada and is an essential tool for a cheap trip across North America. The handbook is edited by Jim Williams at the Sugar Hill International House in Harlem, New York City. The Hostel Handbook listings are provided by permission. *The Hostel Handbook* is copyrighted material, and the name is trademarked.

For the complete, updated handbook, contact: Jim Williams, c/o The Hostel Handbook, 722 Saint Nicholas Avenue, New York, NY 10031; (212) 926-7030. Send a $3 U.S. check (includes shipping) payable to Jim Williams. E-mail: InfoHostel@aol.com.

Another source for those in the digital age is *The Internet Guide to Hostelling*. This web site provides the updated version of *The Hostel Handbook* plus information on hostels worldwide. *The Internet Guide to Hostelling* is edited by Darren Overby at the Pacific Tradewinds Hostel in San Francisco. E-mail: http://www.hostels.com/hostels/.

● This symbol indicates listings taken from either *Hostelling U.S.A.: The Official Guide to Hostels in the United States of America* or *Hostelling North America* (Canada listings). These listings include Hostelling International—American Youth Hostels (HI-AYH) hostels.

Hostelling U.S.A. and *Hostelling North America* are published by Hostelling International—American Youth Hostels, 733 15th Street, NW, Suite 840, Washington, D.C. 20005; (202) 783-6161/(800) 444-6111.

How the Affiliations Are Listed

AAIH—American Association of International Hostels
BHC—Backpackers Hostels Canada
HI-AYH—Hostelling International–American Youth Hostels
HI-C—Hostelling International–Canada
IC—InterClub
U—Unaffiliated
(S—Summer Rates)

UNITED STATES

ALASKA

CITY OF ANCHORAGE

▼ ANCHORAGE BACKPACKERS INN
U $13
3601 Peterkin Avenue
Anchorage, AK 99508
(907) 274-3870

● HI-ANCHORAGE
HI-AYH $15 U.S.
700 H Street
Anchorage, AK 99501
(907) 276-3635

CITY OF FAIRBANKS

▼ FAIRBANKS SHELTER & SHOWER
U $12.50
248 Madcap Lane
Fairbanks, AK 99709
(907) 479-5016
In-state: (800) 499-5016, limited private rooms $18 per person. No curfew; no lock-out. Kitchen. Linen available.

▼ ALASKA HERITAGE INN
AAIH $12
1018 22nd Avenue
Fairbanks, AK 99701
(907) 451-6587
Member discounts (all affiliations). Laundry. Camping. Fifteen minutes to downtown. Cabins, wilderness, canoe, horseback riding, fishing and more.

DENALI PARK

▼ MOUNT MCKINLEY GOLD CAMP
U $22
P.O. Box 149
McKinley, AK 99755
(907) 479-2277
In the heart of Denali National Park. Cabins, tents, cookout buildings. No minimum/maximum stay. Transportation information: (800) 770-7275.

OTHER ALASKA LOCATIONS

▼ CIRCLE HOTSPRING RESORT
U $22
Central, AK 99730
(907) 520-5113

● DELTA JUNCTION INTERNATIONAL HOSTEL
HI-AYH $7 U.S.
P.O. Box 971
Delta Junction, AK 99737
(907) 895-5074

● HI-JUNEAU
HI-AYH $10 U.S.
614 Harris Street
Juneau, AK 99801
(907) 586-9559

● HI-KETCHIKAN
HI-AYH $8 U.S.
Grant and Main Streets
P.O. Box 8515
Ketchikan, AK 99901
(907) 225-3319

● HI-NINILCHIK, THE EAGLE WATCH
HI-AYH $10 U.S.+tax
Mile 3, Oil Well Road
Ninilchik, AK 99639
(907) 567-3905

● HI-SNOW RIVER
HI-AYH $15 U.S.
Alaskan Hwy 9, Milepost 16
HCR 64, P.O. Box 425
Seward, AK 99664
(907) 566-2480

● HI-SITKA
HI-AYH $7 U.S.
P.O. Box 2645, 303 Kimsham Street
Sitka, AK 99835
(907) 747-8356

▼ SKAGWAY INTERNATIONAL HOSTEL
BHC $12
P.O. Box 231, Third Avenue
Skagway, AK 99840
(907) 983-2131
A friendly, family atmosphere in the Klondike tradition!

▼ NATAT CREEK HOSTEL
U $15
P.O. Box 905
Slana, AK 99586
(907) 822-3427
Off-road hiking and canoeing access. Cabins, sauna. Quiet. Call ahead.

● TOK INTERNATIONAL YOUTH HOSTEL
HI-AYH $7.50 U.S.
Mile 1322 1/2 Alaska Hwy
P.O. Box 532
Tok, AK 99780
(907) 883-3745

ARIZONA

CITY OF FLAGSTAFF

▼ GRAND CANYON INTERNATIONAL HOSTEL
U $12
100 North San Francisco Street
Flagstaff, AZ 86001
(520) 779-6971

● HI-FLAGSTAFF
HI-AYH $12
23 North Leroux Street
Flagstaff, AZ 86001
(520) 774-2731

▼ MOTEL DU BEAU
AAIH $12
19 West Phoenix Avenue
Flagstaff, AZ 86001
(800) 332-1944
Price includes tax, linen and breakfast! Free pickup and delivery from bus and train stations and airport. Blue Goose Tours to the Grand Canyon. Phone: (520) 774-6731; fax: (520) 774-4060.

OTHER ARIZONA LOCATIONS

● HI-PHOENIX, THE METCALF HOUSE
HI-AYH $10
1026 North Ninth Street
Phoenix, AZ 85006
(602) 254-9803

▼ TUCSON INTERNATIONAL HOSTEL (CONGRESS HOTEL)
AAIH $14
311 East Congress
Tucson, AZ 85701
(520) 622-8848
Dorms with few beds in historic railroad hotel! Convenient café; hot local nightclub with live music nightly.

▼ CANYON RAILCAR HOSTEL
U $18
1900 Rodeo Road & Old Route 66
Williams, AZ 86046
(520) 635-9371
58 miles to the Grand Canyon. On historic Route 66. Swimming pool.

ARKANSAS

▼ KELLER'S HOME HOSTEL
U $11
Route 62
Eureka Springs, AR 72632
(501) 253-8418

CALIFORNIA

CITY OF SAN FRANCISCO

▼ EUROPEAN GUEST HOUSE
AAIH $12
761 Minna Street
San Francisco, CA 94103
(415) 861-6634

▼ GLOBE HOSTEL
IC $15
10 Hallam Place
San Francisco, CA
(415) 431-0540
We offer a clean, modern, friendly hostel with private bathrooms and two cats. Bar, pool table, café. Central location; open 24 hours. Proof of international travel required. E-mail: globe@2ch.Ch.Com

▼ GLOBETROTTER'S INN
U $12
225 Ellis Street
San Francisco, CA 94102
(415) 346-5786

▼ GRAND CENTRAL HOSTEL
U $12 & up
1412 Market Street
San Francisco, CA 94102
(415) 703-9988
Fun, downtown hostel. Free breakfast, tea, coffee. Close to attractions, pubs and clubs. Open 24 hours. No curfew or chores.

▼ GREEN TORTOISE HOSTEL–SAN FRANCISCO
AAIH $10
494 Broadway
San Francisco, CA 94133
(415) 834-9060
In the heart of Nosh Beach!

▼ HI-SAN FRANCISCO–DOWNTOWN
HI-AYH $13–$15
312 Mason Street
San Francisco, CA 94102
(415) 788-5604

▼ HI-SAN FRANCISCO–FORT MASON
HI-AYH $13–$15
Fort Mason Building 240
San Francisco, CA 94123
(415) 771-7277
Large, beautiful hostel overlooking the Golden Gate Bridge. Spacious kitchen and common areas. Free linen. No curfew. Daily activities! Safest neighborhood in San Francisco. Convenient and super clean. Fun international atmosphere.

▼ INTERNATIONAL GUEST HOUSE
U $12
2976 23rd Street
San Francisco, CA 94110
(415) 641-1411
Uncrowded beautiful Victorian house with 30 guests. Com-

mon room with fireplace; two fully equipped kitchens. Couples' rooms for $24. No curfew. 5-day minimum stay.

▼ INTERNATIONAL STUDENT CENTER
U $12
1188 Folsom Street
San Francisco, CA 94103
(415) 487-1463

▼ MISSION HOSTEL AT EL CAPITAN HOTEL
U $20/2
2361 Mission Street
San Francisco, CA 94110
(415) 695-1597
Privacy at hostel rates is what we provide. Take a break and try our room for two at $22. We provide remodeled rooms. No curfew. Group rates too! Two for twenty-two!

▼ PACIFIC TRADEWINDS GUEST HOUSE
U $12–$14
680 Sacramento Street
San Francisco, CA 94111
(415) 433-7970
Great location; kitchen; free tea/coffee, linen. Service laundry, safety deposit, luggage storage, long-term storage. No curfew. No lockout and free sock wash! Fax: (415) 291-8801, email: OverbyEcH.com

CITY OF LOS ANGELES

(Travelers arriving at Los Angeles Airport are warned against accepting rides at the airport by individuals saying they represent a hostel. So-called "runners" at the airport will promise anything, and you may end up at an inconvenient or unethical location—or at a different hostel than the one they represented to you. Telephone your hostel(s) of choice and follow that hostel's instructions.)

▼ BACKPACKERS PARADISE
U $16
4200 West Century Boulevard
Los Angeles, CA 90302
(310) 672-3090

▼ BANANA BUNGALOW–HOLLYWOOD
AAIH $14
2775 Cahuenga Boulevard West
Los Angeles, CA, 90068
(800) 4-HOSTEL
Free airport, train and bus pickup. Free shuttle to the beach, Disneyland and Universal Studios. Pool, café, kitchen, arcade, weight room, library room, theater, store, TVs.

▼ CADALAC HOTEL
IC $18
401 Ocean Front Walk
Venice, CA 90291
(310) 399-8876

▼ COLONIAL INN HOSTEL
AAIH $12–$14
421 8th Street
Huntington Beach, CA 92648
(714) 536-3315
The Beach is hot—LA is not! Walk to the beach, movies, shops.

▼ HI-FULLERTON—DISNEYLAND
HI-AYH $14
1700 North Harbor Boulevard
Fullerton, CA 92635
(714) 738-3721
Closest hostel to Disneyland and Knott's Berry Farm! 1.5 miles from Amtrak. Small—22 beds, clean, kitchen, porch swing. Coffee houses, restaurants, bars, grocery store nearby.

▼ HI-LOS ANGELES–SOUTH BAY
HI-AYH $11.50
3601 South Gaffey Street #613
San Pedro, CA 90733
(310) 831-8109

▼ HI-SANTA MONICA
HI-AYH $15+tax
1436 Second Street
Santa Monica, CA 90401
(310) 393-9913
LA's best! Great beach location.

▼ HOLLYWOOD HILLS HOSTEL
U $15
6772 Hawthorn Avenue
Hollywood, CA 90028
(213) 850-7733

▼ JIM'S AT THE BEACH
U $15
17 Brooks Avenue
Venice, CA 90921
(310) 399-4018

▼ LINCOLN INTERNATIONAL HOSTEL
IC $14
2221 Lincoln Boulevard
Venice, CA 90291
(310) 305-0250

The Frugal Globetrotter

▼ LOS ANGELES SURF CITY HOSTEL
U $12
26 Pier Avenue
Hermosa Beach, CA 90254
(310) 798-2323

▼ OBAN HOTEL & HOSTEL
U $25
6364 Yucca
Hollywood, CA
(310) 466-0524

▼ VENICE BEACH HOTEL
IC $14
25 Windsward Avenue
Venice, CA 90291
(310) 399-7649

▼ VENICE BEACH HOSTEL
U $13
701 Washington Boulevard
Venice Beach, CA 90292
(310) 306-5180

▼ VENICE MARINA HOSTEL
U $12–$13
2915 Yale Avenue
Marina Del Rey, CA 90292
(310) 301-3983
Free airport pickup. Free breakfast. Daily tours.

▼ ZEN HOSTEL OF LOS ANGELES
U $14
1041 S. Elden Avenue
Los Angeles, CA 90006
(310) 204-6626

CITY OF SAN DIEGO

● HI-ELLIOTT HOSTEL
HI-AYH $12–$13
3790 Udall Street
San Diego, CA 92107-2414
(619) 223-4778

● HI-SAN DIEGO
HI-AYH $12–$14
500 West Broadway
San Diego, CA 92101
(619) 525-1531

OTHER CALIFORNIA LOCATIONS

● HI-REDWOOD NATIONAL PARK
HI-AYH $10–$12

14480 CA Hwy 101 at Wilson Creek Road
Klamath, CA 95548
(707) 482-8265

▼ EEL RIVER REDWOODS HOSTEL
AAIH $12+tax
70400 North Hwy 101
Leggett, CA 95455
(707) 925-6469
Between San Francisco and Oregon. Redwoods, sauna, jacuzzi, pub.

● HI-HIDDEN VILLA
HI-AYH $9.50
26870 Moody Road
Los Altos Hills, CA 94022
(415) 949-8648
(Closed June–August)

● HI-POINT MONTARA LIGHTHOUSE
HI-AYH $10–$12
16th Street at California Hwy 1
P.O. Box 737
Montara, CA 94037
(415) 728-7177

▼ ALPENROSE COTTAGE HOSTEL
U $13
204 East Hinkley Street
Mount Shasta, CA 96067
(916) 926-6724
Small bed & breakfast–type retreat. Gardens in four seasons. Alpine village. Ski, hike, etc. Sheets, towels, tax included.

▼ BILL'S HOME HAVEN
U
1040 Ceilo Lane
Nipomo, CA 93444
(805) 929-3647
Between Los Angeles and San Francisco. Non-smokers, go to Mobil. Horses.

● HI-PIGEON POINT LIGHTHOUSE
HI-AYH $10–$12
210 Pigeon Point Road
Pescadero, CA 94060
(415) 879-0633

● HI-POINT REYES
HI-AYH $10–$12
P.O. Box 247
Point Reyes, CA 94956
(415) 663-8811

▼ SANTA BARBARA INTERNATIONAL HOSTEL
AAIH $12
409 State Street
Santa Barbara, CA 93101
(805) 963-0154
Palm trees, beautiful beaches, hiking in the mountains! Everything a California holiday should be! On the Western Stagecoach Hostel shuttle run. Paradise awaits you!

● HI-SANTA CRUZ
HI-AYH $12–$14
321 Main Street
P.O. Box 1241
Santa Cruz, CA 95061
(408) 423-8304

● HI-SANBORN PARK HOSTEL
HI-AYH $8.50
15808 Sanborn Road
Saratoga, CA 95070
(408) 741-0166

● HI-MARIN HEADLANDS
HI-AYH $10–$12
941 Fort Barry, Building 941
Sausalito, CA 94965
(415) 331-2777

COLORADO

CITY OF DENVER

▼ DENVER INTERNATIONAL HOSTEL
AAIH $8.50
630 East 16th Avenue
Denver, CO 80201
(303) 832-9996
Kitchens, food, library, showers, local and international information. TV, games, no curfew, linens, laundry, storage, sundecks, parking, family room, cheap air/train tickets, vehicle purchase assistance, driveaways, cameras and film, ski/athletic equipment.

▼ STANDISH
U $14
1530 California Street
Denver, CO 80201
(303) 534-3231

OTHER COLORADO LOCATIONS

● HI-CONEJOS RIVER AYH HOSTEL
HI-AYH $9+tax
3591 County Road E. 2
Antonito, CO 81120
(719) 376-2518

▼ LITTLE RED SKI HAUS
U $20
118 East Cooper
Aspen, CO 81611
(303) 925-3333

▼ FIRESIDE INN
HI-AYH $15+tax
P.O. BOX 2252, 114 North French Street
Breckenridge, CO 80424
(970) 453-6456

● GARDEN OF THE GODS CAMPGROUND
HI-AYH $14+tax
3704 West Colorado Avenue
Colorado Springs, CO 80904
(719) 475-9450

▼ DURANGO HOSTEL
U $10
543 East 2nd Avenue, P.O. Box 1445
Durango, CO 81301
(970) 247-9905

● H-BAR-G RANCH HOSTEL
HI-AYH $8–$10+tax
(HI members only)
3500 H-BAR-G Road, P.O. Box 1260
Estes Park, CO 80517
(970) 586-3688

● HI-SHADOWCLIFF
HI-AYH $8
405 Summerland Park Road
P.O. Box 658
Grand Lake, CO 80447
(970) 627-9220

● HI-GRAND JUNCTION
HI-AYH $10+tax
337 Colorado Avenue
Grand Junction, CO 81501
(800) 430-4555

● HI-GLENWOOD SPRINGS HOSTEL
HI-AYH $9.50+tax
1021 Grand Avenue
Glenwood Springs, CO 81601
(970) 945-8545/(800) 9HOSTEL

● HI-PITKIN HOSTEL
HI-AYH $10+tax
329 Main Street
P.O. Box 164

Pitkin, CO 81241
(970) 641-2757

● HI-ALPEN HÜTTE
HI-AYHS$11–$16; W$14–25
471 Rainbow Drive
P.O. Box 919
Silverthorne, CO 80498
(970) 468-6336

▼ HI-WINTER PARK AYH
HI-AYH   S$8–$13
P.O. Box 3323
Winter Park, CO 80482
(970) 726-5356
In the heart of the Rocky Mountains at 9,000 meters above sea level. $8 ski rental. $9 mountain bike rental. 10 private rooms. 4 dorms. 5 kitchens. No curfew; no lockout. On Greyhound and Amtrak.

CONNECTICUT

● HI-HARTFORD, THE MARK TWAIN HOSTEL
HI-AYH $13
131 Tremont Street
Hartford, CT 06105
(203) 523-7255

● WINDSOR HOME HOSTEL
HI-AYH $13–$15
(call for street address)
Windsor, CT
(203) 683-2847

FLORIDA

CITY OF FORT LAUDERDALE

▼ FLOYD'S HOSTEL & CREW HOUSE
U $10
(call for street address)
Ft. Lauderdale, FL 33316
(305) 462-0631
Friendly, quiet, near Mannas. Phone, TV. Free pickup. No curfew.

▼ FT. LAUDERDALE INTERNATIONAL YOUTH HOSTEL
U $12
905 NE 17th Terrace
Ft. Lauderdale, FL 33304
(305) 467-0452
Call first. Longest established, friendly staff.

● HI-FT. LAUDERDALE, INTERNATIONAL HOUSE
HI-AYH $12+tax
3811 North Ocean Boulevard
Ft. Lauderdale, FL 33308
(305) 568-1615

CITY OF MIAMI

▼ HI-MIAMI BEACH AT THE CLAY HOTEL
HI-AYH $12–$13
1438 Washington Avenue
Miami Beach, FL 33139
(305) 534-2988
Open 24 hours. Friendly, international atmosphere. In the heart of the art deco district—minutes from the beach. Near nightlife and shopping. Couple rooms available. Fax: (305) 673-0346. Toll-free reservation number: (800) 379-2529. Best spot in Miami!

▼ MIAMI BEACH INTERNATIONAL TRAVELERS HOSTEL
AAIH $12
236 9th Street
Miami Beach, FL 33139
(305) 534-0268
Fantastic location, only seconds to the beach and nightlife. Clean. Friendly international atmosphere. All rooms have air conditioning and a private bath. Linen provided. 4-person maximum. Private rooms available.

▼ TROPICS
U $12
1550 Collins Avenue
Miami Beach, FL 33139
(305) 531-0361

OTHER FLORIDA LOCATIONS

▼ CLEAR WATER BEACH HOSTEL
AAIH $11–$13
606 Bay Esplanade Avenue
Clear Water Beach, FL 34630
(813) 443-1211
Pool, hammocks, free bikes, canoes, tv, game room, kitchen.

● HI-KEY WEST
HI-AYH $15.25
718 South Street
Key West, FL 33040
(305) 296-5719

● HI-ORLANDO, DOWNTOWN
HI-AYH $8–10+tax
227 North Eola Drive

Orlando, FL 32801
(407) 843-8888

▼ SAINT AUGUSTINE
U $12
32 Treasury Street
St. Augustine, FL 32084
(904) 829-6163
Miles of sandy beaches; the rest is history!

GEORGIA

▼ HAWKS NEST HOSTEL
U $10
1760 McRee Mill Road
Athens (Watkinsville), GA 30677
(706) 769-0563

● HI-ATLANTA
HI-AYH $12.50+tax
223 Ponce de Leon Avenue
Atlanta, GA 30308
(404) 875-2882

▼ HOSTEL IN THE FOREST
U $9
P.O. Box 1496, U.S. Hwy 82 West
Brunswick, GA 31521
(912) 264-9738
Rustic, tranquil accommodation in dorms and tree houses!

HAWAII

OAHU: WAIKIKI AND HONOLULU

▼ HI-HONOLULU
HI-AYH $12
2323A Seaview Avenue
Honolulu, HI 96822
(808) 946-4591

▼ HI-WAIKIKI
HI-AYH $15
2417 Prince Edward Street
Honolulu, HI 96815
(808) 926-8313

▼ POLYNESIAN BEACH CLUB HOSTEL
AAIH $15
134 Kapahulu Avenue #615
Waikiki, HI 96815
(808) 922-1340

▼ WAIKIKI INTERCLUB HOSTEL
IC $15
2413 Kuhio Avenue
Waikiki, HI 96815
(808) 924-2636

▼ WAIKIKI HAWAIIAN SEASIDE HOSTEL
U $13–$15
419 East Seaside Avenue
Waikiki, Honolulu, HI 96815
(808) 924-3306

OAHU–NORTH SHORE

▼ BACKPACKER'S VACATION INNS
U $12–$16
59-788 Karn Hwy
Haleiwa, HI 96712
(808) 638-7838

BIG ISLAND (HAWAII)

▼ AL'S VOLCANO RANCH HOSTEL
U $16
13-3775 Kalapana Hwy
Pahoa, HI 96778
(808) 965-8800

MAUI

▼ BANANA BUNGALOW
U $15
310 North Market Street
Wailuku, Maui, HI 96793
(800) 8-HOSTEL

IDAHO

● HI-GOODING
HI-AYH $10+tax
112 Main Street
Gooding, ID 83330
(208) 934-4374

▼ HI-KELLOGG
HI-AYH $12
834 McKinley Avenue
Kellogg, ID 83837
(208) 783-4171

● HI-NAPLES
HI-AYH $10
Idaho Highway 2
Naples, ID 83847
(208) 267-4118

ILLINOIS

▼ ARLINGTON INTERNATIONAL HOUSE
AAIH $13–$16
616 West Arlington Place
Chicago, IL 60614
(312) 929-5380
No curfew, upscale, fun neighborhood, near downtown.

▼ CHICAGO INTERNATIONAL HOSTEL
U $13
6318 North Winthrop Avenue
Chicago, IL 60660
(312) 262-1011
Everyone $13, including tax and linen. Picture ID required. Well worth the trip per 1995 Let's Go U.S.A. A full-time hostel catering to travelers only.

● HI-CHICAGO SUMMER HOSTEL
HI-AYH $15–$17
731 South Plymouth Court
Chicago, IL 60605
(312) 327-5350

● HI-INTERNATIONAL HOUSE OF CHICAGO
HI-AYH $19
1414 East 59th Street
Chicago, IL 60637
(312) 753-2270

INDIANA

I HI-AYH COUNCIL OFFICES:

Indiana Council
P.O. Box 30048
Indianapolis, IN 46230
(317) 844-5320

Metropolitan Chicago Council
3036 N. Ashland Avenue
Chicago, IL 60657
(312) 327-8114

IOWA

● HI-WESLEY HOUSE
HI-AYH $12
120 North Dubuque Street
Iowa City, IA 52245
(319) 338-1179

KANSAS

▼ MODERN AIR MOTEL
U $25/5
117 West U.S. 36
Smith Center, KS 66967
(800) 727-7332

KENTUCKY

▼ EMILY BOONE GUEST HOME
U $10
1027 Franklin Street
Louisville, KY 40206
(502) 585-3430

LOUISIANA

▼ INDIA HOUSE INTERNATIONAL HOSTEL
U $12
124 South Lopez Street
New Orleans, LA 70119
(504) 821-1904
Seven minutes to the French Quarter. Free airport, bus, train pickup. Kitchen, free linens, swimming pool, free parking, swamp tours.

● HI-NEW ORLEANS MARQUETTE HOUSE
HI-AYH $12.62+tax
2253 Carondelet Street
New Orleans, LA 70130
(504) 523-3014

MAINE

● HI-BAR HARBOR
HI-AYH $12
27 Kennebec Street
P.O. Box 32
Bar Harbor, ME 04609-0032
(207) 288-5587

● WADSWORTH BLANCHARD FARM HOSTEL
HI-AYH $10
R.R. 2, P.O. Box 5992
Hiram, ME 04041
(207) 625-7509

▼ LOON ECHO CAMPGROUND & BUNKHOUSE
U
P.O. Box 711
Jackman, ME 04945
(207) 668-4829

● HI-PORTLAND SUMMER HOSTEL
HI-AYH $15
645 Congress Street
Portland, ME
Mail to:
Portland Summer Hostel
c/o HI-AYH
1020 Commonwealth Avenue
Boston, MA 02215
(207) 874-3281

MARYLAND

● HI-BALTIMORE
HI-AYH $13
17 West Mulberry Street
Baltimore, MD 21201
(410) 576-8880/(800) 898-2246

▼ HI-HARPER'S FERRY
HI-AYH $10–$12
19123 Sandy Hook Road
Knoxville, MD 21758
(301) 834-7652

MASSACHUSETTS

CITY OF BOSTON

▼ ABERCROMBIE'S INN
U $18
23 Farrington Avenue
Boston, MA 02134
(800) 767-5337
Private rooms $35. Call ahead.

▼ HI-BACK BAY SUMMER HOSTEL
HI-AYH $15–$17
519 Beacon Street
Boston, MA
(617) 731-8096

▼ BOSTON'S IRISH EMBASSY HOSTEL
U $15
232 Friend Street
Boston, MA 02114
(617) 973-4841

▼ HI-BOSTON
HI-AYH $15–$17
12 Hemingway Street
Boston, MA 02115
(617) 536-9455

OTHER MASSACHUSETTS LOCATIONS

▼ IRVING HOUSE
U $30
24 Irving Street
Cambridge, MA 02138
(617) 547-4600

● DUDLEY HOME HOSTEL
HI-AYH $10
(closed December–March)
(call for street address)
Dudley, MA
(508) 943-6520

● HI-MID-CAPE
HI-AYH $12
75 Goody Hallet Drive
Eastham, MA 02642
(508) 255-2785

▼ HI-FRIENDLY CROSSWAYS
HI-AYH $10–$15
Whitcomb Avenue
Littleton, MA 01460-3266
(508) 456-3649
Rest in the country while visiting six national parks!

● HI-NANTUCKET
HI-AYH $12
Surfside Nantucket
31 Western Avenue
Nantucket, MA 02554
(508) 228-0433

● HI-MONROE AND ISABEL SMITH HOSTEL
HI-AYH $13
91 Highland Avenue
Northfield, MA
Mail to:
204 Main Street
NMH P.O. Box 2602
Northfield, MA 01360-1089
(413) 498-3505 (in season)
(413) 498-5983 (off season)

▼ ALICE DUNHAM'S GUEST HOUSE
U $40
3 Dyer Street
Provincetown, MA 02657
(508) 487-3330

▼ THE OUTERMOST HOSTEL
AAIH $14
28 Windslow Street
Provincetown, MA 02657
(508) 487-4378
Come to the tip of Cape Cod. Stay in one of our small cottages just minutes from the beach. Visit the National Seashore, go whale-watching, sailing, windsurfing . No curfew.

● HI-TRURO
HI-AYH $12
P.O. Box 402
Truro, MA 02666
(508) 349-3889

● HI-MARTHA'S VINEYARD
HI-AYH $12
Edgartown West Tisbury Road
P.O. Box 3158
West Tisbury, MA 02575
(508) 693-2665

MICHIGAN

▼ TEAHOUSE/GOLDEN DRAGON
U $5
8585 Harding Avenue
Centerline, MI 48015
(313) 756-2676

▼ PARK AVENUE HOSTEL
U $12
2305 Park Avenue
Detroit, MI 48230
(313) 961-8310

MINNESOTA

▼ BELMONT HOUSE HOME HOSTEL
U $10
1420 Belmont Road
Duluth, MN 55805
(218) 728-6206

▼ DULUTH PORT CITY INTERNATIONAL HOSTEL
U $13
(call for street address)
Duluth, MN
(612) 871-3210

● HI-MISSISSIPPI HEADWATERS
HI-AYH $12–S14
Itasca State Park

Mail to:
HC 05, P.O. Box 5A
Lake Itasca, MN 56460
(218) 266-3415

● HI-SPIRIT OF THE LAND HOSTEL
HI-AYH $15–17
Boundary Waters Canoe Area
Mail to:
940 Gunflint Trail
Grand Marais, MN 55604
(218) 388-2241

● HI-CAECILIAN HALL
HI-AYH $14
2004 Randolph Avenue
St. Paul, MN 55105
(612) 690-6604

▼ LANESBORO OLD BARN RESORT HOSTEL
U $10–$13
Route 3, P.O. Box 57
Preston, MN 55965
(507) 467-2512
53 beds. Bathroom, showers, kitchenettes, swimming pool, rentals.

MISSOURI

▼ LEWIS & CLARK INTERNATIONAL HOSTEL
U $12
1500 South Fifth Street
St. Charles, MO 63303
(314) 946-1000

● HI-THE HUCKLEBERRY FINN YOUTH HOSTEL
HI-AYH $14
1904-08 South 12th Street
St. Louis, MO 63104
(314) 241-0076

MONTANA

▼ INTERNATIONAL BACKPACKERS HOSTEL
U $10
405 West Olive Street
Bozeman, MT 59715
(406) 586-4659

▼ BACKPACKER'S INN
U $8

29 Dawson Avenue, P.O. Box 94
East Glacier, MT 59434
(406) 226-9392

● HI-BROWNIE'S
HI-AYH $10+tax
P.O. Box 229
East Glacier Park, MT 59434
(406) 226-4426

▼ BIRCHWOOD HOSTEL
U $9
600 South Orange Street
Missoula, MT 59801
(406) 728-9799
Our 11th year! One couple's room, kitchen and laundry.

▼ BIKING BUNKS, TENT AND R.V. CAMP
U $S9
P.O. Box 91
St. Ignatius, MT 59865
(406) 745-3959
Hike-bike mission wilderness film in the Bison Range.

NEBRASKA

● HI-CORNERSTONE
HI-AYH $8
640 North 16th Street
Lincoln, NE 68508
(402) 476-0926 (Please leave message)

NEVADA

▼ NEVADA HOTEL
U $18
235 South Main Street
Las Vegas, NV 89114
(702) 385-7311

NEW HAMPSHIRE

● HI-PETERBOROUGH MANOR
HI-AYH $15+tax
50 Summer Street
Peterborough, NH 03458
(603) 924-9832

▼ BOWMAN BASE CAMP
U   S$11
U.S. Route 2
Randolph, NH 03570
(603) 466-5130

NEW JERSEY

● HI-OLD MINE ROAD HOSTEL
HI-AYH $10–$12
P.O. Box 172
Layton, NJ 07851
(201) 948-6750

NEW MEXICO

▼ ROUTE 66 HOSTEL
U $11–$13
1012 West Central Avenue S.W.
Albuquerque, NM 87102
(505) 247-1813
Free food; walk to local sites. See the real New Mexico.

● HI-TAOS
HI-AYH $10–$12.50
Taos Ski—Valley Road
Mail to:
P.O. Box 3271
Taos, NM 87571
(505) 776-8298

▼ OSCURO HIGH DESERT HOSTEL RANCH
U $12–$14
Country Road A002
Oscuro, NM 88301
(505) 648-4007
Hiking, camping, gold panning on a 250-acre working ranch in Billy-the-Kid country!

● HI-RIO GRANDE GORGE, THE PLUM TREE HOSTEL
HI-AYH $9–$10+tax
P.O. Box B-4
Pilar, NM 87531
(505) 758-0090

● HI-THE CARTER HOUSE
HI-AYH $12
101 North Cooper Street
Silver City, NM 88061
(505) 388-5485

● HI-RIVERBEND HOT SPRINGS
HI-AYH $11
100 Austin Avenue
Truth or Consequences, NM 87901
(505) 894-6183

▼ CARLSBAD CAVERNS HOSTEL
U $12
31 Carlsbad Caverns SW
White City, NM 88268
(505) 785-2291

NEW YORK

CITY OF NEW YORK

New York City—the Big Apple. You know. Great public transportation: $ 1.25 per trip on train or bus. Pay attention as you would in any big city; it's the same. Most hostels provide security for your documents, etc., so use it. It's a fun city. There is a free bus from JFK Airport to the a train of the subway system. Phone first to confirm the price and get directions.

▼ CHELSEA CENTER
U $18
313 West 29th Street
New York, NY 10001
(212) 643-0214
Very friendly and helpful international staff. Small hostel with garden. Free breakfast and linen. Five-minute walk from bus and train stations. No curfew. Office hours: 8:30 A.M.–11 P.M. Near Broadway theatres, Greenwich Village, Empire State Building and more.

● HI–NEW YORK
HI-AYH $20–$22
891 Amsterdam Avenue
New York, NY 10025-4403
(212) 932-2300

● HI-NIAGARA FALLS
HI-AYH $12-$14
1101 Ferry Avenue
Niagara Falls, NY 14301
(716) 282-3700

▼ INTERNATIONAL HOUSE
U $25
500 Riverside Drive
New York, NY 10027
(212) 316-8436

▼ INTERNATIONAL STUDENT CENTER
U $12
8 West 88th Street
New York, NY 10024
(212) 787-7706

▼ MID-CITY GUEST HOUSE
U $15–$18
608 8th Avenue
New York, NY 10018
(212) 704-0562

▼ NEW YORK BED AND BREAKFAST
U $20

134 West 119th Street
New York, NY 10026
(212) 666-0559

▼ UPTOWN HOSTEL
U $12
239 Lenox Avenue (at 122nd Street)
New York, NY 10027
(212) 666-0559

OTHER NEW YORK LOCATIONS
(See also Niagara Falls, Ontario, Canada)

▼ PINE HAVEN HOSTEL
U $12+tax
531 Western Avenue
Albany, NY 12203
(518) 482-1574

● HI-TIBBETTS POINT LIGHTHOUSE HOSTEL
HI-AYH $10
33439 County Route 6
Cape Vincent, NY 13618
(315) 654-3450

● HI-LAKEGEORGE
HI-AYH $10
Montcalm Street
P.O. Box 176
Lake George, NY 12845
(518) 668-2634

▼ ALL TUCKED INN
U $30
574 3rd Street
Niagara Falls, NY 14301
(716) 282-0919

▼ BELLEAYRE HOSTEL
U $9–$12
P.O. Box J. Main Street
Pine Hill, NY 12465
(914) 254-4200
In beautiful Catskill Mountains Park. Hike, bike, ski and swim. Bunks, lockers, kitchen, laundry, sports equipment: linens extra. Private rooms and efficiency cabins available.

● HI-DOWNING INTERNATIONAL HOSTEL
HI-AYH $10
535 Oak Street
Syracuse, NY 13203-1609
(315) 472-5788

▼ PODUNK HOME HOSTEL
U   S$6
(call for street address)
Trumansburg, NY
(607) 387-9277

NORTH CAROLINA

▼ BLOWING ROCK HOSTEL
U $11
P.O. Box 2350, Goforth Road
Blowing Rock, NC 28605
(704) 295-2350

▼ SMOKESEEGE LODGE
U $10
P.O. Box 179
Dillsboro, NC 28725
(704) 586-8658

● HI-PEMBROKE HOUSE
HI-AYH $7
Odum Street
Mail to:
Baptist Student Center
Pembroke State University
Pembroke, NC 28372
(910) 521-8777/(800) 484-4037, code 2274

OHIO

● HI-COLUMBUS
HI-AYH $10
95 E. 12th Avenue
Columbus, OH 43201
(614) 294-7157

● HI-MALABAR FARM
HI-AYH $10
3954 Bromfield Road
Lucas, OH 44843
(419) 892-2055

● HI-STANFORD HOUSE
HI-AYH $10
6093 Stanford Road
Peninsula, OH 44264
(216) 467-8711

OREGON

● HI-THE ASHLAND HOSTEL
HI-AYH $12–$14
150 North Main Street
Ashland, OR 97520
(541) 482-9217

● HI-SEA STAR
HI-AYH $12
375 2nd Street
Bandon, OR 97411
(503) 347-9632

▼ BEND CASCADE HOSTEL
U $13
19 Southwest Century Drive
Bend, OR 97702
(503) 389-3813
While skiing, hiking or mountain biking, stay in our new hostel.

● HI-LOST VALLEY HOSTEL
HI-AYH $9
81868 Lost Valley Lane
Dexter, OR 97431
(503) 937-3351

▼ EUGENE LITTLE COUGAR HOSTEL
U $10
1955 West 9th Place
Eugene, OR 97402
(503) 343-8398

▼ BROWN SQUIRREL HOSTEL
U $12
44 SW Brook Street
Newport, OR 97365
(503) 265-3729

▼ HI-PORTLAND
HI-AYH $12
3031 SE Hawthorne Boulevard
Portland, OR 97214
(503) 236-3380
All the pancakes you can eat for only $1!

● HI-SEASIDE
HI-AYH $12–$14
930 N. Holladay Drive
Seaside, OR 97138
(503) 738-7911

PENNSYLVANIA

CITY OF PHILADELPHIA

▼ BANK STREET HOSTEL
U $14
32 South Bank Street
Philadelphia, PA 19106
(215) 922-4222

The Frugal Globetrotter

● HI-CHAMOUNIX MANSION PHILADELPHIA
HI-AYH $11
Chamounix Drive
West Fairmont Park
Philadelphia, PA 19131
(215) 878-3676/(800) 379-0017

▼ OLD FIRST REFORMED CHURCH
U   S$11
4th and Race Street
Philadelphia, PA 19106
(215) 922-9663

OTHER PENNSYLVANIA LOCATIONS

● HI-EVANSBURG STATE PARK
HI-AYH $12
837 Mayhall Road
Collegeville, PA 19426
(610) 409-0113

● HI-POCONOS
HI-AYH $10–$12
R.R. 2, P.O. Box 1026
Cresco, PA 18326
(717) 676-9076

● HI-IRONMASTER'S MANSION
HI-AYH $10–$12
1212 Pine Grove Road
Gardners, PA 17324
(717) 486-7575

● HI-GEIGERTOWN
HI-AYH $8.50
P.O. Box 49-B
Geigertown, PA 19523
(610) 286-9537

● HI-MARSH CREEK STATE PARK
HI-AYH $10–$12
P.O. Box 376
Lyndell, PA 19354
(610) 458-5881

● HI-TYLER STATE PARK
HI-AYH $10–$12
P.O. Box 94
Newtown, PA 18940
(215) 968-0927

● HI-OHIOPYLE
HI-AYH $9–$11
P.O. Box 99

Ohiopyle, PA 15470
(412) 329-4476

● HI-WEISEL
HI-AYH $8
7347 Richlandtown Road
Quakertown, PA 18951
(215) 536-8749

● HI-LIVING WATERS HOSTEL
HI-AYH $10
RD 1, P.O. Box 206
Schellsburg, PA 15559
(814) 733-4212/(814) 733-2162

SOUTH CAROLINA

▼ KING GEORGE IV
U   S$15
(call for street address)
Charleston, SC 29401
(803) 723-9339
By reservation only. Historic district. Shared student rooms.

▼RUTLEDGE VICTORIAN INN & GUESTHOUSE
U   S$15
(call for street address)
Charleston, SC 29401
(803) 722-7551
By reservation only. Historic district. Shared student rooms.

SOUTH DAKOTA

● HI-PLEASANT VALLEY
HI-AYH $12
R.R. 1, P.O. Box 256
Gary, SD 57237
(605) 272-5614/(507) 223-5492

▼ RAPID CITY YMCA
HI-AYH $10
815 Kansas City Street
Rapid City, SD 57701
(605) 342-8538

TENNESSEE

▼ MEMPHIS CASTLE HOSTEL
U $10
1084 Poplar
Memphis, TN 38105
(901) 527-7174

● HI-GREAT SMOKEY MOUNTAINS
HI-AYH $13.25
3248 Manis Road
Sevierville, TN 37862
(615) 429-8563/(800) 851-6715

TEXAS

CITY OF AUSTIN

● HI-AUSTIN
HI-AYH $12
2200 South Lakeshore Boulevard
Austin, TX 78741
(512) 444-2294/(800) 725-2331

▼ TAOS HALL
U   S$10
2612 Guadalupe
Austin, TX 78767
(512) 474-6905

OTHER TEXAS LOCATIONS

▼ COUNTRY INN MOTEL & HOSTEL
U $15
Hwy 17, P.O. Box 295
Balmorhea, TX 79718
(915) 375-2477

▼ DALLAS INTERNATIONAL HOSTEL
U $15
10230 Harry Hines Boulevard
Dallas, TX 75201
(214) 358-3211

▼ DALLAS INTERNATIONAL HOSTEL
U
901 Ft. Worth Avenue
Dallas, TX 76208
(214) 747-8978

● HI-EL PASO
HI-AYH $12.50–$14.50
311 East Franklin Avenue
El Paso, TX 79901
(915) 532-3661

▼ COMANCHE MOTEL AND HOSTEL
U $10+tax
1301 East Dickinson Boulevard
Fort Stockton, TX 79735
(915) 336-8447

West Texas, low humidity. Limo tours of Big Bend, Judge Roy Bean's place and the Alamo Village, Sonora and Carlsbad Caves. Fifth largest winery in the United States. Cooking, common rooms, dorms, single and double rooms, 88 beds, game room. Call to make reservations: (800) 530-3793.

● HI-HOUSTON INTERNATIONAL HOSTEL INC.
HI-AYH $11.39
5302 Crawford
Houston, TX 77004
(713) 523-1009

● HI-SAN ANTONIO INTERNATIONAL HOSTEL
HI-AYH $12.85+tax
621 Pierce Street
P.O. Box 8059
San Antonio, TX 78208
(210) 223-9426

▼ TRAVELER'S HOTEL
U $16
220 North Broadway
San Antonio, TX 78205
(512) 226-4381

UTAH

SALT LAKE CITY

▼ AVENUES YOUTH HOSTEL
U $12
107 F Street
Salt Lake City, UT 84103
(801) 359-3855
No smoking in the building. Homey atmosphere. Convenient location for skiers and visitors. Private parking. Kitchen facilities. Laundry room. Cable T.V. Private rooms too!

OTHER UTAH LOCATIONS

▼ LAZY LIZARD INTERNATIONAL HOSTEL
AAIH $7
1213 South Hwy 191
Moab, UT 84532
(801) 259-6057

VERMONT

▼ AUGERGE ALBURG
U
RD 1, P.O. Box 3
Alburg, VT 05440
(802) 796-3169

● HI-GREENWOOD LODGE AYH
HI-AYH   S$14
Vermont Hwy 9
P.O. Box 246
Bennington, VT 05201
(802) 442-2547

● HI-VAGABOND
HI-AYH $12+tax
Vermont Route 30
P.O. Box 224
East Jamaica, VT 05343
(802) 874-4096

▼ KILLINGTON FIRESIDE
U $18
P.O. Box 69
Killington, VT 05751
(802) 422-3361

▼ TURN OF THE RIVER LODGE
U $20
P.O. Box 257
Killington, VT 05751
(802) 422-3766

● HI-TROJAN HORSE HOSTEL
HI-AYHS$12+tax; W$17+tax
44 Andover Street
Ludlow, VT 05149
(802) 228-5244/(800) 547-7475

● CAPITOL HOME HOSTEL
HI-AYH $10–$12
RD 1, P.O. Box 2750
Montpelier, VT 05602 (include SASE)
(802) 223-2104 (no calls after 9 P.M.)

● SLEEPER'S RIVER HOME HOSTEL
HI-AYH $13–$14
(call for street address)
St. Johnsbury, VT
(802) 748-1575 (do not call or arrive after 8 P.M.)

▼ STOWE-BOUND LODGE
U $15
673 South Main Street
Stowe, VT 05672
(802) 253-4515

● HI-GREENMONT FARMS
HI-AYH   S$15
P.O. Box 148, Old West Bolton Road
Underhill Center, VT 05490
(802) 899-1796

VIRGINIA

● HI-BEAR'S DEN LODGE
HI-AYH $12
R.R. 1, P.O. Box 288
Bluemont, VA 22012
(540) 554-8708

● HI-BLUE RIDGE MOUNTAINS
HI-AYH $11.50+tax
R.R. 2, P.O. Box 449
Galax, VA 24333
(540) 236-4962

● HI-SANGRAAL BY-THE-SEA
HI-AYH $15+tax
Mill Creek Landing Road
P.O. Box 187
Urbanna, VA 23175
(804) 776-6500

● HI-ANGIE'S GUEST COTTAGE HOSTEL
HI-AYH $8.50–$11
302 24th Street
Virginia Beach, VA 23451
(804) 428-4690

▼ MRS. H. J. CARTER
U $20
903 Lafayette Street
Williamsburg, VA
(804) 229-1117

WASHINGTON, D.C.

▼ ALLEN LEE HOTEL
U $25
2224 F Street NW
Washington, D.C. 20037
(202) 331-1224

● HI-WASHINGTON, D.C.
HI-AYH $16–$18
1009 11th Sreet NW
Washington, D.C. 20001
(202) 737-2333

▼ INTERNATIONAL STUDENT CENTER
U $15
2451 18th Street NW
Washington, D.C. 20009
(202) 265-6555

▼ SIMKINS' BED & BREAKFAST AND HOSTEL
U $15–$25
1601 19th Street NW
Washington, D.C. 20009
(202) 387-1328
Safe, fun area. Half block from Dupont Metro. Walk to sites. Air conditioning.

WASHINGTON

CITY OF SEATTLE

▼ AMERICAN BACKPACKER'S HOSTEL
U $11–$14
126 Broadway East
Seattle, WA 98102
(206) 720-2965/(800) 600-2965
No curfew. Free pickups from Amtrak, Greyhound, downtown. Airport pickup for 3 or more people. Free breakfast. Pool table.

▼ COMMODORE HOTEL
U $11
2013 2nd Avenue
Seattle, WA 98121
(206) 448-8868

▼ GREEN TORTOISE BACKPACKER'S HOSTEL
AAIH $10
715 2nd Avenue North
Seattle, WA 98109
(206) 322-1222

● HI-SEATTLE
HI-AYH $15–$17+tax
84 Union Street
Seattle, WA 98101
(206) 622-5443

OTHER WASHINGTON LOCATIONS

● HI-BELLINGHAM
HI-AYH $11–$13
Fairhaven Park
107 Chuckanut Drive
Bellingham, WA 98225-8934
(360) 671-1750

▼ THE INN AT BINGEN SCHOOL
U
P.O. Box 155
Bingen, WA 98605
(509) 493-3363

● HI-BIRCH BAY
HI-AYH $10–$12
7467 Gemini Street
Blaine, WA 98230-9674
(360) 371-2180

● HI-FORT COLUMBIA
HI-AYH $10–$12
Fort Columbia State Park
P.O. Box 224
Chinook, WA 98614-0224
(360) 777-8755

▼ NORTH STAR FARM HOSTEL
U
518 Monumental Road
Coltville, WA 99114
(509) 684-4418

▼ GRAYS HARBOR HOSTEL
U $10+tax
6 Ginny Lane
Elma, WA 98541
(360) 482-3119
Hot tub, self-service bike shop, close to bus service. 25 miles to Olympia. 42 miles ot ocean beaches. 100 miles to Mt. Rainier.

▼ RAIN FOREST HOSTEL
U $10
169312 Hwy 101
Forks, WA 98331
(360) 374-2270
In the middle of Olympic National Park. Ocean beaches, rain forest!

● HI-FORT FLAGLER
HI-AYH $10–$12
Fort Flager State Park
10621 Flagler Road
Nordland, WA 98358-9699
(360) 385-1288

▼ DOE BAY VILLAGE RESORT HOSTEL
U
Star Route 86
Olga, WA 98331
(206) 376-2291

● HI-THE OLYMPIC HOSTEL, PORT TOWNSEND
HI-AYH $9
Fort Worden State Park
272 Battery Way
Port Townsend, WA 98368-3699
(360) 385-0655

● HI-SPOKANE
HI-AYH $11
930 South Lincoln
Spokane, WA 99204-3856
(509) 838-5968

▼ PEONE PRARIE BIKE HOSTEL
U $10
Route 3, P.O. Box 11
Spokane (Mead), WA 99021
(509) 466-6315

l HI-VASHON !SLAND AYH RANCH HOSTEL
HI-AYH $9
12119 SW Cove Road
Vashon Island, WA 98070
(206) 463-2592

WISCONSIN

▼ HI-FOLKLORE VILLAGE FARM
HI-AYH $8
3210 Hwy BB
Dodgeville, WI 53533
(608) 924-4000

● HI-RED BARN
HI-AYH   S$10+tax
6750 West Loomis Road
Greendale, WI 53129
(414) 529-3299

● HI-LAONA, WISCONSIN
HI-AYH $12+tax
5397 Beech Street
P.O. Box 325
Laona, WI 54541
(715) 674-2615

▼ HI-WELLSPRING
HI-AYH $12
4382 Hickory Road, P.O. Box 72
Newburg, WI 53060
(414) 675-6755

WYOMING

▼ PIONEER HOTEL
U $14
208 West 17th Street
Cheyenne, WY 82001
(307) 634-3010

▼ BUNKHOUSE AT THE ANVIL MOTEL
U
215 North Cache
Jackson, WY 83001
(307) 733-3668

CANADA

ALBERTA

CITY OF BANFF

▼ HI-C BANFF INTERNATIONAL HOSTEL
HI-C $15–$16
Tunnel Mountain Road
Banff, AB T0L 0C0
(403) 762-4122

● CASTLE MOUNTAIN HOSTEL
HI-C $11 CDN
Hwy 1A, Bow Valley Parkway
P.O. Box 1358
Banff, AB T0L 0C0
(403) 762-2367

● HILDA CREEK HOSTEL
HI-C $9 CDN
Hwy 93
P.O. Box 1358
Banff, AB T0L 0C0
(no phone)

▼ HI-C MOSQUITO CREEK HOSTEL
HI-C $10
Hwy 93, P.O. Box 1358
Banff, AB T0L 0C0
(no phone)

● RAMPART CREEK HOSTEL
HI-C $9 CDN
Hwy 93
P.O. Box 1358
Banff, AB T0L 0C0
(no phone)

CITY OF CALGARY LOCATIONS

● CALGARY INTERNATIONAL HOSTEL
HI-C $13 CDN
520 Seventh Avenue SE
Calgary, AB T2G 0J6
(403) 269-8239

▼ SAINT LOUIS HOTEL
U $16
430 8th Avenue SE
Calgary, AB
(403) 262-6341

CITY OF EDMONTON

● EDMONTON INTERNATIONAL HOSTEL
HI-C $12.50 CDN
10422 91st Street
Edmonton, AB T5H 1S6
(403) 429-0140

▼ HI-C JASPER ATHABASCA FALLS HOSTEL
HI-C $9
10926 88th Avenue
Edmonton, AB T6G OZ1
(403) 852-5959

● BEAUTY CREEK HOSTEL
HI-C S$9 CDN
Hwy 93
10926 88th Avenue
Edmonton, AB T6G 0Z1
(no phone)

▼ HI-C JASPER MT. EDITH CAVELL HOSTEL
HI-C S$8
10926 88th Avenue
Edmonton, AB T6G OZ1
(no phone)

● MALIGNE CANYON HOSTEL
HI-C $9 CDN
Maligne Canyon Road
10926 88th Avenue
Edmonton, AB T6G 0Z1
(403) 852-3584

▼ HI-C WHISTLER'S MOUNTAIN HOSTEL
HI-C $13
10926 88th Avenue
Edmonton, AB T6G 0Z1
(403) 852-3215

OTHER ALBERTA LOCATIONS

▼ CLUBHOUSE ALPINE CLUB
U
P.O. Box 2042
Canmore, AB TOL OMO
(403) 678-3224

▼ HI-C GRAND UNION INTERNATIONAL HOSTEL
HI-C $10
7719 17th Avenue
Coleman, AB TOK OMO
(403) 563-3433

BRITISH COLUMBIA

CITY OF VANCOUVER

▼ AMERICAN BACKPACKER'S HOSTEL
U $10
347 West Pender Street
Vancouver, BC V6B 6T3
(604) 688-0112

▼ HARBOURFRONT HOSTEL
U $15
209 Heatly Street
Vancouver, BC V6A 3GI
(604) 254-0733

● VANCOUVER INTERNATIONAL HOSTEL
HI-C $15 CDN
1515 Discovery Street
Vancouver, BC V6R 4K5
(604) 224-3208

▼ VINCENTS BACKPACKER'S HOSTEL
U $10
927 Main
Vancouver, BC V6A 2VB
(604) 682-2441

CITY OF VICTORIA

● VICTORIA INTERNATIONAL HOSTEL
HI-C $14 CDN
516 Yates Street
Victoria, BC V8W 1K8
(604) 385-4511

▼ RENOUF HOUSE B&B
U $18.25
2010 Stanley Avenue
Victoria, BC V8R 3X6
(604) 595-4774
Includes linen and breakfast. Kayaking and sailing tours!

▼ SELKIRK GUESTHOUSE
U $13.50
934 Selkirk Avenue
Victoria, BC V9A 2V1
(604) 389-1213

▼ VICTORIA BACKPACKERS
U $10
1418 Fernwood Road
Victoria, BC V8V 4P7
(604) 386-4471

The Frugal Globetrotter

OTHER BRITISH COLUMBIA LOCATIONS

● PACIFIC HOSTELRY
HI-C $15 CDN
549 Fir Street
P.O. Box 302
Alert Bay, BC V0N 1A0
(604) 974-2026

● WHISKEY JACK HOSTEL
HI-C S$11 CDN
Yoho National Park
P.O. Box 1358
Banff, AB T0L 0C0
(403) 762-4122

● SQUILAX GENERAL STORE AND HOSTEL
HI-C $12.50 CDN
R.R. 2
Chase, BC V0E 1M0
(604) 675-2977

● FERNIE HOSTEL
HI-C $10 CDN
892 6th Avenue
P.O. Box 580
Fernie, BC V0B 1M0
(604) 423-6811

● RED GOAT LODGE
HI-C S$12 CDN
Hwy 37
P.O. Box 101
Iskut, BC V0J 1K0
(604) 234-3261

● KAMLOOPS "OLD COURTHOUSE" HOSTEL
HI-C $13.50 CDN
7 West Seymour Street
Kamloops, BC V2C 1E4
(604) 828-7991

▼ KELOWNA BACKPACKER
U $10
2343 Pandosy Street
Kelowna, BC V1Y 1T5
(604) 763-6024

▼ NICOL STREET HOSTEL
U   S$13
65 Nicol Street
Nanaimo, BC V9R 4S7
(604) 753-1188
Hub of Vancouver. Many discounts. Parks, islands. Private rooms.

▼ THOMSON'S HOSTEL
U $12
R.B. 3, R.R. 2
Nanaimo, BC V9R 5K2
(604) 722-2251

● ALLEN HOTEL/HOSTEL
HI-C $14.50 CDN
171 Baker Street
Nelson, BC V1L 4H1
(604) 352-7573

▼ INJO'S KOOTENAY COUNTRY HOSTEL
BHC $12.50
R.R. 2, South 18, C. 9
Nelson, BC V1L 5PS
(604) 354-4417

● CARPENTER CREEK HOSTEL
HI-C $13.50 CDN
606 Kildare Street
P.O. Box 97
New Denver, BC V0G 1S0
(604) 358-2242

▼ PINK HOUSE RETREAT
U $15
4323 Bedwell Harbour Road
North Pende Island, BC V0N 2N0
(604) 629-6485

▼ OSOYOOS BACKPACKERS HOSTEL
U $10
6902 62nd Avenue
Osoyoos, BC
(604) 495-2512

● PENTICTON HOSTEL
HI-C $13.50 CDN
464 Ellis Street
Penticton, BC V2A 4M2
(604) 492-3992

● FIDDLEHEAD FARM
HI-C $20 CDN
P.O. Box 421
Powell River, BC V8A 5C2
(604) 334-8044
(includes all meals; reduced rate for long-term stays)

▼ PIONEER ROOMS
U
167 3rd Avenue East
Prince Rupert, BC V8J 1 K4
(604) 624-2334

● CUSHEON CREEK HOSTEL
HI-C $13 CDN
640 Cusheon Lake Road
Saltspring Island, BC V8K 2C2
(604) 537-4149

▼ TOFINO BACKPACKERS HOSTEL
U
241 Campbell Street
Tofino, BC
(604) 725-2288

● WHISTLER HOSTEL
HI-C $14.50–$17.50
5678 Alta Lake Road
P.O. Box 128
Whistler, BC V0N 1B0
(604) 932-5492

▼ SHOESTRING LODGE
U $16
7124 Nancy Grene Drive, P.O. Box 779
Whistler, BC V0N 1 B0
(604) 932-3336

MANITOBA

CITY OF WINNIPEG

▼ GUEST HOUSE INTERNATIONAL
U $11
168 Maryland Street
Winnipeg, MB R3G 1L3
(204) 772-1272

● IVEY HOUSE INTERNATIONAL HOSTEL
HI-C $12 CDN
210 Maryland Street
Winnipeg, MB R3G 1L6
(204) 772-3022

▼ MANITOBA INTERFAITH HOUSE
U $10
159 Mayfair Avenue
Winnipeg, MB R3L OA1
(204) 477-4483

OTHER MANITOBA LOCATIONS

● THE MASKWA PROJECT
HI-C $9.50 CDN
P.O. Box 130
Powerview, MB R0E 1P0
(204) 367-4390

NEW BRUNSWICK

● FUNDY NATIONAL PARK HOSTEL
HI-C   S$8.50 CDN
General Delivery
Alma, NB E0A 1B0
(506) 887-2216

▼ HI-C CAMPBELLTON LIGHTHOUSE HOSTEL
HI-C   S$10
1 Ritchie Street
Campbellton, NB E3N 3G1
(506) 753-7044

● YORK HOUSE HOSTEL
HI-C   S$10 CDN
193 York Street
Fredericton, NB E3B 3N8
(506) 454-1233

▼ HI-C BEAUBEAR MANOR HOSTEL
HI-C $12
Beaubear Manor
Nelson, NB EOC 1TO
(506) 622-3036

NEWFOUNDLAND

▼ HI-C WOODY POINT HOSTEL
HI-C   S$10
Community Hall, P.O. Box 159
Bonne Bay, NF AOK 1PO
(709) 453-2442

NOVA SCOTIA

● SANDY BOTTOM LAKE HOSTEL
HI-C   S$10
Virginia Road
R.R. 4
Annapolis Royal, NS B0S 1A0
(902) 532-2497

▼ CHESLEY HOUSE
U $14
304 Granville Street 3
Bridgetown, NS B0S 1C0

● HALIFAX HERITAGE HOUSE HOSTEL
HI-C $13.75 CDN
1253 Barrington Street
Halifax, NS B3J 1Y3
(902) 422-3863

● GLENMORE INTERNATIONAL HOSTEL
HI-C   S$10 CDN
R.R. 1, Whycocomagh
Twin Rock Valley
Cape Breton, NS B0E 3M0
(902) 258-3622

● LAHAVE MARINE HOSTEL
HI-C   S$9 CDN
c/o LaHave Outfitters
P.O. Box 92
Lahave, NS B0R 1C0
(902) 688-2908

● JOYCE'S MOTEL AND COTTAGES
HI-C   S$12 CDN
P.O. Box 193
St. Peters, NS B0E 3B0
(902) 535-2404

▼ HI-C ICE HOUSE HOSTEL
HI-C   S$8.50
Hwy 1, Evangeline Trail R.R. 1
Yarmouth, NS BSA 4A5
(902) 649-2818

● WENTWORTH HOSTEL
HI-C $9.50 CDN
Wentworth Station
R.R. 1
Wentworth, NS B0M 1Z0
(902) 548-2379

▼ BURNSIDE HOME HOSTEL
U
R.R. 3, 830 Gaspereau River
Wolfville, NS B0P 1X0
(902) 542-7214

ONTARIO

CITY OF NIAGARA FALLS
(See also Niagara Falls, NY, in United States listings.)

▼ FALLS VIEW TOURIST HOME
BHC $14
4745 River Road
Niagara Falls, ON L2G 3G3
(905) 374-8051

● HI-NIAGARA FALLS INTERNATIONAL HOSTEL
HI-C $12 CDN

4699 Zimmerman Avenue
Niagara Falls, ON L2E 3M7
(905) 357-0770

CITY OF OTTAWA

● OTTAWA INTERNATIONAL HOSTEL
HI-C $14.70 CDN
75 Nicholas Street
Ottawa, ON K1N 7B9
(613) 235-2595

▼ SOMERSET HOUSE
U
568 Somerset Street West
Ottawa, ON
(613) 232-0040

CITY OF TORONTO

● HI-TORONTO
HI-C $15.24 CDN
223 Church Street
Toronto, ON M5B 1Y7
(416) 368-0207

▼ LESLIEVILLE HOME HOSTEL
U $13
185 Leslie Street
Toronto, ON M4M 3C6
(416) 461-7258
*Includes linens and towels. Intimate atmosphere. No curfew.
$2 breakfast. 24-hour check-in; 24-hour transportation. Near
downtown. Cheap tours to Niagara Falls. Includes tax. Call
toll-free for reservations: (800) 280-3965; fax: (416) 469-
9938.*

▼ MARIGOLD INTERNATIONAL TRAVELLERS'
HOSTEL
BHC $18+tax
2011 Dundas Street West
Toronto, ON M6R 1W7
(416) 536-8824

▼ NEILL-WYCIK COLLEGE HOTEL
BHC $16.50 (U.S.)
96 Gerrard Street East
Toronto, ON MSB 1tB7
(416) 977-2320
*Toll-free number: (800) 268-4358; fax: (416) 977-2809.
Downtown Toronto. $16.50 a night for students, hostel mem-
bers. Bus from airport stops at our doors. Open May 5–August
29. Sundecks, sauna, laundry room, T.V. lounge. No curfews!*

OTHER ONTARIO LOCATIONS

● ARDEN (BLUE ECHO) INTERNATIONAL HOS-
TEL
HI-C $15 CDN
R.R. 4
Arden, ON K0H 1B0
(613) 335-2841

▼ HI-C AIR BASE ISLAND INTERNATIONAL
HOSTEL
HI-C   S$8
Biscotasing, ON POM 1CO
(705) 674-0104

● HI-GODERICH
HI-C   S$10 CDN
R.R. 2
Goderich, ON N7A 3X8
(519) 524-8428

▼ LIVING WATERS CABINS
U   S$15 and up
392 Queen Street
Kincardine, ON N2Z 2R2
(519) 396-3887

● KINGSTON INTERNATIONAL HOSTEL
HI-C $12 CDN
210 Bagot Street
Kingston, ON K7L 3G1
(613) 546-7203

▼ RED DEER LODGE
U
P.O. Box 201
Madawaska, ON K0J 2C0
(613) 637-5215

▼ SUMMER HOUSE PARK
U
Miller Lake
Miller Lake, ON N0H 1Z0
(519) 795-7712

● ALGONQUIN HOTEL
HI-C $19 CDN
864 Queen Street East
Sault Ste. Marie, ON P6A 2B4
(705) 253-2311

▼ BURNSYDE YOUTH HOSTEL
U $25
139 William Street
Stratford, ON NSA 4X9
(519) 271-7076

▼ HI-C ROCKY MOUNTAIN INTERNATIONAL
HOSTEL
U $12
2881 Valleyview Road
Sudbury, ON POM 1EO
(705) 887-4931

● CONFEDERATION COLLEGE—SIGLEY HALL
RESIDENCE
HIC   S$19.50 CDN
960 William Street
Confederation College
Sibley Hall Residence
Thunder Bay, ON P7C 4W1
(807) 475-6381

▼ LAKEHEAD UNIVERSITY RESIDENCE
U
955 Oliver Road
Thunder Bay, ON P78 5E1
(807) 343-8812

▼ WATERLOO INTERNATIONAL HOME HOSTEL
U $14
102b Albert Street
Waterloo, ON N2L 3S8
(519) 725-5202

PRINCE EDWARD ISLAND

▼ HI-C CHARLOTTETOWN HOSTEL
HI-C   S$13
153 Mount Edward Road
Charlottetown, PEI C1A 7N4
(902) 894-9696

QUEBEC

CITY OF MONTREAL

▼ CHEZ JEAN AUBERGE
U $14
4136 rue Henn Julien
Montreal, QC H2W 2K3
(514) 843-8279
Super sympa, cool, centre ville, breakfast. Bienvenue.

● AUBERGE DE MONTREAL
HI-C $16 CDN
1030 Mackay Street
Montreal, QC H3G 2H1
(514) 843-3317

The Frugal Globetrotter

▼ VACANCES CANADA 4 SAISONS
U $11.50
5155 rue de Gaspe
Montreal, QC H2T 2A1
(514) 495-2581

CITY OF QUEBEC

▼ AUBERGE DE LA PAIX
U $17
31 rue Couillard
Quebec City, QC GIR 3T4
(418) 694-0735
Open year-round. Breakfast, bike rental, near Chateau Frontenac.

▼ BATTLEFIELDS BACKPACKERS
U
820 Eymard Street
Quebec City, QC G1S 4A1
(418) 681-6804

● CENTRE INTERNATIONAL DE SÉJOUR DE OUEBEC
HI-C $15 CDN
19 Rue Ste-Ursula
Quebec, QC G1R 4E1
(418) 694-0755

OTHER QUEBEC LOCATIONS

▼ AUBERGE LE BALCONVERT
U
CP 442, Route 362
Bae St. Paul, QC JOA 1BO
(418) 435-5587

▼ AUGERGE JEUNESSE SAGUENAY
U $15
27 Bosse Ouest
Chicoutimi, QC G74 1K9
(418) 543-1123

● AUBERGE DE CAP-AUX-OS
HI-C $13 CDN
2095 b. Grande-Grève
Gaspe, QC G0E 1J0
(418) 892-5153

● AUBERGE ILE-DU-REPOS DE PÉRIBONKA
HI-C $12.50 CDN
C.P. 38
Ste- Monique
de Honfleur, QC G0W 2T0
(418) 347-5649

▼ HEBERGEMENT MONTREAL
U
1391 rue Beauregard
Longueuil, QC
(514) 495-2581

● AUBERGE DU CHATEAU BAHIA
HI-C $13 CDN
152 Boulevard Perron
Pointe-à-la-Garde, QC G0C 2M0
(418) 788-2048

● AUBERGE DE LA GRANDE LIGNE
HI-C $14.50 CDN
318 Chemin de la grande Ligne
Racine, QC JOE 1Y0
(514) 532-3177

● HI-C AUBERGE LA VOILE
HI-C $12 CDN
58 St. Germain Est
Rimouski, QC GSL 1A4
(418) 722-8002

● HI-C AUBERGE INTERNATIONAL DE RIVIERE-DU-LOUP
HI-C $12 CDN
46 Hotel de Ville
Rivière-du-Loup, QC GSR 1L5
(418) 862-7566

● AUBERGE INTERNATIONAL LE TANGON
HI-C   S$12 CDN
555 Cartier
C.P. 902
Sept-lles, QC G4R 4L2
(418) 962-8180

● LE DOMAINE FRASER
HI-C $12 CDN
684 Route 165,
Bernierville, QC G0N 1N0
(418) 428-9551

▼ LAURENTIAN HOSTEL
BHC $14
39 Chemin des Lilas
S-Anne-Des-Lacs, QC JOR 1BO
(514) 224-5401

● LA MAISON MAJORIQUE & LA MAISON ALEXIS
HI-C $12 CDN
158 Bateau Passeur
Tadoussac, QC G0T 2A0
(418) 235-4372

● AUBERGE LA FLOTILLE
HI-C $14.50 CDN
497 rue Radisson
Trois-Rivières, QC G9A 2C7
(819) 378-8010

● LE CHALET BEAUMONT
HI-C $14 CDN
1451 Beaumont
Val-David, QC J0T 2N0
(819) 322-1972

SASKATCHEWAN

▼ KIKINAK FRIENDSHIP CENTER
U
P.O. Box 254
La Ronge, SK 50J 1T0
(306) 425-2051

● TURGEON INTERNATIONAL HOSTEL
HI-C $12 CDN
2310 McIntyre Street
Regina, SK S4P 2S2
(306) 791-8165

● WASKESIU INTERNATIONAL HOSTEL
HI-C   S$12 CDN
Montreal Road
P.O. Box 85
Waskesiu Lake, SK S0J 2Y0
(306) 663-5450

YUKON

HI-C DAWSON CITY RIVER HOSTEL
HI-C   S$12.50
West Dawson
P.O. Box 32
Dawson City, YK Y0B 1G0
(no phone)

ABOUT THE AUTHOR

Bruce writes for *Details* magazine. His offbeat adventure seminar, "Bargain Hunting for Global Adventure," enlightens and amuses university and continuing education audiences nationwide. The lecture offers an unusual perspective on travel by giving those with big plans and small budgets detailed reasons and strategies (*rat-race exit blueprints*) for exploring the world.

He has circled the globe five times and continues traveling, inspiring adventurers and writing. Allergic to cubicle-infested offices and corporate culture, he prefers rambling onto uncharted territory, especially small villages in the middle of nowhere. His second book, *Tales to Close the Century,* is nearly complete. He graduated with a B.S. in physics (1984) and has been interviewed on CNN.

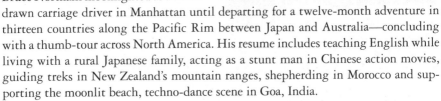

Bruce Northam moonlighted as a horse-drawn carriage driver in Manhattan until departing for a twelve-month adventure in thirteen countries along the Pacific Rim between Japan and Australia—concluding with a thumb-tour across North America. His resume includes teaching English while living with a rural Japanese family, acting as a stunt man in Chinese action movies, guiding treks in New Zealand's mountain ranges, shepherding in Morocco and supporting the moonlit beach, techno-dance scene in Goa, India.

After consuming volumes of shoestring-adventure travel books and attending dozens of "travel-cheap" seminars, he developed these "drop-out Cliffs Notes." A seasoned world traveler, he details several economic travel imaginations. His most recent furlough: New York–Ireland–Turkey–Pakistan–Nepal–Thailand–the Philippines–Hawaii–San Francisco.

Bruce can't seem to completely quit Manhattan.

What do you suppose will satisfy the soul, except to walk free?
—Walt Whitman

INDEX- ->

NOTES ----------------------->

The Frugal Globetrotter

The Frugal Globetrotter